THE LOS ANGELES
OLD-TIME RADIO
SCHEDULE BOOK

VOLUME 1
1929-1937

KEITH D. LEE

The Los Angeles Old-Time Radio Schedule Book — Volume 1, 1929-1937
© 2013 Keith D. Lee. All Rights Reserved.

No part of this book may be reproduced in any form or by any means, electronic, mechanical, digital, photocopying or recording, except for the inclusion in a review, without permission in writing from the publisher.

Published in the USA by:
BearManor Media
PO Box 1129
Duncan, Oklahoma 73534-1129
www.bearmanormedia.com

ISBN 978-1-59393-237-4

Printed in the United States of America.
Book design by Brian Pearce | Red Jacket Press.

TABLE OF CONTENTS

Introduction 5

Listings for 1929 7

Listings for 1930 23

Listings for 1931 81

Listings for 1932 139

Listings for 1933 197

Listings for 1934 255

Listings for 1935 313

Listings for 1936 371

Listings for 1937 429

INTRODUCTION

This series of books are a listing of national and local Los Angeles-based OTR shows from Fall, 1929 through Summer, 1954, in an easy-to-read grid format. Each section lists the OTR shows that were playing during that particular calendar season in that particular OTR year. The shows that are listed were on the four major OTR networks (Blue/ABC, CBS, MBS, and NBC) and their local Los Angeles affiliates from 8AM to 11PM Monday through Sunday.

KNX was primarly an independent station until Fall 1936 when it took over for KHJ as the primary Los Angeles-based CBS affiliate. Then, KHJ became the primary Los Angeles-based Mutual affiliate. (Please note that there was a legal dispute between the *Los Angeles Times* and KNX from summer of 1934 through summer of 1935. That is why there is a "(N/A)" in the KNX Listings for those parts of those years.)

In reading any of the sample chapters, please note the following:

Each cell in the grid represents a fifteen minute block of time.

Each blank cell means that the preceding show is still on. I deferred from using quotation marks because it looked too unreadable.

A slash between the names of two or more daily shows either in the same cell or adjoining cells signifies that those shows shared that timeslot on intermittant days for each week during that particular calendar season. In the case of weekly shows, a slash signifies that the shows shared the same timeslot for part of that particular calendar season.

Such generic show titles as "Songs," "Music," "News," "Public Affairs," "Sports," and "Talk" and any combination thereof are used.

In the case of a daily show, such a generic title signifies the type of show on during the week. In the case of a weekly show, the networks or their affiliated stations couldn't find a sponsor for that timeslot and filled it with a generic show of music, talk, etc.

The information printed has been thoroughly checked for absolute correctness based on the OTR sources that still exist; contradictions and errors in them notwithstanding.

The book is the summation of one year of research using the following sources:

JJ's Radio Logs: *http://www.jjonz.us/RadioLogs/*

The New York Old-Time-Radio Schedule Book, Volumes 1-3 by Keith D. Lee. BearManor Media, OK, 2011.

Because there aren't very many OTR sources anymore, and many of them contradict one another, many thanks are necessary to JJ for allowing me access to his wonderfully entertaining and informative Radio Log Web Page. Hopefully, this will inspire the next generations to research even more into the history of OTR.

LISTINGS FOR 1929

EVENING — FALL, 1929

Sunday

	BLUE	CBS	KNX	NBC
5pm	(Off the Air)	Rabbi Magnin, religion (4:30PM)	Dr. Matthews' Radio Church (4:00PM)	New York Studio Program
5:15				
5:30		Kahn Orchestra		
5:45				
6pm		The Majestic Theater Hour	Ernest Holmes: Theodore C. Abel	
6:15				
6:30				
6:45				
7pm		The First Methodist Church of Hollywood	The Lubovsiki Trio	Goldkette Orchestra
7:15				
7:30				
7:45				
8pm		The KFRC Concert	The First Presbyterian Church of Hollywood	Pryor Moore Orchestra
8:15				
8:30				
8:45				
9pm			The KNX String Ensemble	Music
9:15				
9:30				
9:45				
10pm		The Ten o'Clock Wire		
10:15		The KFRC Program		Dance Orchestra
10:30				
10:45				

EVENING — FALL, 1929

Monday

BLUE	CBS	KNX	NBC	
(Off the Air)	The Story Man	Talk and Music	The Children's Hour (4:30PM)	5pm
				5:15
	Dance Orchestra			5:30
				5:45
		Mood Music	Jubilee	6pm
				6:15
	Charles Hamp, organ			6:30
				6:45
	Light Opera	Jane Purcell, songs	NBC Chain Program	7pm
				7:15
		One-Act Playlet		7:30
				7:45
	The Blue Monday Jamboree	The Lubovsiki Trio	Rudy Siegler's Symphonists	8pm
				8:15
				8:30
				8:45
		Feature Program	Bert Dolan Orchestra	9pm
				9:15
			Music	9:30
				9:45
	The Ten o'Clock Wire		Pyror Moore Orchestra	10pm
	Anson Weeks Orchestra	Ted Lewis Orchestra		10:15
				10:30
				10:45

EVENING — FALL, 1929

Tuesday

	BLUE	CBS	KNX	NBC
5pm	(Off the Air)	The Story Man	Travelogue	The Children's Hour (4:30PM)
5:15				
5:30		Dance Orchestra		
5:45				
6pm		The Old Gold Hour	Lucie Lee, organ	The Eveready Hour
6:15				
6:30				
6:45				
7pm		Dance Orchestra	Dr. Mars Baumgarten, astrology	The Clicquot Club Eskimos
7:15				
7:30				
7:45				
8pm		The KFRC Concert	Music	Rudy Sieger's Symphonists
8:15				
8:30				
8:45				
9pm			Records	Music
9:15				
9:30		The Sierra Symphonists		
9:45			Ferner and His Cello	
10pm		The Ten o'Clock Wire	String Quartet	Delores Del Riio, songs
10:15		Earl Burtnett Orchestra		
10:30				
10:45				

EVENING — FALL, 1929

Wednesday

BLUE	CBS	KNX	NBC	
(Off the Air)	The Voice of Columbia	Spanish Lessons (3:15pm)	The Children's Hour (4:30pm)	*5pm*
		Big Brother		*5:15*
				5:30
				5:45
	Organ Recital	Lucie Lee, organ		*6pm*
				6:15
			The Palmolive Hour	*6:30*
				6:45
	Ben Selvin Orchestra	Radio Skit		*7pm*
				7:15
	Music	Records	Rochester Civic Orchestra	*7:30*
				7:45
	The Movie Club	The KNX Frolics	Jack and Ethel, songs	*8pm*
				8:15
				8:30
				8:45
	Music	William Hatch Orchestra	The Schoenberg Trio	*9pm*
				9:15
				9:30
				9:45
	The Ten o'Clock Wire	Ted Lewis Orchestra	The Cotton Blossom Minstrels	*10pm*
	Earl Burtnett Orchestra			*10:15*
				10:30
				10:45

EVENING — FALL, 1929

Thursday

	BLUE	CBS	KNX	NBC
5pm	(Off the Air)	The Story Man	Talk and Records	The Children's Hour (4:30pm)
5:15				
5:30				
5:45				
6pm		Organ Recital	Organ Recital	Music
6:15				
6:30				
6:45				
7pm		The Sierra Symphonists	Wally Erickson Orchestra	New York Studio Program
7:15				
7:30				Music
7:45				
8pm		Studio Program	Studio Program	
8:15				
8:30				New York Studio Program
8:45				
9pm		The KFRC Concert	The Lubovsiki Trio	
9:15				
9:30				
9:45				
10pm		The Ten o'Clock Wire	Taylor Orchestra	Dance Orchestra
10:15		Earl Burtnett Orchestra		
10:30				
10:45				

EVENING — FALL, 1929

Friday

BLUE	CBS	KNX	NBC	
(Off the Air)	The Story Man	Talk and Records	The Children's Hour (4:30PM)	*5pm*
				5:15
				5:30
				5:45
	Organ Recital	Organ Recital	New York Studio Program	*6pm*
				6:15
	Sunset Ensemble			*6:30*
				6:45
		Dance Orchestra		*7pm*
				7:15
	Light Opera			*7:30*
				7:45
		The KNX Frolics	Winifred Donaldson, songs	*8pm*
				8:15
	Musical Suggestions			*8:30*
				8:45
	Mary and Bob's True Story Hour			*9pm*
				9:15
				9:30
				9:45
	The Ten o'Clock Wire	The Hollywood Legion Fight	Jean Dunn, songs	*10pm*
	Earl Burtnett Orchestra			*10:15*
				10:30
				10:45

EVENING — FALL, 1929

Saturday

	BLUE	CBS	KNX	NBC
5pm	(Off the Air)	The CBS Commodore Ensemble	Music	New York Studio Program
5:15				
5:30				
5:45				
6pm		Mr. and Mrs.	Lucie Lee, organ	General Electric Orchestra
6:15				
6:30		Organ Recital		
6:45				
7pm		The New York Theater Hour	The Theater Hour	Lucky Strike Dance Orchestra
7:15				
7:30				
7:45				
8pm		Raymond Paige Orchesrra	Music	Ensemble and Vocal Quartet
8:15				
8:30				
8:45				
9pm		Night Court	Studio Program	Felipe Delgado, songs
9:15				
9:30				
9:45				
10pm		The Ten o'Clock Wire	Jackie Taylor Orchestra	Music
10:15		Earl Burtnett Orchestra		
10:30				
10:45				

DAYTIME — FALL, 1929

Sunday

	BLUE	CBS	KNX	NBC
8am	(Off the Air)	(Off the Air)	(Off the Air)	(Off the Air)
8:15				
8:30				
8:45				
9am		Records	Records	
9:15				
9:30				
9:45				
10am		The KFRC Concert		Los Angeles Church Federation Services
10:15				
10:30				
10:45				
11am		The First Methodist Church of Los Angeles	First Presbyterian Church of Hollywood	Temple Baptist Church
11:15				
11:30				
11:45				
12pm				
12:15				
12:30		Music	Music	
12:45				
1pm			The IBSA Watchtower	
1:15				
1:30				
1:45				

DAYTIME — FALL, 1929

Monday-Friday

BLUE	CBS	KNX	NBC	
(Off the Air)	The Alarm Clock	Prayer, Records, and Talk	Home Talk	*8am*
				8:15
				8:30
				8:45
				9am
				9:15
	Julie Wintz Orchestra			*9:30*
				9:45
			Music / Studio Program	*10am*
				10:15
	The Times Forum			*10:30*
				10:45
				11am
				11:15
	Charlie Hamp, organ			*11:30*
				11:45
	Talk and Music		Talk and Music	*12pm*
				12:15
				12:30
				12:45
				1pm
				1:15
		The Bookworm		*1:30*
				1:45

DAYTIME — FALL, 1929

Sunday

	BLUE	CBS	KNX	NBC
2pm		Newsreel	The Park Board Program	
2:15				
2:30		Records		Music
2:45				
3pm				
3:15				
3:30				
3:45				
4pm			Dr. Matthews' Radio Church	
4:15				
4:30		Rabbi Magnin, religion		
4:45				

DAYTIME — FALL, 1929

Monday-Friday

BLUE	CBS	KNX	NBC	
	Records	Studio Orchestra	Studio Program	*2pm*
				2:15
		(Off the Air)		*2:30*
				2:45
	Music	Studio Orchestra		*3pm*
				3:15
				3:30
				3:45
		Talk and Music		*4pm*
				4:15
	Music / The Melody Makers		The Children's Hour	*4:30*
				4:45

DAYTIME — FALL, 1929

Saturday

	BLUE	CBS	KNX	NBC
8am	(Off the Air)	Music	Prayer, Records, and Talk	Home Talk
8:15				
8:30				
8:45				
9am				
9:15				
9:30				The National Farm and Home Hour
9:45				
10am				
10:15				
10:30		The Times Forum		
10:45				
11am		Sports	Records	Sports
11:15				
11:30				
11:45				
12pm				
12:15				
12:30				
12:45				
1pm				
1:15				
1:30				
1:45				

DAYTIME — FALL, 1929

Saturday

	BLUE	CBS	KNX	NBC
2pm			Sports	
2:15				
2:30				
2:45				
3pm				
3:15				
3:30				
3:45				
4pm				
4:15				
4:30				
4:45				

LISTINGS FOR 1930

EVENING — WINTER, 1930

Sunday

	BLUE	CBS	KNX	NBC
5pm	The Vagabonds Quartet	The World's Business	Dr. Matthews' Radio Church (4:30PM)	Enna Jettick Melodies
5:15				The Collier Hour
5:30		Rabbi Magnin, religion	Scriptural Research	
5:45				
6pm	The Three Sisters	The Majestic Theater Hour	Records	
6:15			Ernest Holmes: Theodore C. Abel	The Atwater-Kent Hour
6:30	Bob and Jimmy, songs	The KFRC Melody Hour		
6:45				
7pm	Noreen Gamill, drama	Virginia and Andy, songs	Music	
7:15	Margaret Kernan, songs			The Studebaker Champions
7:30	Ray Van Dyne Orchestra	Professor Lindsley and Walter Tourtellote	The Arizona Wranglers	
7:45				Frank Kneeland, songs
8pm		Music	The First Presbyterian Church of Hollywood	Evelyn Snow, songs
8:15				The Sarah Padden Players
8:30	The KECA Symphonette	The Old Scrap Book		
8:45				Purcel Mayer, violin
9pm		The Chevrolet Chronicles	The Lubovsiki Trio	The Borden Milk Program
9:15				
9:30	Enna Jettick Melodies	Val Valenti Orchestra		Songs
9:45	The Schonberger Trio			
10pm		The Ten o'Clock Wire		The Slumber Program
10:15		Val Valenti Orchestra		
10:30	Concert Jewels		The Hollywood Pantages Theater	Dance Orchestra
10:45				

EVENING — WINTER, 1930

Monday

BLUE	CBS	KNX	NBC	
Half-Hour in the Nation's Capitol	Mac and His Gang	Travelogue	Baron Keyes, stories	5pm
		Big Brother		5:15
Piano Recital	Records			5:30
			Stock Market Reports	5:45
Maytag Orchestra		The KNX String Ensemble	Songs	6pm
	Sport-O-Log	Frank Watanabe and Honorable Archie		6:15
Piano Recital	An Evening in Paris	The Airizona Wranglers	The Family Party	6:30
				6:45
Songs	Guy Lombardo Orchestra		Stromberg-Carlson Orchestra	7pm
				7:15
The Empire Builders	Don Amalzo, songs	Don Amalzo, songs	Los Caballeros Orchestra	7:30
				7:45
Ballads	The Blue Monday Jamboree	Public Affairs	Sign of the Shell	8pm
				8:15
Amos 'n' Andy		One-Act Playlet		8:30
Music				8:45
Ray Van Dyne Orchestra		Piano Twins	Songs	9pm
			The Emperor of Crime	9:15
			The Memorial Park Concert	9:30
				9:45
Musical Echoes	The Ten o'Clock Wire			10pm
	Earl Burtnett Orchestra	Gus Arnheim Orchestra		10:15
News	Anson Weeks Orchestra		Music	10:30
Health Talk				10:45

EVENING — WINTER, 1930

Tuesday

	BLUE	CBS	KNX	NBC
5pm	South American Melodies	Ted White and Mel Larsen, songs	Travelogue	Baron Keyes, stories
5:15			Big Brother	
5:30	Talk			
5:45	Jack Baldwin, piano	The Columbia Program		Stock Market Reports
6pm	Wedgewood Nowell, songs	Peggy Hamilton, fashion	Spanish Ensemble	Fireside Revelry
6:15				Hollywood Hams
6:30	The Happy Wonder Bakers	Pianoville	Lucie Lee, organ	Cotten Pickers Orchestra
6:45				
7pm	Westinghouse Salute	Jo and Vi	Frank Watanabe and Honorable Archie	Music
7:15		Paramount Symphony Orchestra	The Paramount Publix Hour	
7:30	Lucky Strike Dance Orchestra			
7:45				
8pm	Ron and Don, Two Pianos	The John Manville Fire Fighters	The Arizona Wranglers	The Violet Ray Music Box
8:15	The Yellow Caballeros	Song Parade		
8:30	Amos 'n' Andy			Music
8:45	The Sperry Smiles	What's Wrong with This Picture		
9pm	Florsheim Frolics		Hap and Sap	Songs
9:15		Song Symphonettes		The Emperor of Crime
9:30	Memory Lane	The KFRC Fashion Parade	Classic Song Recital	Music
9:45		The West Coast Theater		
10pm	Music	The Ten o'Clock Wire	Gus Arnheim Orchestra	Organ Recital
10:15		Earl Burtnett Orchestra		
10:30	News			
10:45	Health Talk			

EVENING — WINTER, 1930

Wednesday

BLUE	CBS	KNX	NBC	
Bob and Jimmy, songs (4:45 PM)	Records	Travelogue	Baron Keyes, stories	5pm
		Big Brother		5:15
Piano Recital				5:30
Reginald Ellis			Stock Market Reports	5:45
Los Angeles Fire Department Orchestra	Gold Medal Fast Freight	Lucie Lee, organ	The Halsey Stuart Concert	6pm
		Frank Watanabe and Honorable Archie		6:15
	Virginia and Andy, songs	The Hollywood Pantages Theater	The Palmolive Hour	6:30
				6:45
Noreen Gamill, drama	Music	Music		7pm
				7:15
The Coca-Cola Hour		Mr. and Mrs.	The Schoenberger Trio	7:30
				7:45
Music	George Olsen, gossip	Bert Butterworth, stories	Jack and Ethel, songs	8pm
				8:15
Amos 'n' Andy	The MJB Demi-Tasse Revue	KNX Little Symphony Orchestra	Music	8:30
Jack and Jill			The Popcorn Review	8:45
Nick Harris	The Ascot Auto Races	The Serenaders and Drury Lane	Songs	9pm
			The Emperor of Crime	9:15
The Camel Pleasure Hour			Music	9:30
				9:45
	The Ten o'Clock Wire	Gus Arnheim Orchestra		10pm
	Earl Burtnett Orchestra			10:15
News			Songs	10:30
Health Talk				10:45

EVENING — WINTER, 1930

Thursday

	BLUE	CBS	KNX	NBC
5pm	The Fleischman Yeast Hour, Rudy Vallee	Organ Recitial	Organ Recital (4:00pm)	Baron Keyes, stories
5:15			Big Brother	
5:30				Songs
5:45		Wesley Tourtellote, songs		Stock Market Reports
6pm	The Arco Birthday Party		Jesse Crawford, organ	Nick Harris
6:15		Piano Instruction	Frank Watanabe and Honorable Archie	
6:30	The Maxwell House Concerts	Raymond Paige Orchestra	Theo K. Hay, songs	The Purcell Mayer Trio
6:45				Arthur Lang, songs
7pm	Winnie Fields Moore, songs	The Lutheran Hour	Dr. Baumgarten, astrology	The RCA Victor Hour
7:15				
7:30		The KFRC Opera	The Blunt Familiy	The Standard Symphony Hour
7:45				
8pm	Hollywood Hams	The Violet Ray Music Box	Songs	
8:15	Oscar Ploetz, songs			
8:30	Amos 'n' Andy	Raymond Paige Orchestra	The Arizona Wrangler	Music
8:45	The Sperry Smiles			
9pm	Lucky Strike Dance Orchestra	Folgeria	Songs	Songs
9:15				The Emperor of Crime
9:30		Sports of the Air	The Lubovsiki Trio	Packard Orchestra
9:45				
10pm	Harold Spaulding, songs	The Ten o'Clock Wire	Gus Arnheim Orchestra	
10:15		Earl Burtnett Orchestra		
10:30	News			The KFI Symphonette
10:45	Health Talk			

EVENING — WINTER, 1930

Friday

BLUE	CBS	KNX	NBC	
The Cities Service Concerts	The KFRC Dance Band	Records (4:00PM)	Baron Keyes, stories	5pm
		Big Brother		5:15
			Garden Talk	5:30
			Stock Market Reports	5:45
The RKO Revue	Sport-O-Log	KNX Little Symphony Orchestra	The Interwoven Pair	6pm
	Songs	Frank Watanabe and Honorable Archie		6:15
Eva Olivotti, songs	Andy and Virginia, songs	The Lubovsiki Trio	Armour Orchestra	6:30
				6:45
Manny Stein Orchestra	Radio Follies	Country Jane, songs	Armstrong Quakers Orchestra	7pm
				7:15
	Songs of a Decade		The RKO Theater	7:30
		Phoenix Hosiery		7:45
The Elgin Program	Nights in the Old World	The Optimistic Do-Nuts	Ray West Orchestra	8pm
Oscar Ploetz, songs			Brown-bilt Footlites	8:15
Amos 'n' Andy	Raymond Paige Orchestra		Music	8:30
Jack and Jill			The Rounders	8:45
The KECA String Ensemble	Henry Cantor Orchestra	The Lion Tamers		9pm
			The Emperor of Crime	9:15
Modern Melodies	Public Affairs		Music	9:30
		The Hollywood Legion Fight		9:45
The KECA String Ensemble	The Ten o'Clock Wire			10pm
	Earl Burtnett Orchestra			10:15
News			Bob and Jimmy, songs	10:30
Health Talk		Gus Arnheim Orchesra		10:45

EVENING — WINTER, 1930

Saturday

	BLUE	CBS	KNX	NBC
5pm	Haven Johnson, songs	News	Travelogue	Sports (2:00 PM)
5:15	Ynez Allen, violin	The Columbia Male Chorus	Records	Football Gossip
5:30	The Fuller Brush Man	Studio Program		Piano Recital
5:45				Stock Market Reports
6pm	Music	Sports	Public Affairs	General Electric Orchestra
6:15			Frank Watanabe and Honorable Archie	
6:30			Lucie Lee, organ	
6:45				
7pm	The Song and String Trio		The Lubovsiki Trio	Lucky Strike Dance Orchestra
7:15				
7:30			The Arizona Wranglers	
7:45				
8pm	Rainbow Harmonies	The Jonathan Chorus	The KNX Night Club	The Gilmore Circus
8:15				
8:30	Amos 'n' Andy	Raymond Paige Orchestra		
8:45	The Sperry Smiles			
9pm	Virginia Fiohri, songs	The Show Shop		George Leibling, piano
9:15	The KECA String Ensemble			
9:30		White's Night Club		Pyror Moore Orchestra
9:45			One-Act Playlet	
10pm	Gordon Berger, songs	The Ten o'Clock Wire	Gus Arnheim Orchestra	
10:15		Earl Burtnett Orchestra		
10:30				The Associated Spotlight Review
10:45				

DAYTIME — WINTER, 1930

Sunday

	BLUE	CBS	KNX	NBC
8am	(Off the Air)	Records	(Off the Air)	(Off the Air)
8:15				
8:30		Come Into the Garden		The Breakfast Frolic
8:45				
9am		Home, Sweet Home	Records and Studio Music	
9:15				
9:30				
9:45	The Schonberger Trio			Everton Stidham, songs
10am				Los Angeles Church Federation Services
10:15				
10:30				
10:45				
11am	Third Church of Christian Science	First Methodist Church of Los Angeles	First Presbyterian Church of Hollywood	Temple Baptist Church
11:15				
11:30				
11:45				
12pm				Helen Guest, songs
12:15		New York Philharmonic Orchestra		
12:30			Louise Johnson, astrology	Temple of the Golden Hour
12:45				
1pm			The IBSA Watchtower	
1:15				
1:30				Sylvia's Happy Hour
1:45				

DAYTIME — WINTER, 1930

Monday-Friday

BLUE	CBS	KNX	NBC	
(Off the Air)	Hallelujah	Prayer, Records, and Talk	The Shell Happy Time Hour	8am
				8:15
Exercises				8:30
				8:45
The Vermont Lumberjacks	Talk and Music		Music / Beauty Talk	9am
			Music	9:15
Music	Feminine Fancies			9:30
				9:45
		Be Young and Happy, Eddie Albright	Stock Market Reports	10am
			The Heinz Program	10:15
	Music		Talk and Music / Woman's Magazine of the Air	10:30
				10:45
		Music	Music / The Standard School Broadcast	11am
				11:15
Music / California Federation of Women's Clubs	Music / American School of the Air	Talk and Music / Dr. Matthews' Radio Church		11:30
			Language Lesson	11:45
		Music	Stock Market Reports	12pm
			Music	12:15
	Biltmore Concert Orchestra			12:30
		Records		12:45
	The Ballad Hour			1pm
				1:15
	The Times Forum	The Bookworm		1:30
				1:45

DAYTIME — WINTER, 1930

Sunday

	BLUE	CBS	KNX	NBC
2pm		The Rose Hills Concert	The Park Board Program	
2:15				
2:30				
2:45				
3pm	The Catholic Hour	The KFRC Studio Program		Old Lamps for New
3:15				
3:30				Alexander Reilly, organ
3:45				
4pm	The Three Skippers	Public Affairs	Records	
4:15				
4:30	Piano Recital		Dr. Matthews' Radio Church	Advanced Thought
4:45				

DAYTIME — WINTER, 1930

Monday-Friday

BLUE	CBS	KNX	NBC	
Music	The Happy Go Lucky Hour	Music / The Jingle Man	Talk and Music	*2pm*
				2:15
		Music	Music / Winnie Fields Moore, songs	*2:30*
				2:45
US Agricultural Talk	Talk and Music		Talk and Music / Sylvia's Happy Hour	*3pm*
Music				*3:15*
		Music / The Hollywood Civic Theater	Music	*3:30*
				3:45
Music / The Melody Man		Music		*4pm*
Talk and Music / Sing a Song of Safety Club			News	*4:15*
The Quaker Man, Phil Cook			Big Brother	*4:30*
Talk and Music	News			*4:45*

DAYTIME — WINTER, 1930

Saturday

	BLUE	CBS	KNX	NBC
8am	(Off the Air)	The New York Philharmonic Children's Concert	Prayer, Records, and Talk	The Shell Happy Time Hour
8:15				
8:30	Exercises			
8:45				
9am	The Vermont Lumberjacks	The Adventures of Helen and Mary	The Arizona Wranglers	Beauty Talk
9:15	Ballads			Stock Market Reports
9:30		Feminine Fancies		The National Farm and Home Hour
9:45				
10am		Cheer Up and Smile		
10:15				
10:30		Sports	The Jingle Man	Woman's Magazine of the Air
10:45				The Three Coeds
11am	Sports		Be Young and Happy, Eddie Albright	
11:15				
11:30				Ballads
11:45				Spanish Lesson
12pm			Records	Stock Market Reports
12:15				
12:30				
12:45				
1pm		Manhattan Towers	Dr. Matthews' Radio Church	
1:15				
1:30		The Times Forum	Be Young and Happy, Eddie Albright	Sports
1:45				

DAYTIME — WINTER, 1930

Saturday

	BLUE	CBS	KNX	NBC
2pm		Sports		
2:15				
2:30			Sports	
2:45				
3pm	US Agricultural Talk			
3:15	Piano and Song Duo			
3:30	The Paramount Trio			
3:45				
4pm	Diversified Melodies			
4:15				
4:30	The Sunny Four Quartet			
4:45				

EVENING — SPRING, 1930

Sunday

	BLUE	CBS	KNX	NBC
5pm	Disc Duo (4:30PM)	Rabbi Magnin, religion (4:30PM)	Dr. Matthews' Radio Church	Leila Castberg, songs (4:30PM)
5:15		Tea Time for Three		The Collier Hour
5:30	Norcei Gamill, stories	Around the Samovar		
5:45				
6pm	The Rhythm Kings	The Majestic Theater Hour	Ernest Holmes: Theodore C. Abel	
6:15				The Atwater-Kent Hour
6:30				
6:45				
7pm	Margaret Kernan, songs	The Will Rogers Program	Scriptural Research	
7:15				The Studebaker Champions
7:30	Campus Orchestra	The KHJ Concert	Music	
7:45				Modest Altshuler Orchestra
8pm	Grace Hamilton and Jack Stern, songs		The First Presbyterian Church of Hollywood	
8:15				
8:30	The Capitol B's Trio	Dance Orchestra		
8:45				Maurine Dyer, songs
9pm	The KECA String Ensemble	Val Valenti Orchestra	The Lubovsiki Trio	The Borden Milk Program
9:15				
9:30				Violin Recital
9:45				
10pm	Gay Classics	The Ten o'Clock Wire		Music
10:15		Val Valenti Orchestra		
10:30			Dance Marathon	
10:45				

EVENING — SPRING, 1930

Monday

BLUE	CBS	KNX	NBC	
Ballads	Charlie Wellman, songs	Travelogue	Baron Keyes, stories	5pm
		Big Brother		5:15
	Don Lee Symphony Orchestra			5:30
				5:45
Ted Fio Rito Orchestra		Lucie Lee, organ	Hawaiian Trio	6pm
				6:15
	Charles Hamp, organ	KNX Little Symphony Orchestra	The Family Party	6:30
				6:45
	The Inglewood Park Concert		Rochester Civic Orchestra	7pm
				7:15
Spanish Music	Concert Classics	One-Act Playlet	The Empire Builders	7:30
				7:45
William Don, stories	The Blue Monday Jamboree	The Lubovsiki Trio	Light Classics	8pm
				8:15
Amos 'n' Andy				8:30
Music				8:45
The KECA String Ensemble		Piano Twins	The Voice of Firestone	9pm
				9:15
		The Radio Detective	The Cigar Band	9:30
				9:45
Ray West Orchestra	The Ten o'Clock Wire		Songs	10pm
	Anson Weeks Orchestra	Johnny Hamp's Kentucky Serenaders		10:15
			Max Fisher Orchestra	10:30
				10:45

EVENING — SPRING, 1930

Tuesday

	BLUE	CBS	KNX	NBC
5pm	Carmen Ray, songs (4:00 PM)	Charlie Wellman, songs	Travelogue	Baron Keyes, stories
5:15			Big Brother	
5:30	Around the World	Sunset Ensemble		
5:45				Stock Market Reports
6pm	Dance Orchestra	The Old Gold Hour	Lucie Lee, organ	The Eveready Hour
6:15				
6:30	The Happy Wonder Bakers		KNX Little Symphony Orchestra	Bob and Monte, songs
6:45				
7pm	Westinghouse Salute	Mr. and Mrs.	Dr. Baumgardten, health	Arthur Lang, songs
7:15				
7:30	The RKO Hour	Musical Memories	The Old Cedar Chest	Ray West Orchestra
7:45				
8pm		The Ice Carnival	Hap and Sap	Grand Opera
8:15				
8:30	Amos 'n' Andy	Music	Piano Twins	Packard Orchestra
8:45	Anna and Oscar, songs			
9pm	Florsheim Frolics	Don Lee Symphony Orchestra	The Adventurers	Grand Opera
9:15				
9:30	Nick Harris	Ballad Crooners	Glenn and Gene, the Harmony Boys	
9:45				
10pm	Ray West Orchestra	The Ten o'Clock Wire	Johnny Hamp's Kentucky Serenaders	
10:15	Literary Digest	Earl Burtnett Orchestra		
10:30				Max Fisher Orchestra
10:45				

EVENING — SPRING, 1930

Wednesday

BLUE	CBS	KNX	NBC	
Ballads	Charlie Wellman, songs	Travelogue	Baron Keyes, stories	5pm
		Big Brother		5:15
				5:30
			Stock Market Reports	5:45
Dance Orchestra	Peggy Hamilton, fashions	Lucie Lee, organ	The Halsey Stuart Concert	6pm
				6:15
	Charlie Hamp, organ	The Musical Calingas Family	The Palmolive Hour	6:30
				6:45
	Don Lee Symphony Orchestra	The Lubovsiki Trio		7pm
				7:15
The Coca-Cola Hour		Radio Skit	Ray West Orchestra	7:30
	Male Quartet			7:45
The Happy Chappies	Romantic California	Bert Butterworth, stories	Jack and Ethel, songs	8pm
				8:15
Amos 'n' Andy	Studio Program	KNX Little Symphony Orchestra	The Three Skippers	8:30
Travelogue			The Sunkist Serenaders	8:45
The Three Skippers		Gold Medal Fast Freight		9pm
			Packard Orchestra	9:15
	Paramount Previews	Musical Suggestions		9:30
				9:45
Literary Digest	The Ten o'Clock Wire	Johnny Hamp's Kentucky Serenaders		10pm
Ray West Orchestra	Earl Burtnett Orchestra		Piano Recital	10:15
			Max Fisher Orchestra	10:30
				10:45

EVENING — SPRING, 1930

Thursday

	BLUE	CBS	KNX	NBC
5pm	The Fleischman Yeast Hour, Rudy Vallee	News and Views (4:45 PM)	Travelogue	Baron Keyes, stories
5:15			Big Brother	
5:30				
5:45		Frederick William Wile, news		Stock Market Reports
6pm	The Arco Birthday Party	Charlie Wellman, organ	Country Jane, songs	Songs
6:15				
6:30	The Maxwell House Concerts	Elvia Allman, songs		Nick Harris
6:45				
7pm		The Forest Lawn Concert	KNX Little Symphony Orchestra	The RCA Victor Hour
7:15				
7:30	Organ Recital		Lute Duets	The Standard Symphony Hour
7:45				
8pm		The Merry Makers	The Lubovsiki Trio	
8:15				
8:30	Amos 'n' Andy			Arthur Lang, songs
8:45	The Happy Chappies			
9pm	Memory Lane	Kodak Orchestra		Ray West Orchestra
9:15			The Musical Musketeers	
9:30	Eddie Armstrong, songs	Mood Pictures		Packard Orchestra
9:45				
10pm	Literary Digest	The Ten o'Clock Wire	Johnny Hamp's Kentucky Serenaders	
10:15	Ray West Orchestra	Earl Burtnett Orchestra		
10:30				Max Fisher Orchestra
10:45				

EVENING — SPRING, 1930

Friday

BLUE	CBS	KNX	NBC	
The Cities Service Concerts	News and Views (4:45 PM)	Musical Program (4:00 PM)	Baron Keyes, stories	5pm
		Big Brother		5:15
	Viennese Quartet			5:30
			Stock Market Reports	5:45
Buster Wilson Orchestra	Tropical Inn	Lucie Lee, organ	The Interwovan Pair	6pm
				6:15
Molly Wilbur, songs	Charlie Hamp, organ	KNX Little Symphony Orchestra	Armour Orchestra	6:30
				6:45
Six Clouds of Joy	Sign of the Green and White	Country Jane, songs	Armstrong Quakers Orchestra	7pm
				7:15
The Raleigh Revue	Don Lee Symphony Orchestra		The Schonberger Trio	7:30
				7:45
The Hamilton Sketchbook	Vaudeville	The Optimistic Do-Nuts	Ray West Orchestra	8pm
Bridge Lesson				8:15
Amos 'n' Andy	The History of Sacramento		Mart and Lill, songs	8:30
Anne and Oscar, songs			Tone Pictures	8:45
	Mary and Bob's True Story Hour	The Lion Tamers	The Three Coeds	9pm
Kodak Orchestra			Studio Program	9:15
				9:30
Winifred Donaldson, songs		The Hollywood Legion Fight		9:45
LIterary Digest	The Ten o'Clock Wire		Russian Quartet	10pm
Ray West Orchestra	Earl Burtnett Orchestra			10:15
			Max Fisher Orchestra	10:30
				10:45

EVENING — SPRING, 1930

Saturday

	BLUE	CBS	KNX	NBC
5pm	Around the World	Exploring the Jungle for Science	Travelogue	Two Shades of Blue
5:15				
5:30		Dixie Echoes		Hollywood Gossip
5:45				
6pm	Los Angeles Fire Department Orchestra	Hank Simmons' Show Boat	Lucie Lee, organ	General Electric Orchestra
6:15				
6:30				
6:45			The KNX String Ensemble	
7pm	Jack Parker, songs	Paramount Symphony Orchestra	The Paramount Publix Hour	Lucky Strike Dance Orchestra
7:15				
7:30	Music			
7:45				
8pm	Helen Guest, songs	Dance Orchestra	The Musical Comedy Hour	The Gilmore Circus
8:15				
8:30	Amos 'n' Andy	Night Carnival		
8:45	Songs			
9pm	The KECA String Ensemble		Lucie Lee, organ	
9:15				
9:30				Mixed Quartet
9:45				
10pm	Literary Digest	The Ten o'Clock Wire	Johnny Hamp's Kentucky Serenaders	
10:15	Ray West's Cafe	Earl Burtnett Orchestra		
10:30				Max Fisher Orchestra
10:45				

DAYTIME — SPRING, 1930

Sunday

	BLUE	CBS	KNX	NBC
8am	(Off the Air)	Records	Hollywood Bowl Church Services	Mount Davidson Church Services
8:15				
8:30				
8:45				
9am		Home, Sweet Home		
9:15				
9:30		Naval Parley	Records and Studio Music	
9:45				
10am				Los Angeles Church Federation Services
10:15				
10:30				
10:45				
11am		First Methodist Church of Los Angeles	First Presbyterian Church of Hollywood	Temple Baptist Church
11:15				
11:30				
11:45				
12pm				Violin Melodies
12:15				
12:30		The Conclave of Nations	Louise Johnson, astrology	Temple of the Golden Hour
12:45				
1pm		Music	The IBSA Watchtower	
1:15				
1:30				Sylvia's Happy Hour
1:45				

DAYTIME — SPRING, 1930

Monday-Friday

BLUE	CBS	KNX	NBC	
(Off the Air)	Music	Prayer, Records, and Talk	The Shell Happy Time Hour	*8am*
				8:15
				8:30
				8:45
			Talk and Music	*9am*
				9:15
	Feminine Fancies			*9:30*
				9:45
		Be Young and Happy, Eddie Albright		*10am*
				10:15
	Records		Talk and Music / Woman's Magazine of the Air	*10:30*
				10:45
	Charlie Hamp, organ	Talk and Music		*11am*
				11:15
Musical Memories	Music / American School of the Air	Music / Dr. Matthews' Radio Church		*11:30*
Home of the Canny Cook			Language Lesson	*11:45*
	Biltmore Concert Orchestra	Music / The Sackett Trio	US Agricultural Talk	*12pm*
				12:15
	News			*12:30*
	Talk and Music			*12:45*
				1pm
				1:15
		The Bookworm		*1:30*
				1:45

DAYTIME — SPRING, 1930

Sunday

	BLUE	CBS	KNX	NBC
2pm		News Reel of the Air		
2:15				
2:30		Charles Lindsay, songs	The Park Board Program	
2:45				
3pm	The Catholic Hour	The Cathedral Hour		The Salvation Army Band
3:15				
3:30				
3:45				
4pm	Claire Dudley, songs	The Globetrotters	Dr. Matthews' Radio Church	The Science of Life
4:15				
4:30	Disc Duo	Rabbi Magnin, religion		Leila Castberg, songs
4:45				

DAYTIME — SPRING, 1930

Monday-Friday

BLUE	CBS	KNX	NBC	
Music	The Happy Go Lucky Hour	Studio Orchestra	Talk and Music	*2pm*
				2:15
	Talk and Music		Music / Pacific School of the Air	*2:30*
				2:45
Music / Jerome Powers, piano			Talk and Music	*3pm*
				3:15
Music				*3:30*
Music / California Federation of Women's Clubs				*3:45*
Music / The Sing-A-Song of Safety Club			Music / Mothers' Legion of the Air	*4pm*
			News	*4:15*
Music / Back of the News in Washington			Big Brother	*4:30*
				4:45

DAYTIME — SPRING, 1930

Saturday

	BLUE	CBS	KNX	NBC
8am	(Off the Air)	The US Army Band	Prayer, Records, and Talk	The Shell Happy Time Hour
8:15				
8:30				
8:45				
9am		The Adventures of Helen and Mary		
9:15				Spanish Lesson
9:30		Victor Young Orchestra		
9:45				The National Farm and Home Hour
10am		Harry Tucker Orchestra	Be Young and Happy, Eddie Albright	
10:15				
10:30				Woman's Magazine of the Air
10:45				
11am		Ann Leaf at the Organ	KNX Little Symphony Orchestra	
11:15				
11:30		The Dominion Male Quartet		
11:45				French Lesson
12pm		Bilmore Concert Orchestra	Guitar and Songs	Stock Market Reports
12:15				
12:30		The Manilus School Band		
12:45				
1pm		The Times Forum		
1:15				
1:30		Peggy Hamilton, fashion	Be Young and Happy, Eddie Albright	
1:45				

DAYTIME — SPRING, 1930

Saturday

	BLUE	CBS	KNX	NBC
2pm		Music		
2:15				Alma and Adele, songs
2:30			Music	
2:45				Songs
3pm	Ray West's Cafe			
3:15				The Masked Minstrels
3:30		Ted Husing's Sportslants		
3:45				
4pm	Paul McNally, guitar	Music		Music
4:15				
4:30	The Fuller Brush Man			
4:45		News		

EVENING — SUMMER, 1930

Sunday

	BLUE	CBS	KNX	NBC
5pm	Manny Hall, psychology	The Majestic Theater Hour	Dr. Matthews' Radio Church (4:30PM)	Sacred Songs
5:15				The Atwater-Kent Hour
5:30	Unity Talk		Scriptural Research	
5:45	Mamie Stark, songs			
6pm	Ray West's Cafe	Mayhew Lake Orchestra	Ernest Holmes: Theodore C. Abel	
6:15				The Studebaker Champions
6:30		Around the Samovar		
6:45				Los Cabelleros Orchestra
7pm	Margaret Kernan, songs	The Back Home Hour	Horsefly and His Wranglers	
7:15	Noreen Gamill, drama			Purcell Mayer, violin
7:30		Professor Lindsay, readings		
7:45	The KECA String Ensemble			Songs
8pm	Enna Jettick Melodies	Music	The First Presbyterian Church of Hollywood	
8:15	The KECA String Ensemble			The Sarah Padden Players
8:30				
8:45				
9pm	The KECA Symphonette	Fifty-Five Piece Orchestra	The Lubovsiki Trio	The Borden Milk Program
9:15				
9:30				Jane Green, songs
9:45				
10pm	Gay Classics	The Ten o'Clock Wire	Music	Cliff Perrins Orchestra
10:15		Val Valenti Orchestra		
10:30				
10:45				

EVENING — SUMMER, 1930

Monday-Friday

BLUE	CBS	KNX	NBC	
Music	The KFRC Concert	Travelogue	Baron Keyes, stories	5pm
		Big Brothers		5:15
The Family Party	Records			5:30
			Stock Market Reports	5:45
Dance Orchestra	Don Lee Symphony Orchestra	Lucie Lee, organ	Stromberg-Carlson Orchestra	6pm
				6:15
	Jesse Crawford, organ	Music	Piano Recital	6:30
				6:45
	The Inglewood Park Concert	Under the Make-Up	Governor Young, comment	7pm
				7:15
Amos 'n' Andy	Mayor Rolph, comment	Music	Swedish Sketches	7:30
Jack and Jill, songs			Senator Tubbs, comment	7:45
The Cotton Blossom Minstrels	The Blue Monday Jamboree	One-Act Playlet	Sign of the Shell	8pm
				8:15
		The Luvoski Trio		8:30
				8:45
Ray Van Dyne Orchestra		Piano Twins	The A&P Gypsies	9pm
				9:15
			Mildred Laughlin, songs	9:30
				9:45
Songs	The Ten o'Clock Wire	Gus Arnheim Orchestra	Music	10pm
	Anson Weeks Orchestra			10:15
Exercises				10:30
				10:45

EVENING — SUMMER, 1930

Tuesday

	BLUE	CBS	KNX	NBC
5pm	Songs	Music	Travelogue	Baron Keyes, stories
5:15			Big Brother	
5:30	The Happy Wonder Bakers			
5:45				Stock Market Reports
6pm	Westinghouse Salute	Mr. and Mrs.	Hungarian Ensemble	Songs
6:15				Anna and Oscar, songs
6:30	The RKO Hour	Grand Opera	Lucie Lee, organ	Cotton Pickers Orchestra
6:45				
7pm	Moments Inpromptu	Broadway Melodies	Dr. Baumgarten, astrology	
7:15	The Happy Chappies			
7:30	Amos 'n' Andy	Fred Waring Orchestra	Music	
7:45	The Sperry Sweetheart			
8pm	The Royal Hildalgos	The Raymond Paige Feature	Horsefly and His Wranglers	
8:15				
8:30	Nick Harris	The Women's Forum	KNX Little Symphony Orchestra	Music
8:45				
9pm	Ray Van Dyne Orchestra		The Royal Vagabonds	The Happy Chappies
9:15				
9:30		One-Act Playlet	The Radio Detective	
9:45				
10pm	Songs	The Ten o'Clock Wire	Gus Arnheim Orchestra	The Aeolian Organ Recital
10:15		Earl Burtnett Orchestra		
10:30	Exercises			
10:45				

EVENING — SUMMER, 1930

Wednesday

BLUE	CBS	KNX	NBC	
The Halsey Stuart Concert	Philco Concert Orchestra	Travelogue	Baron Keyes, stories	*5pm*
		Big Brother		*5:15*
The Palmolive Hour				*5:30*
			Stock Market Reports	*5:45*
	Peggy Hamilton, fashions	Lucie Lee, organ	Nick Harris	*6pm*
				6:15
The Coca-Cola Hour	Professor Lindsey, readings	The Lyric Trio	The Sierra Male Quartet	*6:30*
				6:45
Noreen Gammill, drama	Music	Radio Skit	Tom Terris: Vagabond Adventures	*7pm*
Otto Ploetz, dialects				*7:15*
Amos 'n' Andy	California Melodies	Cycle of Song	Music	*7:30*
Jack and Jill, songs			Governor Young, comment	*7:45*
Parisian Quintet	Romantic California	Music	Jack and Ethel, songs	*8pm*
				8:15
Will Round String Ensemble	The MJB Demi-Tasse Revue		Purcell Mayer, violin	*8:30*
The Nomad Novelist				*8:45*
The KECA String Symphony	Mood Pictures		Eva Olivetti, songs	*9pm*
				9:15
The Camel Pleasure Hour	White's Night Club			*9:30*
				9:45
Songs	The Ten o'Clock Wire	Gus Arnheim Orchestra		*10pm*
	Earl Burtnett Orchestra			*10:15*
Exercises				*10:30*
				10:45

EVENING — SUMMER, 1930

Thursday

	BLUE	CBS	KNX	NBC
5pm	The Arco Birthday Party	The KFRC Organ	Travelogue	Baron Keyes, stories
5:15			Big Brother	
5:30	Jack Frost Melody Moments	Arabesque		
5:45				Stock Market Reports
6pm	The Maxwell House Concerts	Dance Orchestra	Music	The RCA Victor Hour
6:15				
6:30	Songs	Pianoville		
6:45				
7pm	Wedgewood Nowell, songs	Music	Laf-O-Grafs	Speedway to Happiness
7:15	Vincent and Howard, songs	Heywood Broun, sports		
7:30	Amos 'n' Andy	Music	Music	Survey of World Conditions
7:45	The Happy Chappies			The Standard Symphony Hour
8pm	The Lucky Strike Hour	The Merry Makers	Horsefly and His Wranglers	
8:15				
8:30			KNX Little Symphony Orchestra	
8:45				Circumstantial Evidence
9pm	Memory Lane	Music	The Nomads	
9:15				The Three Skippers
9:30	Eddie Armstrong, songs		Music	Packard Orchestra
9:45				
10pm	Songs	The Ten o'Clock Wire	Gus Arnheim Orchestra	
10:15		Earl Burtnett Orchestra		
10:30	Exercises			The KFI Symphonette
10:45				

EVENING — SUMMER, 1930

Friday

BLUE	CBS	KNX	NBC	
The Interwoven Pair	Music	Travelogue	Baron Keyes, stories	5pm
		Big Brother		5:15
Armour Orchestra	Records		Garden Talk	5:30
			Stock Market Reports	5:45
Nick Harris	Music	KNX Little Symphony Orchestra	Armstrong Quakers Orchestra	6pm
				6:15
The Raleigh Revue	Gold Medal Fast Freight		The Slavick Trio	6:30
			Radio Interference	6:45
The Elgin Program	In Old Vienna	Country Jane, songs	Winifred Donaldson, songs	7pm
Otto Ploetz, dialects			Mayor Rolph, comment	7:15
Amos 'n' Andy	Wilbur Osbourne Orchestra		Songs	7:30
Jack and Jill, songs				7:45
The National Bridge Review	Vaudeville	The Optimistic Do-Nuts	Music	8pm
Arthur Blanco, songs				8:15
	Music		Songs	8:30
Anne and Oscar, songs			Walter O' Keefe, songs	8:45
Winifred Donaldson, songs		The Lion Tamers		9pm
Kodak Orchestra			The Three Coeds	9:15
	Organ Recital		Packard Orchestra	9:30
Piano Recital		The Hollywood Legion Fight		9:45
Songs	The Ten o'Clock Wire			10pm
	Earl Burtnett Orchestra			10:15
Exercises			Songs	10:30
		Coconut Grove Orchestra		10:45

EVENING — SUMMER, 1930

Saturday

	BLUE	CBS	KNX	NBC
5pm	The Melody Man	Hank Simmons' Show Boat	Travelogue	Hollywood Gossip
5:15	Ynez Allan, violin			
5:30	General Electric Orchestra		Records	Malvern Christie, songs
5:45				Stock Market Reports
6pm	Virginia Ballroom Orchestra	Paramount Symphony Orchestra	The Paramount Publix Hour	Lucky Strike Dance Orchestra
6:15				
6:30	Old Timer's Orchestra			
6:45				
7pm	Eddie Armstong, songs	Will Osborne Orchestra	The Lubovsiki Trio	The Musical Comedy Album
7:15				
7:30	Amos 'n' Andy	The KHJ Revue		
7:45	The Sperry Sweetheart			
8pm	The KECA String Ensemble	The Oil-O-Matics	Horsefly and His Wranglers	The Gilmore Circus
8:15				
8:30		Musical Cocktails	KNX Little Symphony Orchestra	The Hollywood Bowl Concert
8:45				
9pm	The Rainbow Harmonies	The Ascot Auto Races	The Musical Calangis Family	
9:15				
9:30	Will Round Orchestra			
9:45				
10pm	The Associated Spotlight Review	The Ten o'Clock Wire	Gus Arnheim Orchestra	
10:15		Earl Burtnett Orchestra		Violin Recital
10:30				Lou Gordon, songs
10:45				

DAYTIME — SUMMER, 1930

Sunday

	BLUE	CBS	KNX	NBC
8am	(Off the Air)	Records	(Off the Air)	(Off the Air)
8:15		Anthony Euwer, songs		
8:30		Pubilc Affairs		
8:45				
9am		Home, Sweet Home	Records	
9:15				
9:30				
9:45				
10am				Personal Experiences in India
10:15				Grace Mead, songs
10:30			Musicale	Temple Baptist Church
10:45				
11am	Third Church of Christian Science	First Methodist Church of Los Angeles	First Presbyterian Church of Hollywood	
11:15				
11:30				
11:45				
12pm				
12:15				
12:30		The Cathedral Hour	Louise Johnson, astrology	Helen Guest, songs
12:45				
1pm		The Gauchos	The IBSA Watchtower	Temple of the Golden Hour
1:15				
1:30		Whittier Memorial Park Concert		
1:45				

DAYTIME — SUMMER, 1930

Monday-Friday

BLUE	CBS	KNX	NBC	
(Off the Air)	Is He Right	Prayer, Records, and Talk	The Shell Happy Time Hour	*8am*
				8:15
	Stock Market Reports			*8:30*
	Manhattan Towers			*8:45*
				9am
				9:15
	Feminine Fancies		Beauty Talk	*9:30*
			Music	*9:45*
		Be Young and Happy, Eddie Albright	Stock Market Reports	*10am*
				10:15
			Woman's Magazine of the Air	*10:30*
	Agnes White, songs			*10:45*
	The Columbia Revue			*11am*
	Records	Music		*11:15*
			Talk	*11:30*
Musical Memories			Language Lesson	*11:45*
	Biltmore Concert Orchestra		Stock Market Reports	*12pm*
				12:15
	News		Talk	*12:30*
	Talk and Music			*12:45*
				1pm
				1:15
	The Times Forum	The Bookworm		*1:30*
				1:45

DAYTIME — SUMMER, 1930

Sunday

	BLUE	CBS	KNX	NBC
2pm	The Catholic Hour		The Park Board Program	Sylvia's Happy Hour
2:15				
2:30		The Globetrotters		
2:45				
3pm	The Trio Half-Hour	Collumbia Symphony Orchestra		
3:15				
3:30	Helen Lambert, piano	The Round Towners		Advanced Thought
3:45		Dr. Klein, health		
4pm	The Blue Boys	Jesse Crawford, organ	The Golden State Band	
4:15				The Happy Chappies
4:30			Dr. Matthews' Radio Church	
4:45		The KFRC Concert		

DAYTIME — SUMMER, 1930

Monday-Friday

BLUE	CBS	KNX	NBC	
Music	The Happy Go Lucky Hour	Records / The Jingle Man	Talk and Music	*2pm*
				2:15
		Talk and Music	Music / Winnie Fields Moore, songs	*2:30*
				2:45
		Music / Lucie Lee, organ	Talk and Music	*3pm*
Music / Sing a Song of Safety Club				*3:15*
The Quaker Man, Phil Cook	Talk and Music			*3:30*
The Melody Man				*3:45*
Music /	The Nit-Wit Hour /	Records		*4pm*
Half Hour in the Nation's Capitol /	Charlie Wellman, Songs		News	*4:15*
The Fleischman Yeast Hour, Rudy Vallee /			Big Brother	*4:30*
The Cities Service Concert	News			*4:45*

DAYTIME — SUMMER, 1930

Saturday

	BLUE	CBS	KNX	NBC
8am	(Off the Air)	Is He Right	Prayer, Records, and Talk	The Happy Chappies
8:15				Morning Melodies
8:30		Records		Log of the Day
8:45				
9am				
9:15				Stock Market Reports
9:30				
9:45				The National Farm and Home Hour
10am		Elvia Allman's Spelling Bee		
10:15				
10:30			The Jingle Man	Woman's Magazine of the Air
10:45				
11am				
11:15			Be Young and Happy, Eddie Albright	
11:30		Records		Hollywood Bowl Talk
11:45				
12pm		Bilmore Concert Orchestra	KNX Little Symphony Orchestra	Stock Market Reports
12:15				
12:30		News	The Silver Slipper Cafe'	
12:45		French Trio		
1pm		Peggy Hamilton, fashion	Dr. Matthews' Radio Church	
1:15				
1:30		Salvador Baquez, songs	Be Young and Happy, Eddie Albright	
1:45				

DAYTIME — SUMMER, 1930

Saturday

	BLUE	CBS	KNX	NBC
2pm		Tom, Dick and Harry, songs	Louise Lee, organ	
2:15				
2:30		Ted Husing's Sportslants	Opera	
2:45		The Couple Next Door		Kelly Alexander, songs
3pm		Melomaniacs		
3:15	Songs			The Masked Minstrels
3:30	The Fuller Brush Man			Annette Petite, songs
3:45				
4pm	Manny Stein Orchestra	Exploring the Jungle for Science		
4:15		Records		News
4:30				Don Abbott, songs
4:45		News		Gerturde Gusselle, songs

EVENING — FALL, 1930

Sunday

	BLUE	CBS	KNX	NBC
5pm	The Vagabonds Quartet	The World's Business	Dr. Matthews' Radio Church (4:30PM)	Enna Jettick Melodies
5:15				The Collier Hour
5:30		Rabbi Magnin, religion	Scriptural Research	
5:45				
6pm	The Three Sisters	The Majestic Theater Hour	Records	
6:15			Ernest Holmes: Theodore C. Abel	The Atwater-Kent Hour
6:30	Bob and Jimmy, songs	The KFRC Melody Hour		
6:45				
7pm	Noreen Gamill, drama	Virginia and Andy, songs	Music	
7:15	Margaret Kernan, songs			The Studebaker Champions
7:30	Ray Van Dyne Orchestra	Professor Lindsley and Walter Tourtellote	The Arizona Wranglers	
7:45				Frank Kneeland, songs
8pm		Music	The First Presbyterian Church of Hollywood	Evelyn Snow, songs
8:15				The Sarah Padden Players
8:30	The KECA Symphonette	The Old Scrap Book		
8:45				Purcel Mayer, violin
9pm		The Chevrolet Chronicles	The Lubovsiki Trio	The Borden Milk Program
9:15				
9:30	Enna Jettick Melodies	Val Valenti Orchestra		Songs
9:45	The Schonberger Trio			
10pm		The Ten o'Clock Wire		The Slumber Program
10:15		Val Valenti Orchestra		
10:30	Concert Jewels		The Hollywood Pantages Theater	Dance Orchestra
10:45				

EVENING — FALL, 1930

Monday

BLUE	CBS	KNX	NBC	
Half-Hour in the Nation's Capitol	Mac and His Gang	Travelogue	Baron Keyes, stories	5pm
		Big Brother		5:15
Piano Recital	Records			5:30
			Stock Market Reports	5:45
Maytag Orchestra		The KNX String Ensemble	Songs	6pm
	Sport-O-Log	Frank Watanabe and Honorable Archie		6:15
Piano Recital	An Evening in Paris	The Airizona Wranglers	The Family Party	6:30
				6:45
Songs	Guy Lombardo Orchestra		Stromberg-Carlson Orchestra	7pm
				7:15
The Empire Builders	Don Amalzo, songs	Don Amalzo, songs	Los Caballeros Orchestra	7:30
				7:45
Ballads	The Blue Monday Jamboree	Public Affairs	Sign of the Shell	8pm
				8:15
Amos 'n' Andy		One-Act Playlet		8:30
Music				8:45
Ray Van Dyne Orchestra		Piano Twins	Songs	9pm
			The Emperor of Crime	9:15
			The Memorial Park Concert	9:30
				9:45
Musical Echoes	The Ten o'Clock Wire			10pm
	Earl Burtnett Orchestra	Gus Arnheim Orchestra		10:15
News	Anson Weeks Orchestra		Music	10:30
Health Talk				10:45

EVENING — FALL, 1930

Tuesday

	BLUE	CBS	KNX	NBC
5pm	South American Melodies	Ted White and Mel Larsen, songs	Travelogue	Baron Keyes, stories
5:15			Big Brother	
5:30	Talk			
5:45	Jack Baldwin, piano	The Columbia Program		Stock Market Reports
6pm	Wedgewood Nowell, songs	Peggy Hamilton, fashion	Spanish Ensemble	Fireside Revelry
6:15				Hollywood Hams
6:30	The Happy Wonder Bakers	Pianoville	Lucie Lee, organ	Cotten Pickers Orchestra
6:45				
7pm	Westinghouse Salute	Jo and Vi	Frank Watanabe and Honorable Archie	Music
7:15		Paramount Symphony Orchestra	The Paramount Publix Hour	
7:30	Lucky Strike Dance Orchestra			
7:45				
8pm	Ron and Don, Two Pianos	The John Manville Fire Fighters	The Arizona Wranglers	The Violet Ray Music Box
8:15	The Yellow Caballeros	Song Parade		
8:30	Amos 'n' Andy			Music
8:45	The Sperry Smiles	What's Wrong with This Picture		
9pm	Florsheim Frolics		Hap and Sap	Songs
9:15		Song Symphonettes		The Emperor of Crime
9:30	Memory Lane	The KFRC Fashion Parade	Classic Song Recital	Music
9:45		The West Coast Theater		
10pm	Music	The Ten o'Clock Wire	Gus Arnheim Orchestra	Organ Recital
10:15		Earl Burtnett Orchestra		
10:30	News			
10:45	Health Talk			

EVENING — FALL, 1930

Wednesday

BLUE	CBS	KNX	NBC	
Bob and Jimmy. songs (4:45PM)	Records	Travelogue	Baron Keyes, stories	*5pm*
		Big Brother		*5:15*
Piano Recital				*5:30*
Reginald Ellis			Stock Market Reports	*5:45*
Los Angeles Fire Department Orchestra	Gold Medal Fast Freight	Lucie Lee, organ	The Halsey Stuart Concert	*6pm*
		Frank Watanabe and Honorable Archie		*6:15*
	Virginia and Andy, songs	The Hollywood Pantages Theater	The Palmolive Hour	*6:30*
				6:45
Noreen Gamill, drama	Music	Music		*7pm*
				7:15
The Coca-Cola Hour		Mr. and Mrs.	The Schoenberger Trio	*7:30*
				7:45
Music	George Olsen, gossip	Bert Butterworth, stories	Jack and Ethel, songs	*8pm*
				8:15
Amos 'n' Andy	The MJB Demi-Tasse Revue	KNX Little Symphony Orchestra	Music	*8:30*
Jack and Jill			The Popcorn Review	*8:45*
Nick Harris	The Ascot Auto Races	The Serenaders and Drury Lane	Songs	*9pm*
			The Emperor of Crime	*9:15*
The Camel Pleasure Hour			Music	*9:30*
				9:45
	The Ten o'Clock Wire	Gus Arnheim Orchestra		*10pm*
	Earl Burtnett Orchestra			*10:15*
News			Songs	*10:30*
Health Talk				*10:45*

EVENING — FALL, 1930

Thursday

	BLUE	CBS	KNX	NBC
5pm	The Fleischman Yeast Hour, Rudy Vallee	Organ Recital	Organ Recital (4:00 PM)	Baron Keyes, stories
5:15			Big Brother	
5:30				Songs
5:45		Wesley Tourtellote, songs		Stock Market Reports
6pm	The Arco Birthday Party		Jesse Crawford, organ	Nick Harris
6:15		Piano Instruction	Frank Watanabe and Honorable Archie	
6:30	The Maxwell House Concerts	Raymond Paige Orchestra	Theo K. Hay, songs	The Purcell Mayer Trio
6:45				Arthur Lang, songs
7pm	Winnie Fields Moore, songs	The Lutheran Hour	Dr. Baumgarten, astrology	The RCA Victor Hour
7:15				
7:30		The KFRC Opera	The Blunt Familiy	The Standard Symphony Hour
7:45				
8pm	Hollywood Hams	The Violet Ray Music Box	Songs	
8:15	Oscar Ploetz, songs			
8:30	Amos 'n' Andy	Raymond Paige Orchestra	The Arizona Wrangler	Music
8:45	The Sperry Smiles			
9pm	Lucky Strike Dance Orchestra	Folgeria	Songs	Songs
9:15				The Emperor of Crime
9:30		Sports of the Air	The Lubovsiki Trio	Packard Orchestra
9:45				
10pm	Harold Spaulding, songs	The Ten o'Clock Wire	Gus Arnheim Orchestra	
10:15		Earl Burtnett Orchestra		
10:30	News			The KFI Symphonette
10:45	Health Talk			

EVENING — FALL, 1930

Friday

BLUE	CBS	KNX	NBC	
The Cities Service Concerts	The KFRC Dance Band	Records (4:00PM)	Baron Keyes, stories	5pm
		Big Brother		5:15
			Garden Talk	5:30
			Stock Market Reports	5:45
The RKO Revue	Sport-O-Log	KNX Little Symphony Orchestra	The Interwoven Pair	6pm
	Songs	Frank Watanabe and Honorable Archie		6:15
Eva Olivotti, songs	Andy and Virginia, songs	The Lubovsiki Trio	Armour Orchestra	6:30
				6:45
Manny Stein Orchestra	Radio Follies	Country Jane, songs	Armstrong Quakers Orchestra	7pm
				7:15
	Songs of a Decade		The RKO Theater	7:30
		Phoenix Hosiery		7:45
The Elgin Program	Nights in the Old World	The Optimistic Do-Nuts	Ray West Orchestra	8pm
Oscar Ploetz, songs			Brown-bilt Footlites	8:15
Amos 'n' Andy	Raymond Paige Orchestra		Music	8:30
Jack and Jill			The Rounders	8:45
The KECA String Ensemble	Henry Cantor Orchestra	The Lion Tamers		9pm
			The Emperor of Crime	9:15
Modern Melodies	Public Affairs		Music	9:30
		The Hollywood Legion Fight		9:45
The KECA String Ensemble	The Ten o'Clock Wire			10pm
	Earl Burtnett Orchestra			10:15
News			Bob and Jimmy, songs	10:30
Health Talk		Gus Arnheim Orchesra		10:45

EVENING — FALL, 1930

Saturday

	BLUE	CBS	KNX	NBC
5pm	Haven Johnson, songs	News	Travelogue	Sports (2:00PM)
5:15	Ynez Allen, violin	The Columbia Male Chorus	Records	Football Gossip
5:30	The Fuller Brush Man	Studio Program		Piano Recital
5:45				Stock Market Reports
6pm	Music	Sports	Public Affairs	General Electric Orchestra
6:15			Frank Watanabe and Honorable Archie	
6:30			Lucie Lee, organ	
6:45				
7pm	The Song and String Trio		The Lubovsiki Trio	Lucky Strike Dance Orchestra
7:15				
7:30			The Arizona Wranglers	
7:45				
8pm	Rainbow Harmonies	The Jonathan Chorus	The KNX Night Club	The Gilmore Circus
8:15				
8:30	Amos 'n' Andy	Raymond Paige Orchestra		
8:45	The Sperry Smiles			
9pm	Virginia Fiohri, songs	The Show Shop		George Leibling, piano
9:15	The KECA String Ensemble			
9:30		White's Night Club		Pyror Moore Orchestra
9:45			One-Act Playlet	
10pm	Gordon Berger, songs	The Ten o'Clock Wire	Gus Arnheim Orchestra	
10:15		Earl Burtnett Orchestra		
10:30				The Associated Spotlight Review
10:45				

DAYTIME — FALL, 1930

Sunday

	BLUE	CBS	KNX	NBC
8am	(Off the Air)	Records	(Off the Air)	(Off the Air)
8:15				
8:30		Come Into the Garden		The Breakfast Frolic
8:45				
9am		Home, Sweet Home	Records and Studio Music	
9:15				
9:30				
9:45	The Schonberger Trio			Everton Stidham, songs
10am				Los Angeles Church Federation Services
10:15				
10:30				
10:45				
11am	Third Church of Christian Science	First Methodist Church of Los Angeles	First Presbyterian Church of Hollywood	Temple Baptist Church
11:15				
11:30				
11:45				
12pm				Helen Guest, songs
12:15		New York Philharmonic Orchestra		
12:30			Louise Johnson, astrology	Temple of the Golden Hour
12:45				
1pm			The IBSA Watchtower	
1:15				
1:30				Sylvia's Happy Hour
1:45				

DAYTIME — FALL, 1930

Monday-Friday

BLUE	CBS	KNX	NBC	
(Off the Air)	Hallelujah	Prayer, Records, and Talk	The Shell Happy Time Hour	*8am*
				8:15
Exercises				*8:30*
				8:45
The Vermont Lumberjacks	Talk and Music		Music / Beauty Talk	*9am*
			Music	*9:15*
Music	Feminine Fancies			*9:30*
				9:45
		Be Young and Happy, Eddie Albright	Stock Market Reports	*10am*
			The Heinz Program	*10:15*
	Music		Talk and Music / Woman's Magazine of the Air	*10:30*
				10:45
		Music	Music / The Standard School Broadcast	*11am*
				11:15
Music / California Federation of Women's Clubs	Music / American School of the Air	Talk and Music / Dr. Matthews' Radio Church		*11:30*
			Language Lesson	*11:45*
		Music	Stock Market Reports	*12pm*
			Music	*12:15*
	Biltmore Concert Orchestra			*12:30*
		Records		*12:45*
	The Ballad Hour			*1pm*
				1:15
	The Times Forum	The Bookworm		*1:30*
				1:45

DAYTIME — FALL, 1930

Sunday

	BLUE	CBS	KNX	NBC
2pm		The Rose Hills Concert	The Park Board Program	
2:15				
2:30				
2:45				
3pm	The Catholic Hour	The KFRC Studio Program		Old Lamps for New
3:15				
3:30				Alexander Reilly, organ
3:45				
4pm	The Three Skippers	Public Affairs	Records	
4:15				
4:30	Piano Recital		Dr. Matthews' Radio Church	Advanced Thought
4:45				

DAYTIME — FALL, 1930

Monday-Friday

BLUE	CBS	KNX	NBC	
Music	The Happy Go Lucky Hour	Music / The Jingle Man	Talk and Music	*2pm*
				2:15
		Music	Music / Winnie Fields Moore, songs	*2:30*
				2:45
US Agricultural Talk	Talk and Music		Talk and Music / Sylvia's Happy Hour	*3pm*
Music				*3:15*
		Music / The Hollywood Civic Theater	Music	*3:30*
				3:45
Music / The Melody Man		Music		*4pm*
Talk and Music / Sing a Song of Safety Club			News	*4:15*
The Quaker Man, Phil Cook			Big Brother	*4:30*
Talk and Music	News			*4:45*

DAYTIME — FALL, 1930

Saturday

	BLUE	CBS	KNX	NBC
8am	(Off the Air)	The New York Philharmonic Children's Concert	Prayer, Records, and Talk	The Shell Happy Time Hour
8:15				
8:30	Exercises			
8:45				
9am	The Vermont Lumberjacks	The Adventures of Helen and Mary	The Arizona Wranglers	Beauty Talk
9:15	Ballads			Stock Market Reports
9:30		Feminine Fancies		The National Farm and Home Hour
9:45				
10am		Cheer Up and Smile		
10:15				
10:30		Sports	The Jingle Man	Woman's Magazine of the Air
10:45				The Three Coeds
11am	Sports		Be Young and Happy, Eddie Albright	
11:15				
11:30				Ballads
11:45				Spanish Lesson
12pm			Records	Stock Market Reports
12:15				
12:30				
12:45				
1pm		Manhattan Towers	Dr. Matthews' Radio Church	
1:15				
1:30		The Times Forum	Be Young and Happy, Eddie Albright	Sports
1:45				

DAYTIME — FALL, 1930

Saturday

	BLUE	CBS	KNX	NBC
2pm		Sports		
2:15				
2:30			Sports	
2:45				
3pm	US Agricultural Talk			
3:15	Piano and Song Duo			
3:30	The Paramount Trio			
3:45				
4pm	Diversified Melodies			
4:15				
4:30	The Sunny Four Quartet			
4:45				

LISTINGS FOR 1931

EVENING — WINTER, 1931

Sunday

	BLUE	CBS	KNX	NBC
5pm	Nick Harris	The World's Business	Dr. Matthews' Radio Church (4:30pm)	Enna Jettick Melodies
5:15				The Collier Hour
5:30	Bob and Jimmy, songs	Rabbi Magnin, religion	Records	
5:45				
6pm	George Grandee, songs	Professor Lindsley and Leigh Harline		
6:15	The Vagabonds Quartet			The Atwater-Kent Hour
6:30		Detroit Symphony Orchestra	Ernest Holmes: Theodore C. Abel	
6:45				
7pm		The Royal Poet of the Organ	Wesley Tourtellote, organ	
7:15	Margaret Kernan, songs			The Studebaker Champions
7:30	Ray Van Dyne Orchestra	The Edison String Choir	The Arizona Wranglers	
7:45	Sunday Evenings at Seth Parker			Music
8pm		The KFRC Concert	The First Presbyterian Church of Hollywood	
8:15	Piano Recital			
8:30	The KECA Symphonette	Charlie Hamp, songs		Violin Recital
8:45		Musical Forget-Me-Nots		
9pm		The Chevrolet Chronicles	The Lubovsiki Trio	The Borden Milk Program
9:15				
9:30	Enna Jettick Melodies	Val Valenti Orchestra		Selwyn Harris, songs
9:45	Felipe Delgado, songs			
10pm		The Ten o'Clock Wire		Kaffe Hag Slumber Music
10:15	Paul Carson, organ	Val Valenti Orchestra		
10:30			The Hollywood Pantages Theater	Dance Orchestra
10:45				

EVENING — WINTER, 1931

Monday

BLUE	CBS	KNX	NBC	
How's Business	Mac and His Gang	Travelogue	Baron Keyes, stories	5pm
Fifteen Minutes in the Nation's Capitol		Big Brother		5:15
Piano Recital	Detectives Black and Blue			5:30
			Stock Market Reports	5:45
Maytag Orchestra	The Three Bakers	Wesley Tourtellote, organ	James Anderson, songs	6pm
			Olga Stefani, songs	6:15
Mildred Laughlin, songs	Don Lee Symphony Orchestra	Music	The Family Party	6:30
				6:45
	Guy Lombardo Orchestra	Frank Watanabe and Honorable Archie	Stromberg-Carlson Orchestra	7pm
		Music		7:15
The Empire Builders	Don Amalzo, songs	Don Amalzo, songs	Music	7:30
				7:45
Amos 'n' Andy	The Blue Monday Jamboree	Music	Sign of the Shell	8pm
Rhymes				8:15
Songs				8:30
				8:45
The KECA String Ensemble		The Lubovsiki Trio	Sherlock Holmes	9pm
				9:15
		The Good Samaritan	The Emperor of Crime	9:30
			Songs	9:45
Musical Echoes	The Ten o'Clock Wire		The Vagabond Movie Director	10pm
	Earl Burtnett Orchestra	The Arizona Wranglers		10:15
News	Anson Weeks Orchestra			10:30
Exercises				10:45

EVENING — WINTER, 1931

Tuesday

	BLUE	CBS	KNX	NBC
5pm	Music	Music	Travelogue	Baron Keyes, stories
5:15			Big Brother	
5:30	Jack Baldwin, piano	Detectives Black and Blue		Songs
5:45		The Premier Chef		Stock Market Reports
6pm	Musical Magazine	Peggy Hamilton, fashion	Wesley Tourtellote, organ	Songs
6:15				
6:30	The Happy Wonder Bakers	Music	The Trojan Trio	Harold Spaulding, songs
6:45				
7pm	Westinghouse Salute	Jo and Vi	Frank Watanabe and Honorable Archie	Music
7:15		Charlie Hamp, songs	Sam Coslow Orchestra	
7:30	Lucky Strike Dance Orchestra	Paramount Symphony Orchestra	The Paramount Publix Hour	
7:45				
8pm	Amos 'n' Andy	Tapestries of Life	Music	Elizabeth Jensen, songs
8:15	Songs			The Violet Ray Music Box
8:30			The Lion Tamers	
8:45	The Sperry Smiles			The Royal Hawaiians
9pm	Georgia Starke, songs	Blue Moods	One-Act Playlet	Florsheim Frolics
9:15				
9:30	Memory Lane	Don Lee Symphony Orchestra	The KNX String Ensemble	Songs
9:45				
10pm	The Schonberger Trio	The Ten o'Clock Wire	The Arizona Wrangler	Music
10:15		Earl Burtnett Orchestra		
10:30	News			
10:45	Health Talk			

EVENING — WINTER, 1931

Wednesday

BLUE	CBS	KNX	NBC	
Bobby Jones, golf	Records	Travelogue	Baron Keyes, stories	5pm
Radiotran Varieties		Big Brother		5:15
Piano Recital	Detectives Black and Blue			5:30
Reginald Ellis	Leigh Harline, organ		Stock Market Reports	5:45
Los Angeles Fire Department Orchestra	Gold Medal Fast Freight	Wesley Tourtellote, organ	The Halsey Stuart Concert	6pm
				6:15
	Music	Slim Martin Orchestra	The Palmolive Hour	6:30
				6:45
Music		Frank Watanabe and Honorable Archie		7pm
		Dr. Baumgarten, astrology		7:15
		Music	The Coca-Cola Program	7:30
Otto Ploetz, songs				7:45
Amos 'n' Andy	Guy Lombardo Orchestra	Bert Butterworth, stories	Songs	8pm
The Amphions			The KFI Symphonette	8:15
	The MJB Small Black Revue	Television Orchestra		8:30
Music			Songs	8:45
	Raymond Paige Orchestra	The Serenaders	Jose Bohr, songs	9pm
			The Emperor of Crime	9:15
The Camel Pleasure Hour	Music	The Good Samaritan	Eva Olivotti, songs	9:30
				9:45
	The Ten o'Clock Wire	The Russian Art Club		10pm
	Earl Burtnett Orchestra			10:15
News		The Arizona Wranglers	A Night in Moscow	10:30
Health Talk				10:45

EVENING — WINTER, 1931

Thursday

	BLUE	CBS	KNX	NBC
5pm	The Fleischman Yeast Hour, Rudy Vallee	Leigh Harline, organ	Travelogue	Baron Keyes, stories
5:15			Big Brother	
5:30		Detectives Black and Blue		Songs
5:45		Songs		Stock Market Reports
6pm	The Arco Birthday Party	Savino Tone Pictures	Wesley Tourtellote, organ	Nick Harris
6:15				
6:30	The Maxwell House Concerts	Professor Lindsley and Leigh Harline		The Loveless Twins
6:45			The KNX Trio	The Lyric Trio
7pm	Winnie Fields Moore, songs	The Lutheran Hour	Frank Watanabe and Honorable Archie	Lucky Strike Dance Orchestra
7:15			Records	
7:30		The KFRC Opera	George Gramlich, songs	The Standard Symphony Hour
7:45				
8pm	The Royal Hawaiians	The Violet Ray Music Box	The Philco Classic Symphony	
8:15	Richard and Fink, songs			
8:30	Amos 'n' Andy	Top O' the World Night Club	Soup to Nuts	Arthur Freidman, piano
8:45	The Sperry Smiles			
9pm	Ray Van Dyne Orchestra	Folgeria	The Lubovsiki Trio	The MJB Demi-Tasse Revue
9:15				
9:30		Southern Melodies		Music
9:45				
10pm	Harold Spaulding, songs	The Ten o'Clock Wire	The Arizona Wranglers	Piano Paintings
10:15		Earl Burtnett Orchestra		
10:30	News			Packard Ordhestra
10:45	Exercises		The Hollywood Harmony Boys	

EVENING — WINTER, 1931

Friday

BLUE	CBS	KNX	NBC	
The Cities Service Concerts	Music	Travelogue	Baron Keyes, stories	5pm
		Big Brother		5:15
	Detectives Black and Blue		Garden Talk	5:30
	Organ Recital		Stock Market Reports	5:45
The RKO Revue	The KHJ String Trio	Wesley Tourtellote, organ	The Interwovan Pair	6pm
				6:15
Eva Olivotti, songs	Memoirs of General Pershing	Novelty Orchestra	Armour Orchestra	6:30
				6:45
Manny Stein Orchestra	The Inglewood Park Concert	Frank Watanabe and Honorable Archie	Armstrong Quakers Orchestra	7pm
		Music		7:15
	Charlie Hamp, songs	Metropolitan WaterTalk	The RKO Theater	7:30
Otto Ploetz, songs	The Adventures of a Con Man	Wesley Tourtellote, organ		7:45
Amos 'n' Andy	Callifornia Melodies	The Optimistic Do-Nuts	Songs	8pm
The Stove Poker Philosopher			Brown -bilt Footlites	8:15
	Music		S & W Melodies	8:30
				8:45
	The Sunset Musical Cocktail	KNX Dance Music	Arthur Lang, songs	9pm
			The Emperor of Crime	9:15
	Songology		Music	9:30
Songs		The Hollywood Legion Fight		9:45
Rose Dirmann, songs	The Ten o'Clock Wire			10pm
	Earl Burtnett Orchestra			10:15
News			Sketches in the Trenches	10:30
Health Talk		The Holllywood Harmony Boys		10:45

EVENING — WINTER, 1931

Saturday

	BLUE	CBS	KNX	NBC
5pm	Music (4:30pm)	The KFRC Organ	Travelogue	The Rhythm Masters
5:15	Radiotran Varieties	Ann Leaf at the Organ	Records	Movie Gossip
5:30	The Fuller Brush Man	Fletcher Henderson Orchestra		Songs
5:45				Stock Market Reports
6pm	Los Angeles Fire Department Orchestra	The KHJ Novelties	Wesley Tourtellote, organ	General Electric Orchestra
6:15				
6:30		The National Radio Forum	Petite Ensemble	
6:45				
7pm	Ray Van Dyne Orchestra	Hank Simmons' Show Boat	Frank Watanabe and Honorable Archie	Lucky Strike Dance Orchestra
7:15			June Purcell, songs	
7:30				
7:45				
8pm	Amos 'n' Andy	Vignettes in Symphony	The KNX Revue	George Grandee, songs
8:15	Rainbow Harmonies			The Gilmore Circus
8:30			The Arizona Wranglers	
8:45	The Sperry Smiles			Songs
9pm	The Los Angeles Auto Show	The Merrymakers	The Russian-American Art Club	Music
9:15				
9:30	Harold Spaulding, songs		The Good Samaritan	The Associated Spotlight Review
9:45				
10pm	The KECA String Ensemble	The Ten o'Clock Wire	The Arizona Wranglers	
10:15		Earl Burtnett Orchestra		
10:30				
10:45			The Hollywood Harmony Boys	

DAYTIME — WINTER, 1931

Sunday

	BLUE	CBS	KNX	NBC
8am	The Roxy Symphony Concert	The KFRC Organ	(Off the Air)	(Off the Air)
8:15				
8:30		Come Into the Garden		
8:45				
9am	Music	Home, Sweet Home	Records and Studio Music	The Breakfast Frolic
9:15	John Barclay, songs			
9:30	Neopolitan Days			Pietro Salvatore, violin
9:45				Songs
10am	The National Oratorio Society		The IBSA Watchtower	
10:15				
10:30				
10:45				Temple Baptist Church
11am	Bible Stories	First Methodist Church of Los Angeles	First Presbyterian Church of Hollywood	
11:15				
11:30				
11:45				
12pm	Music	New York Philharmonic Orchestra		
12:15				Barbara Jamieson, piano
12:30			Louise Johnson, astrology	Helen Guest, songs
12:45				
1pm			The IBSA Watchtower	The Golden Hour
1:15				
1:30				
1:45				

DAYTIME — WINTER, 1931

Monday-Friday

BLUE	CBS	KNX	NBC	
(Off the Air)	Hallelujah	Prayer, Records, and Talk	The Shell Happy Time Hour	*8am*
				8:15
Exercises				*8:30*
				8:45
The Vermont Lumberjacks	Talk and Music		Music / Beauty Talk	*9am*
Music			Music	*9:15*
	Feminine Fancies			*9:30*
Music / The Weekly Entertainers				*9:45*
Music / Charlie Wellman, health		Be Young and Happy, Eddie Albright	Stock Market Reports	*10am*
Music				*10:15*
	Talk and Music		Talk and Music / Woman's Magazine of the Air	*10:30*
				10:45
		Music / Jack Carter's Birthday Party	Music / The Standard School Broadcast	*11am*
				11:15
Music / California Federation of Women's Clubs	Music / American School of the Air	Talk and Music / Dr. Matthews' Radio Church		*11:30*
Music / Sisters of the Skillet			Language Lesson	*11:45*
Music / Hotel St. Francis Drake Orchestra	Biltmore Concert Orchestra	Records	Stock Market Reports	*12pm*
The Radio Guild / The National Farm and Home Hour			Talk and Music	*12:15*
	News			*12:30*
	Talk and Music			*12:45*
				1pm
				1:15
Music / Pacific School of the Air	The Times Forum	The Bookworm		*1:30*
				1:45

DAYTIME — WINTER, 1931

Sunday

	BLUE	CBS	KNX	NBC
2pm	Alexander Reilly, organ	The Rose Hills Concert	The Park Board Program	Sylvia's Happy Hour
2:15				
2:30				
2:45				
3pm	The Catholic Hour	The KFRC Studio Program		Old Lamps for New
3:15				
3:30				Alexander Reilly, organ
3:45				
4pm	Music		Wesley Tourtellotte, organ	Advanced Thought
4:15	Molly and Mike, songs			
4:30	Piano Recital		Dr. Matthews' Radio Church	The RCA Victor Hour
4:45		The Vesper Hour		

DAYTIME — WINTER, 1931

Monday-Friday

BLUE	CBS	KNX	NBC	
Music	The Happy Go Lucky Hour	Music / The Jingle Man	Music / The NBC Matinee	2pm
				2:15
Music / The NBC Matinee		Talk and Music	Music / Winnie Fields Moore, songs	2:30
				2:45
US Agricultural Talk	Talk and Music		Talk and Music / Sylvia's Happy Hour	3pm
Music / Kathleen Spengler, whistler				3:15
Music / Paul's Hawaiians			Music	3:30
				3:45
Music / The Italian Lamguage	Music / Frederick Wile, comment	Records		4pm
Talk and Music			News	4:15
			Big Brother	4:30
	News			4:45

DAYTIME — WINTER, 1931

Saturday

	BLUE	CBS	KNX	NBC
8am	(Off the Air)	The New York Philharmonic Children's Concert	(Off the Air)	The Shell Happy Time Hour
8:15				
8:30	Exercises	The Columbia Revue	The Arizona Wranglers	
8:45				
9am	The Vermont Lumberjacks	Music	Records	Beauty Talk
9:15	Sax Appeal			Stock Market Reports
9:30	The Alabama Boys	Paul Treymaine Orchestra		The National Farm and Home Hour
9:45	Music	Music		
10am	A Night in Moscow	Cheer Up and Smile		
10:15				
10:30			The Jingle Man	Woman's Magazine of the Air
10:45				
11am		Organ Recital		
11:15		The National Democratic Forum		
11:30			Be Young and Happy, Eddie Albright	The Three Coeds
11:45				Spanish Lesson
12pm	Hotel St. Francis Drake Orchestra	Biltmore Concert Orchestra	Music	US Agricultural Talk
12:15				
12:30			Records	
12:45				
1pm	Music	News	Dr. Matthews' Radio Church	
1:15	The Pacific Feature Hour	Ann Leaf at the Organ		
1:30		The Times Forum	Be Young and Happy, Eddie Albright,	
1:45				

DAYTIME — WINTER, 1931

Saturday

	BLUE	CBS	KNX	NBC
2pm	Music	Organ Recital	Records	
2:15		Morton Downey, songs		
2:30				Sylvia's Happy Hour
2:45				
3pm	Stock Market Reports	Dance Orchestra		
3:15	The Demaree-Williams Rhythm Masters			
3:30				
3:45	Diversified Melodies	Tony Won's Scrapbook		
4pm		The Camel Quarter Hour		The Tea Timers Band
4:15	The Sing-A-Song of Safety Club	The Romance of American Industry		
4:30	Music			
4:45		News		Betty Burke, songs

EVENING — SPRING, 1931

Sunday

	BLUE	CBS	KNX	NBC
5pm	Nick Harris	Devil, Drugs, and Doctor	Dr. Matthews' Radio Church	Enna Jettick Melodies
5:15		The Vesper Hour		The Collier Hour
5:30				
5:45				
6pm	The Vagabonds Quartet	Rabbi Magnin, religion	Records	
6:15				The Atwater-Kent Hour
6:30		Detroit Symphony Orchestra	Ernest Holmes: Theodore C. Abel	
6:45				The Book Drama Players
7pm	Purcell Mayer, violin	The Royal Poet of the Organ	Dr. Aked, health	
7:15	Charles Francis Coe, comment			
7:30	The Royal Hawaiians	The Fortune Builders	The Arizona Wranglers	
7:45	Sunday Evenings at Seth Parker	The Edison String Choir		Purcell Mayer, violin
8pm		Cadillac-LaSalle Orchestra	The First Presbyterian Church of Hollywood	Beautiful Women of the Ages
8:15	Heel Huggers Harmonies			
8:30	The KECA Symphonette	Dr. Barrows, health		A Night in Moscow
8:45		Musical Forget-Me-Nots		
9pm		The Chevrolet Chronicles	The Lubovsiki Trio	The Borden Milk Program
9:15				
9:30	Enna Jettick Melodies	Dance Orchestra		Maurine Dyer, songs
9:45	Felipe Delgado, songs	Val Velenti Orchestra		
10pm		The Ten o'Clock Wire		Kaffe Hag Slumber Music
10:15	Paul Carson, organ	Val Valenti Orchestra	The Gossipers	
10:30			The Hollywood Pantages Theater	Rose Dirmann, songs
10:45				

EVENING — SPRING, 1931

Monday

BLUE	CBS	KNX	NBC	
The Averill Trio	Mac and His Gang (4:45pm)	Big Brother	Baron Keyes, stories (4:45pm)	5pm
	Detectives Black and Blue			5:15
Gold Medal Express	Music			5:30
			Stock Market Reports	5:45
Maytag Orchestra	The Three Bakers	Tom and Wash, songs	The KFI String Orchestra	6pm
				6:15
The Sperry Serenaders	An Evening in Paris	William Hatch Orchestra	The Family Party	6:30
		Wesley Tourtellote, organ		6:45
The KECA String Ensemble	Guy Lombardo Orchestra	Frank Watanabe and Honorable Archie	Stromberg-Carlson Orchestra	7pm
		The Singing Strings		7:15
The Empire Builders	The Salvation Army Citadel Band	The Serenaders	Real Folks	7:30
				7:45
Amos 'n' Andy	The Blue Monday Jamboree	The Arizona Wranglers	Music	8pm
Thomas Mitchell, stories				8:15
Music		June Pursell, songs		8:30
The Silhouettes				8:45
The KECA String Ensemble		The Lubovsiki Trio	Sherlock Holmes	9pm
				9:15
		The Good Samaritan	The Schonberger Trio	9:30
				9:45
Music	The Ten o'Clock Wire	Nights in Spain	News	10pm
	Anson Weeks Orchestra		Tom Terris, World Traveler	10:15
		Wesley Tourtellote, organ		10:30
Exercises				10:45

EVENING — SPRING, 1931

Tuesday

	BLUE	CBS	KNX	NBC
5pm	Music	Seeing Southern California (4:45pm)	Big Brother	Paul Whiteman Orchestra
5:15		Numerologist		
5:30		Detectives Black and Blue	Records	Dog Stories
5:45	The Nomad Novelist	Music		Stock Market Reports
6pm	Musical Magazine	Peggy Hamilton, fashion	Tom and Wash, songs	KFI Symphony Orchestra
6:15				
6:30	The Happy Wonder Bakers	Moods Moderne	Let's Dance	
6:45				
7pm	The KECA After-Dinner Review	Jo and Vi	Frank Watanabe and Honorable Archie	Lucky Strike Dance Orchestra
7:15		Music	Music	
7:30		Paramount Symphony Orchestra	The Paramount Publix Hour	
7:45	Ranse Valentine, rhymes			
8pm	Amos 'n' Andy	The Sierra Symponists	Music	Songs
8:15	Songs	Pryor's Cremo Band		Memory Lane
8:30		The KFRC Concert	The Gilmore Circus	
8:45	The Sperry Smiles			The Emperor of Crime
9pm	KECA Symphony Orchestra	Richie Craig, Jr., Radio Funster	The Barber Shop Quartet	Florsheim Frolics
9:15		Tapestries of Life		
9:30	The Hill Billies		One-Act Playlet	The Caswell Concert
9:45				Music
10pm	Songs	The Ten o'Clock Wire	Music	News
10:15		Anson Weeks Orchestra		Music
10:30	Exercises			Arthur Lang, songs
10:45				

EVENING — SPRING, 1931

Wednesday

BLUE	CBS	KNX	NBC	
Bobby Jones, golf	Organ Recital (4:45pm)	Big Brother	Baron Keyes, stories (4:45pm)	*5pm*
Radiotran Varieties	Detectives Black and Blue			*5:15*
Music	The Sunkist Musical Cocktail		Music	*5:30*
		Timely Tips	Stock Market Reports	*5:45*
The KECA String Ensemble	KFRC Dinner Music	Wesley Tourtellote, organ	The Halsey Stuart Concert	*6pm*
		Tom and Wash, songs		*6:15*
HI-Lights on Low Brows	Don Lee Symphony Orchestra	The Hollywood Pantages Theater	The Palmolive Hour	*6:30*
The Musical Comedy Album				*6:45*
	Vitality Personalities	Frank Watanabe and Honorable Archie		*7pm*
	Music	Tom Brenneman and Perlwinkle		*7:15*
	The Violet Ray Music Box	The Rosierucian Ensemble	The Coca-Cola Program	*7:30*
John Vale, songs				*7:45*
Amos 'n' Andy	The Columbia Concert Hall	Brown's Airdales	Songs	*8pm*
Ranse Valentine, rhymes	Pryor's Cremo Band		The Camel Pleasure Hour	*8:15*
Music	The MJB Small Black Revue	Music		*8:30*
				8:45
	Bob and Harriet, songs	The Good Samaritan		*9pm*
			Rin-Tin-Tin Thriller	*9:15*
	Gruen Guild Frolics		Music	*9:30*
	Peter Pan Fashions			*9:45*
Music	The Ten o'Clock Wire	Music	News	*10pm*
	Anson Weeks Orchestra		Music	*10:15*
Exercises		The Russian-American Art Club		*10:30*
				10:45

EVENING — SPRING, 1931

Thursday

	BLUE	CBS	KNX	NBC
5pm	The Fleischman Yeast Hour, Rudy Vallee	Sunset Melodies	Big Brother	Baron Keyes, stories (4:45pm)
5:15		Detectives Black and Blue		Music
5:30		Sunset Melodies		
5:45		Organ Recital	Timely Tips	Stock Market Reports
6pm	The Arco Birthday Party	KFRC Dinner Music	Wesley Tourtellote, organ	Nick Harris
6:15		Old Gold Character Reading	Tom and Wash, songs	
6:30	The Maxwell House Concerts	Professor Lindsley and Leigh Harline	Maurice Gunsky, songs	
6:45			Marjorie Healy, songs	The Lyric Trio
7pm	Music	The Lutheran Hour	Frank Watanabe and Honorable Archie	Lucky Strike Dance Orchestra
7:15			Songs	
7:30		The KFRC Opera	The Barber Shop Quartet	The Standard Symphony Hour
7:45			Music	
8pm	The Royal Hawaiians	Hallelujah	The Philco Classic Symphony	
8:15	John Vale, songs	Pryor's Cremo Band		
8:30	Amos 'n' Andy	News	Jane Purcell, songs	The Wandering Minstels
8:45	The Sperry Smiles	The Pabco Trail Blazers		
9pm	Music	Folgeria	The Lubovsiki Trio	The MJB Demi-Tasse Revue
9:15				
9:30		Raymond Paige Orchestra		Beautiful Women of the Ages
9:45				
10pm	The KECA String Ensemble	The Ten o'Clock Wire	The Arizona Wranglers	News
10:15		Anson Weeks Orchestra		Parisian Quintet
10:30	Exercises			Edwin LeMaire, organ
10:45				

EVENING — SPRING, 1931

Friday

BLUE	CBS	KNX	NBC	
The Cities Service Concerts	Seeing Southern California (4:45pm)	Big Brother	Baron Keyes, stories (4:45pm)	*5pm*
	Detectives Black and Blue		Songs	*5:15*
	The Sharnova Trio		Garden Talk	*5:30*
			Stock Market Reports	*5:45*
The RKO Revue	Pat Frayue's Sportslants	Wesley Tourtellote, organ	The Interwovan Pair	*6pm*
	KFRC Dinner Music	Tom and Wash, songs		*6:15*
The Sperry Serenaders	Don Ricardo, songs	The Pennant Knights	Armour Orchestra	*6:30*
	Felix Mills, organ			*6:45*
Music	Songs	Frank Watanabe and Honorable Archie	Armstrong Quakers Orchestra	*7pm*
		Music		*7:15*
	The Inglewood Park Concert	Metropolitan WaterTalk	The RKO Theater	*7:30*
John Vale, songs		Golf Classics		*7:45*
Amos 'n' Andy	Dance Orchestra	The Optimistic Do-Nuts	Music	*8pm*
The Stove Poker Philosopher	Pryor's Cremo Band		Brown-bilt Footlites	*8:15*
	Gilmore College Daze		S & W Melodies	*8:30*
				8:45
Renne Hemery, violin	The Sunset Musical Cocktail	KNX Dance Music	The House of Color	*9pm*
Music		The Arizona Wrangers		*9:15*
	Biltmore Concert Orchestra		Kodak Orchestra	*9:30*
		The Hollywood Legion Fight		*9:45*
Mystery Serial	The Ten o'Clock Wire		News	*10pm*
	Anson Weeks Orchestra		Tales of the Arabian Nights	*10:15*
Exercises				*10:30*
		The Adventures of Bill and Mr. Jackson	Music	*10:45*

EVENING — SPRING, 1931

Saturday

	BLUE	CBS	KNX	NBC
5pm	Juvenile Sketches	Eleanor Allen, organ	Records (2:30pm)	Jack Baldwin, piano (4:45pm)
5:15	Radiotran Varieties	Ann Leaf at the Organ		Movie Gossip
5:30	The Fuller Brush Man	Eleanor Allen, organ		Songs
5:45		Mary Charles, songs	Timely Tips	Stock Market Reports
6pm	Clyde Lehman, piano	Potluck	Wesley Tourtellote, organ	General Electric Orchestra
6:15			Tom and Wash, songs	
6:30	Hi-Lites on Low Brows	The National Radio Forum	Songs	
6:45	Raine Bennett, songs		Wesley Tourtellote, organ	
7pm		Hank Simmons' Show Boat	Frank Watanabe and Honorable Archie	Lucky Strike Dance Orchestra
7:15			Philosophies in Music	
7:30				
7:45	Cecil Wilcox, songs		The Gossipers	
8pm	Amos 'n' Andy	Jack Denny Orchestra	KNX Varieities	The Royal Hawaiians
8:15	Thomas Mitchell, stories	Pryor's Cremo Band		The Gilmore Circus
8:30	George Grandee, songs	The Merrymakers		
8:45	The Sperry Smiles			The Emperor of Crime
9pm	El Sidero Minstrels		The Russian-American Art Club	George Liebling, piano
9:15				
9:30	Harold Spaulding, songs	Town House Orchestra	The Good Samaritan	The Associated Spotlight Review
9:45				
10pm		The Ten o'Clock Wire	The Arizona Wranglers	
10:15		Anson Weeks Orchestra		
10:30	The Modern Music Maids			
10:45				

DAYTIME — SPRING, 1931

Sunday

	BLUE	CBS	KNX	NBC
8am	Neapolitan Days	The Times Comics Pages	The Sharples Breakfast Club (7:00AM)	(Off the Air)
8:15				
8:30	The Roxy Symphony Concert	Come Into the Garden		Lilyan Ariel, piano
8:45				The Pet Clinic
9am		Home, Sweet Home	Records and Studio Music	The Breakfast Frolic
9:15				
9:30	Echoes of the Orient			
9:45				The KFI Ensemble
10am	The National Oratorio Society		Organ Reciital	
10:15				
10:30			Studio Program	.
10:45				Third Church of Christian Science
11am	The Ten-Twenty-Thirty Period of Opera	First Methodist Church of Los Angeles	First Presbyterian Church of Hollywood	
11:15				
11:30	Yeast Foamers Orchestra			
11:45				
12pm	Paul's Hawaiians	New York Philharmonic Orchestra		
12:15				Barbara Jamleson, piano
12:30			Louise Johnson, astrology	Helen Guest, songs
12:45				
1pm			The IBSA Watchtower	Music
1:15				
1:30				
1:45				

LISTINGS FOR 1931 105

DAYTIME — SPRING, 1931

Monday-Friday

BLUE	CBS	KNX	NBC	
(Off the Air)	Hallelujah	The Sharples Breakfast Club (7:00AM)	The Shell Happy Time Hour	8am
Stock Market Reports				8:15
Exercises				8:30
				8:45
Cross-Cuts of the Day	Talk and Music			9am
The Vermont Lumberjacks		Music	The Children's Clinic	9:15
Jack Baldwin, piano	Feminine Fancies		Talk and Music	9:30
				9:45
Music / Radio Ramblings		Be Young and Happy, Eddie Albright	Songs	10am
Songs			Music / The Heinz Program	10:15
	Talk and Music		Talk and Music / Woman's Magazine of the Air	10:30
				10:45
	Music / The Columbia Artist's Recital	Talk and Music / Jack Carter's Birthday Party	Music / The Standard School Broadcast	11am
				11:15
Music / California Federation of Women's Clubs	Music / American School of the Air	Talk and Music / Dr. Matthews' Radio Church		11:30
			Language Lesson	11:45
Luncheon Concert	Biltmore Concert Orchestra	Talk and Music	US Agricultural Talk	12pm
The National Farm and Home Hour				12:15
	News			12:30
	Talk and Music			12:45
Music / Hotel St. Francis Drake Orchestra				1pm
				1:15
	The Times Forum	The Bookworm	Talk / Pacific School of the Air	1:30
				1:45

DAYTIME — SPRING, 1931

Sunday

	BLUE	CBS	KNX	NBC
2pm	Alexander Reilly, organ	Frank Moss, songs	The Park Board Program	Sylvia's Happy Hour
2:15				
2:30		Professor Lindsley and Leigh Harline		
2:45				
3pm	The Catholic Hour	Music		Old Lamps for New
3:15				
3:30				Alexander Reilly, organ
3:45				
4pm	Old Stager's Memories		Wesley Tourtellotte, organ	Leila Castberg, songs
4:15				Songs
4:30	Mattie Crawford, psychology	The Pilgrim Hour		The RCA Victor Hour
4:45				

DAYTIME — SPRING, 1931

Monday-Friday

BLUE	CBS	KNX	NBC	
Music / The NBC Matinee	The Happy Go Lucky Hour		Music / Paul's Hawaiians	2pm
				2:15
		Talk and Music	Music / Winnie Fields Moore, songs	2:30
			Talk and Music	2:45
Talk and Music	Talk and Music		Talk and Music / Sylvia's Happy Hour	3pm
				3:15
			Music	3:30
Stock Market Reports				3:45
Music / The Italian Language	The Camel Quarter Hour / Frederick Wile, comment	Travelogue	News	4pm
Talk and Music	Music	Records	Big Brother	4:15
	Town Topics	Music	Phil Cook, the Quaker Man	4:30
Music / The Averill Trio	News / Seeing Southern California		Baron Keyes, stories	4:45

DAYTIME — SPRING, 1931

Saturday

	BLUE	CBS	KNX	NBC
8am	Van and Don, songs (7:45AM)	Hallelujah	The Sharples Breakfast Club (7:00AM)	The Shell Happy Time Hour
8:15	Stock Market Reports			
8:30	Exercises			
8:45				
9am	Cross-Cuts of the Day	Organ Recital		Margaret Duncan, organ
9:15	The Vermont Lumberjacks			The Children's Clinic
9:30	The Alabama Boys	Beauty Talk		The National Farm and Home Hour
9:45	Piano Recital	Paul Treymaine Orchestra		
10am	A Night in Moscow	Mill's Soothing Sax	Be Young and Happy, Eddie Albright	
10:15				
10:30		Clarence Weaver, science		Woman's Magazine of the Air
10:45		Don Ricardo, songs		
11am		Organ Recital		
11:15		The Columbia Artist's Recital		
11:30	Alexander Reilly, organ	Columbia Salon Orchestra		The Three Coeds
11:45				Spanish Lesson
12pm	Hotel St. Francis Drake Orchestra	Biltmore Concert Orchestra	Music	US Agricultural Talk
12:15				
12:30		News	Travelogue	
12:45		Saturday Syncopators		
1pm	Bits of Melody		Dr. Matthews' Radio Church	
1:15	Music	Margit Aegedus, violin		The Pacific Feature Hour
1:30		The Times Forum	Be Young and Happy, Eddie Albright	
1:45				

DAYTIME — SPRING, 1931

Saturday

	BLUE	CBS	KNX	NBC
2pm	The NBC Matinee	Music	Light Concert Ensemble	Sylvia's Happy Hour
2:15				
2:30			Records	
2:45				
3pm	Music			Matinee Melodists
3:15				
3:30				
3:45				
4pm		Morton Downey, songs		
4:15		Armand Vascey Orchestra		
4:30		Town Topics		
4:45		News		Jack Baldwin, piano

EVENING — SUMMER, 1931

Sunday

	BLUE	CBS	KNX	NBC
5pm	Baldassare Ferlazzo, violin (4:30pm)	The Vesper Hour	Dr. Matthews' Radio Church	Heel Huggers Harmonies
5:15	Concert Jewels			Piano Recital
5:30		The Lewisohn Stadium Concerts		The Alabama Boys
5:45	The Lyric Trio			
6pm	Edwin Franko Goldman Band		Records	Philosophy
6:15				Packard Orchestra
6:30		The Gauchos	Ernest Holmes: Theodore C. Abel	
6:45	Sunday Evenings at Seth Parkers	The Star Revelers		The Wonder Twins
7pm		Cadillac-La Sallle Orchestra	Lucie Lee, organ	Music
7:15	Alvino Rey Orchestra		The Viennese Knights	
7:30	Dance Orchestra	The Edison String Choir		The Carnation Contented Hour
7:45			The Gossipers	
8pm	Gunnar Johansen, piano	Musical Forget-Me-Nots	The First Presbyterian Church of Hollywood	Music
8:15				
8:30	Musical Moods	Nocturne		
8:45				
9pm	The Novelty Trio	The Chevrolet Chronicles	The Lubovsiki Trio	The NBC Special
9:15	Jean Dunn, songs			
9:30	Music			Young Marketer's Symphonette
9:45				
10pm	Helen Guest, songs	The Ten o'Clock Wire	The Arizona Wranglers	Kaffe Hag Slumber Music
10:15		George Wendt Orchestra		
10:30	George Grandee, songs	Tom Gruen Orchestra	The Hollywood Pantages Theater	Dance Orchestra
10:45	William Ross, violin			

EVENING — SUMMER, 1931

Monday

BLUE	CBS	KNX	NBC	
Maytag Orchestra	Music	Big Brother (4:00pm)	Organ Recital (4:30pm)	*5pm*
			Stock Market Reports	*5:15*
Jack Baldwin, piano		Billy Van, songs	The General Motors Concert	*5:30*
				5:45
Music		Music	Gold Medal Express	*6pm*
		Tom and Wash, songs		*6:15*
The Eson Twins	Dinner Music		Dance Orchestra	*6:30*
Violin Recital		Wesley Tourtellote, organ		*6:45*
Amos 'n' Andy	Music	Frank Watanabe and Honorable Archie	The Roamer's Male Quartet	*7pm*
Ranse Valentine, rhymes	Pryor's Cremo Band	Songs		*7:15*
Music	The Camel Quarter Hour	The Los Angeles Realty Board	The MJB Demi-Tasse Revue	*7:30*
	Raymond Paige Orchestra			*7:45*
The Three Coeds	The Blue Monday Jamboree	The Lubovsiki Trio	Hotel Agua Caliente Orchestra	*8pm*
				8:15
The Vagabonds Quartet		The Arizona Wranglers	Music	*8:30*
				8:45
The Ranch Boys		The Question and Answer Lady	Rajput, Hindu Secret Service	*9pm*
		Dance Orchestra	Music	*9:15*
The Pacific Nations Singers				*9:30*
				9:45
	The Ten o'Clock Wire	The USC Band	The Richfield Reporter	*10pm*
	Anson Weeks Orchestra		Packard Orchestra	*10:15*
News				*10:30*
Exercises				*10:45*

EVENING — SUMMER, 1931

Tuesday

	BLUE	CBS	KNX	NBC
5pm	Baldassare Ferlazzo, violin	Music (4:45pm)	Big Brother	The Nash Parade of Progress
5:15		The Buccaneers		
5:30	The Fuller Brush Man	Organ Recital	Records	Nick Harris
5:45		News		
6pm	Instrumental Novelty	Ben Bernie, the Old Maestro	Wesley Tourtellote, organ	Lucky Strike Dance Orchestra
6:15		Fredrick William Wile, comment	Tom and Wash, songs	
6:30		Savino Tone Pictures	Petite Concert	
6:45	Piano Moods			
7pm	Amos 'n' Andy	Music	Frank Watanabe and Honorable Archie	Music
7:15	The Sperry Smiles	Pryor's Cremo Band	Music	
7:30	The Dorie Quartet	The Camel Quarter Hour		
7:45		Ashbury Park Orchestra	Glen Ellison, songs	
8pm	Dance Orchestra	Detectives Black and Blue	The Arizona Wranglers	The Caswell Concert
8:15		Music		Memory Lane
8:30	Kenneth Rundquist, songs	The KFRC Concert	The Gilmore Circus	
8:45				The Emperor of Crime
9pm	The Ranch Boys	The Associated Negro Chorus	Glen Ellison, songs	Dance Orchestra
9:15				
9:30	Songs		One-Act Playlet	James Burroughs, songs
9:45				
10pm	Music	The Ten o'Clock Wire	Hotel Roosevelt Orchestra	The Richfield Reporter
10:15		Earl Burtnett Orchestra		Music
10:30	News			Packard Orchestra
10:45	Exercises			

EVENING — SUMMER, 1931

Wednesday

BLUE	CBS	KNX	NBC	
Violin recital	Organ Recital	Big Brother	The Halsey Stuart Concert	5pm
Songs				5:15
	The Children's Hour		The Palmolive Hour	5:30
	News	Timely Tips		5:45
The KECA String Ensemble	Connee Boswell, songs	Wesley Tourtellote, organ		6pm
	The Rhythm Choristers	Tom and Wash, songs		6:15
The Roamer's Male Quartet	Raymond Paige Orchestra	The KNX Trio	The Coca-Cola Program	6:30
John Vale, songs		Music		6:45
Amos 'n' Andy	Norte Dame's Four Horsemen	Frank Watanabe and Honorable Archie	John Moss Orchestra	7pm
The KECA String Trio	Pryor's Cremo Band	Tom Brenneman and Perlwinkle		7:15
Packard Orchestra	The Camel Quarter Hour	The Serenaders	The MJB Small Black Revue	7:30
	Music			7:45
The Arcadians	Detectives Black and Blue	Brown's Airdales	Felipe Delgado, songs	8pm
	Songs of Edward Lynn		Rin-Tin-Tin Thriller	8:15
Songs	The Violet Ray Music Box	The Philco Classic Symphony	The Hi-Jinks Dance Band	8:30
				8:45
The Ranch Boys	Bob and Harriet, songs	The Question and Answer Lady	Rajput, Hindu Secret Service	9pm
		The Arizona Wranglers	The Roamer's Male Quartet	9:15
Moonlight Matinee	Music		Packard Orchestra	9:30
				9:45
News	The Ten o'Clock Wire	The USC Band	The Richfield Reporter	10pm
Radio Interference	Earl Burtnett Orchestra		Radio Interference	10:15
		The Russian-American Art Club	The Ranch Boys	10:30
				10:45

EVENING — SUMMER, 1931

Thursday

	BLUE	CBS	KNX	NBC
5pm	The Arco Birthday Party	Organ Recital	Big Brother	Organ Recital (4:00pm)
5:15				Songs
5:30	The Maxwell House Concerts			
5:45		News	Timely Tips	Piano Duet
6pm	Dramas from the News	The Lewisohn Stadium Concerts	Wesley Tourtellote, organ	Lucky Strike Dance Orchestra
6:15			Tom and Wash, songs	
6:30	Songs	Barbara Marvel Orchestra	The KNX Trio	
6:45		Irene Beasley, songs	Wesley Tourtellote, organ	
7pm	Amos 'n' Andy	Music	Frank Watanabe and Honorable Archie	Music
7:15	The Sperry Smiles		Songs	
7:30	The KECA After-Dinner Review		Let's Dance	The Standard Symphony Hour
7:45		Radio Round-Up		
8pm		Detectives Black and Blue	The Lubovsiki Trio	
8:15		Your Announcer Has Been		
8:30	Music of All Countries	The Inglewood Park Concert		The Wandering Minstels
8:45				
9pm	The Ranch Boys	One-Act Playlet	The Question and Answer Lady	Packard Orchestra
9:15			The Arizona Wranglers	
9:30	The Story Teller	Manhattan Dreams, Jane Green		James Burroughs, songs
9:45				
10pm	Songs	The Ten o'Clock Wire	Roosevelt Hotel Orchestra	The Richfield Reporter
10:15		Earl Burtnett Orchestra		The Nomad Novelist
10:30	News			Packard Orchestra
10:45	Exercises			

EVENING — SUMMER, 1931

Friday

BLUE	CBS	KNX	NBC	
Music	The Three Cheers (4:45pm)	Big Brother	The Interwoven Pair	*5pm*
	The Sharnova Trio			*5:15*
		Records	Armour Orchestra	*5:30*
	News	The Town Crier		*5:45*
Roy Ringwald, songs	The Pillsbury Pageant	Wesley Tourtellote, organ	Paul Whiteman Orchestra	*6pm*
Nick Harris		Tom and Wash, songs		*6:15*
	The Sunset Musical Cocktail	Music	The RKO Theater	*6:30*
John Vale, songs				*6:45*
Amos 'n' Andy	The Inter-City Radio Contest	Frank Watanabe and Honorable Archie	The Roamer's Male Quartet	*7pm*
Fred Forrest, songs	Pryor's Cremo Band	Music	Brown-bilt Footlites	*7:15*
	The Camel Quarter Hour		The Fearful Seven	*7:30*
John Vale, songs	Ben Bernie, the Old Maestro	Vincent Lopez Orchestra	James Burroughs, songs	*7:45*
	The Singing Strings	The Optimistic Do-Nuts	The House of Color	*8pm*
Arthur Lang, songs				*8:15*
	Gilmore College Daze		The Affliated Negro Chorus	*8:30*
				8:45
The Ranch Boys	Raymond Paige Orchestra	The Question and Answer Lady	Rajput, Hindu Secret Service	*9pm*
		The Arizona Wranglers		*9:15*
The Musical Comedy Album			Kodak Orchestra	*9:30*
		The Hollywood Legion Fight		*9:45*
Songs	The Ten o'Clock Wire		The Richfield Reporter	*10pm*
Jean Dunn, songs	Earl Burtnett Orchestra		Music	*10:15*
News				*10:30*
Exercises		The Adventures of Bill and Mr. Jackson		*10:45*

EVENING — SUMMER, 1931

Saturday

	BLUE	CBS	KNX	NBC
5pm	Bob and Jimmy, songs	The Hernandez Brothers, songs	Blossom Room Dansant (4:00pm)	General Electric Orchestra
5:15	Ballads	News		
5:30	Songs	The Lewisohn Stadium Concerts		Hollywood Word Pictures
5:45			Timely Tips	The Alabama Boys
6pm	Music	Hank Simmons' Show Boat	Wesley Tourtellote, organ	Lucky Strike Dance Orchestra
6:15			Tom and Wash, songs	
6:30				
6:45			Wesley Tourtellote, organ	
7pm	Amos 'n' Andy	Bert Lown Orchestra	Frank Watanabe and Honorable Archie	The Roamer's Male Quartet
7:15	Covered Wagon Days	Pryor's Cremo Band	Sol Hoopl's Hawaiians	The Gilmore Circus
7:30		The Camel Quater Hour		
7:45	The Sperry Smiles		The Gossipers	
8pm	The KECA String Ensemble	Detectives Black and Blue	KNX Varieities	Cactus Kate
8:15		The Merrymakers		
8:30				The Hollywood Bowl Concert
8:45				
9pm	The Ranch Boys		The Question and Answer Lady	
9:15			Music	
9:30	The Associated Spotlight Review			
9:45				
10pm	George Olsen Orchestra	The Ten o'Clock Wire	Blossom Room Dasant	
10:15		Earl Burtnett Orchestra		The Ranch Boys
10:30	Music			
10:45				

DAYTIME — SUMMER, 1931

Sunday

	BLUE	CBS	KNX	NBC
8am	Rochester Civic Orchestra	The Times Comics Pages	The Sharples Breakfast Club (7:00AM)	(Off the Air)
8:15				
8:30	The Troika Bells	Come Into the Garden		
8:45				
9am	Pop Concert	Home, Sweet Home	Judge Rutherford, legal talk	The Breakfast Frolic
9:15				
9:30				The KFI Ensemble
9:45				
10am	Explorer's Talk			
10:15	The Caribbeans			
10:30	Yeast Foamers Orchestra			Helen Guest, songs
10:45				
11am		First Methodist Church of Los Angeles	Third Church of Christian Scientist	
11:15				
11:30				
11:45				
12pm		The Cathedral Hour		
12:15			Records	
12:30			Louise Johnson, astrology	
12:45				
1pm		The KFRC Sunshine Hour		
1:15				
1:30			Pyror Moore Orchestra	
1:45				

DAYTIME — SUMMER, 1931

Monday-Friday

BLUE	CBS	KNX	NBC	
(Off the Air)	Hallelujah	The Sharples Breakfast Club (7:00AM)	The Shell Happy Time Hour	8am
				8:15
Exercises				8:30
				8:45
Cross-Cuts of the Day / Around the House	Talk and Music	Music / George Washington, Jr.	Music / Hints to Housewives	9am
		Music / Shopping Service	Talk and Music	9:15
Talk and Music		Records		9:30
				9:45
		Be Young and Happy, Eddie Albright		10am
			Music / The Heinz Program	10:15
			Talk and Music / Woman's Magazine of the Air	10:30
				10:45
		Talk and Music / Jack Carter's Birthday Party	Music	11am
				11:15
The Birth of Music		Talk and Music		11:30
Music				11:45
Luncheon Concert	Music / Biltmore Concert Orchestra		US Agricultural Talk	12pm
The National Farm and Home Hour		Dr. Matthews' Radio Church		12:15
	News			12:30
	Talk and Music	The Gossipers		12:45
Music		The Paris Inn Frolics		1pm
				1:15
	The Times Forum			1:30
				1:45

DAYTIME — SUMMER, 1931

Sunday

	BLUE	CBS	KNX	NBC
2pm	The Catholic Hour	The Chicago Knights	The Park Board Program	The Aeolian Organ Recital
2:15				
2:30		Piano Recital		
2:45		Speed Demons		
3pm	The Balboa Park Organ	Dr. Klien, health		The KFI String Trio
3:15		Fray and Braggiettti, songs		
3:30		Musical Comedy Shorts		
3:45		The Boswell Sisters, songs		
4pm	Silvio Lavatelli, cello	Devils, Drugs, and Doctors	The Vesper Hour	Enna Jettick Melodies
4:15	The Nomad Novelist	Kate Smith and Her Swanee Music		Blow the Man Down
4:30	Baldassare Ferlazzo, violin	Professor Lindsley, talk		Piano Recital
4:45				Songs

DAYTIME — SUMMER, 1931

Monday-Friday

BLUE	CBS	KNX	NBC	
	The Happy Go Lucky Hour	The Bookworm	The NBC Matinee	2pm
				2:15
		Talk and Music	Talk and Music	2:30
				2:45
Talk and Music	Feminine Fancies			3pm
				3:15
			Music	3:30
				3:45
Talk and Music / The Fleischman Yeast Hour, Rudy Vallee /	Music	Big Brother / Travelogue	Talk and Music / Organ Recital	4pm
The Cities Service Concerts				4:15
				4:30
	Music / Seeing Southern California			4:45

DAYTIME — SUMMER, 1931

Saturday

	BLUE	CBS	KNX	NBC
8am	(Off the Air)	Hallelujah	(Off the Air)	The Shell Happy Time Hour
8:15				
8:30	Exercises			
8:45			Prayer	
9am	Cross-Cuts of the Day	Music	George Washington, Jr.	Polly Hall, piano
9:15	Around the House		The Arizona Wranglers	Music
9:30		Records		The National Farm and Home Hour
9:45			Shopping Service	
10am		Mill's Soothing Sax	Be Young and Happy, Eddie Albright	
10:15				
10:30		Clarence Weaver, science	Records	Woman's Magazine of the Air
10:45		Don Ricardo, songs		
11am			Travelogue	
11:15		Music	Records	
11:30	The Birth of Words			French Lesson
11:45	Alexander Reilly, organ			Hollywood Bowl Talk
12pm	The Entertainers	Biltmore Concert Orchestra		US Agricultural Talk
12:15	Ballads of Approval			
12:30		News	Dr. Matthews' Radio Church	
12:45		Music		
1pm	Hotel St. Francis Drake Orchestra		The Paris Inn Frolics	
1:15				
1:30		The Times Forum		
1:45				

DAYTIME — SUMMER, 1931

Saturday

	BLUE	CBS	KNX	NBC
2pm	Black and Gold Orchestra	Music	The Bookworm	Siesta Melodies
2:15				
2:30		Whispering Smith	Records	
2:45		Songs		
3pm	Gene Austin, songs	Hotel St. Moritz Orchestra		Songs
3:15	Society's Laws			Hollywood Gossip
3:30	Sonata Recital	Reis and Dunn, songs		Organ Recital
3:45	Piano Recital	Music		
4pm	News		Blossom Room Dasant	Rudy Vallee Orchestra
4:15	Music	Kate Smith' and Her Swanee Music		
4:30	Organ Recital	Henry Burbig Orchestra		
4:45		Lavender and Old Lace		

EVENING — FALL, 1931

Sunday

	BLUE	CBS	KNX	NBC
5pm	Music	Devil, Drugs, and Doctor	Dr. Matthews' Radio Church	Enna Jettick Melodies
5:15		The Vesper Hour		The Collier Hour
5:30	The Alabama Boys			
5:45	Manley Hall, songs			
6pm	George Grandel, songs	Rabbi Magnin, religion	Dr. Aked, health	
6:15	Music			The American Album of Familiar Music
6:30		Adventuring with Count Von Luckner	Ernest Holmes: Theodore C. Abel	
6:45				The Buick Revelers
7pm		Texaco Symphony Orchestra	The Arizona Wranglers	
7:15	Wee Kirk o' the Heather			Ted Weems Orchestra
7:30		The Edison String Choir	Dance Orchestra	
7:45	Sunday Evenings at Seth Parker			Music
8pm		Musical Forget-Me-Nots	The First Presbyterian Church of Hollywood	
8:15	The Follies Dance Band	The Continental String Orchestra		Piano Duets
8:30	Music	Brooks Orchestra		The Carnation Contented Hour
8:45				
9pm		The Chevrolet Chronicles	A Night in Paris	The NBC Special
9:15			The Lubovsiki Trio	
9:30	The NBC Special	Harmony Highlights		Music
9:45		Walker's Birthday Party		
10pm	Felipe Delgado, songs			The Richfield Reporter
10:15		The Ten o'Clock Wire		String Quartet
10:30	Billy Ross, violin	Val Valenti Orchestra		Dance Orchestra
10:45				

EVENING — FALL, 1931

Monday

BLUE	CBS	KNX	NBC	
Songs	Songs	Big Brother	Songland	5pm
	News			5:15
Piano Recital	Songs		Death Valley Days	5:30
	The Balto Special			5:45
Maytag Orchestra	Music	News	Music	6pm
		Music		6:15
Dance Orchestra	An Evening in Paris	Louie's Hungry Five	The General Motors Concert	6:30
		Music		6:45
	Guy Lombardo Orchestra	Frank Watanabe and Honorable Archie	Gold Medal Express	7pm
		Music		7:15
The Three Bakers	Bob and Harriet, songs	Dance Orchestra	Real Folks	7:30
Football Preview	Musical Cross-Words			7:45
Amos 'n' Andy	The Blue Monday Jamboree	The Treasure Ship	Music	8pm
Ranse Valentine, rhymes			The Lumberjacks Quartet	8:15
Gretchen Garrett, songs		The Lubovsiki Trio	The MJB Demi-Tasse Revue	8:30
				8:45
Bouquet of Melodies		News	The Roamer's Male Quartet	9pm
Dance Ordchestra		Dance Orchestra	Sherlock Holmes	9:15
		The Question and Answer Lady		9:30
The Canfield Beach Boys			The Prince Albert Quarter Hour	9:45
	The Ten o'Clock Wire	The Embassy Club	The Richfield Reporter	10pm
The Ranch Boys	Hotel Roosevelt Orchestra		Music	10:15
				10:30
News				10:45

EVENING — FALL, 1931

Tuesday

	BLUE	CBS	KNX	NBC
5pm	Baron Keyes, stories	Elvia and Nell, songs (4:45pm)	Big Brother	Coffee Matinee
5:15		News		
5:30	Piano Recital	Mona Content, piano		Heel Hugger Harmonies
5:45		Jack Parker, songs		The Three Bakers
6pm	Dance Orchestra	Ben Bernie, the Old Maestro	News	Musical Magazine
6:15		The Columbians	Music	
6:30	The Fuller Brush Man	Red Goose Adventures	Louie's Hungry Five	Memories
6:45		Detectives Black and Blue	Music	
7pm	Music	To the Ladies	Frank Watanabe and Honorable Archie	Lucky Strike Dance Orchestra
7:15		Mark Warnow Orchestra	Music	
7:30	The Canfield Beach Boys	The KFRC Concert	The Gilmore Circus	
7:45	Dance Orchestra			
8pm	Amos 'n' Andy	Chandu, the Magician	One-Act Playlet	The Emporor of Crime
8:15	Patrol	Pryor's Cremo Band		Memory Lane
8:30		The Camel Quarter Hour	The Arizona Wranglers	
8:45	The Sperry Smiles	The Inglewood Park Concert		The Roamer's Male Quartet
9pm	Music		News	The Caswell Concert
9:15		Beauties of History	Dixie Ensemble	Great Trials of History
9:30		Harmony Highlights		The Dixie Symphony Quartet
9:45		Music	Music	The Prince Albert Quarter Hour
10pm	Music	The Ten o'Clock Wire	The Embassy Club	The Richfield Reporter
10:15		Roosevelt Hotel Orchestra		Songs
10:30				
10:45	News			

EVENING — FALL, 1931

Wednesday

BLUE	CBS	KNX	NBC	
Baron Keyes, stories	Organ Recital (4:45pm)	Big Brother	College Memories	5pm
	News		Dance Orchestra	5:15
The Three Bakers	Frank Gage, songs			5:30
Music	The Balto Special	Amusement Tips	Guitar Recital	5:45
	The Three Cheers	News	The Halsey Stuart Concert	6pm
	The Los Angeles Quartet	Music		6:15
Songs	Songs	Louie's Hungry Five	The Palmolive Hour	6:30
The KECA After-Dinner Review	Detectives Black and Blue	Music		6:45
	Vitality Personalities	Frank Watanabe and Honorable Archie		7pm
	Bringing Up Father	The Rosicrucian String Ensemble		7:15
	Old Friends		The Coca-Cola Program	7:30
John Vale, songs		Songs		7:45
Amos 'n' Andy	Chandu, the Magician	Brown's Airdales	Songs	8pm
The Lyric Trio	Pryor's Cremo Band		The Lumberjacks Quartet	8:15
Songs	The Camel Quarter Hour	The Serenaders	Golden Melodies	8:30
	The Boswell Sisters, songs			8:45
Music	Musc	News	Rin-Tin-Tin Thriller	9pm
		Songs	Great Trials of History	9:15
	Harmony Highlights	The Question and Answer Lady	Songs	9:30
			The Prince Albert Quarter Hour	9:45
	The Ten o'Clock Wire	The Embassy Club	The Richfield Reporter	10pm
	Roosevelt Hotel Orchestra		The Ranch Boys	10:15
			Music	10:30
News				10:45

EVENING — FALL, 1931

Thursday

	BLUE	CBS	KNX	NBC
5pm	The Fleischman Yeast Hour, Rudy Vallee	Organ Recital	Big Brother	Nick Harris
5:15		News		Dance Orchestra
5:30		The Whittier College Hour	Records	
5:45		The Balto Special	Timely Tips	Judge Paonessa, legal talk
6pm	The Arco Birthday Party	Eugene Ormandy Presents	News	Music of All Countries
6:15			Music	
6:30	The Maxwell House Concerts	Music	Louie's Hungry Five	The Wandering Mnstrels
6:45		Detectives Black and Blue	Music	
7pm	Music	Gilmore College Daze	Frank Watanabe and Honorable Archie	Lucky Strike Dance Orchestra
7:15			Smilin' Ed McConnell, songs	
7:30		Bob and Harriet, songs	The Arizona Wrangler	
7:45	Patrol	The Ken Christie Trio		
8pm	Amos 'n' Andy	Chandu, the Magician	The Lubovsiki Trio	The Three Bakers
8:15	The Firestone Band	Pryor's Cremo Band		The Standard Symphony Hour
8:30		The Camel Quarter Hour		
8:45	Music	Songs		
9pm		The KFRC Surprise Program	The Question and Answer Lady	
9:15	The Sperry Smiles		Dance Orchestra	Great Trials of History
9:30	Music	Harmony Highlights		The Roamer's Male Quartet
9:45			News	The Prince Albert Quarter Hour
10pm	Bob and Jimmy, songs	The Ten o'Clock Wire	The Embassy Club	The Richfield Reporter
10:15	The Ranch Boys	Hotel Roosevelt Orchestra		The Hi-Liters Review
10:30				
10:45	News			

EVENING — FALL, 1931

Friday

BLUE	CBS	KNX	NBC	
The Cities Service Concerts	The Three Cheers (4:45pm)	Big Brother	Hollywood Word Pictures	5pm
	News			5:15
	The March of Time		Music	5:30
		The Town Crier	Garden Talk	5:45
Nick Harris	On Twelfth Street	News	The Interwoven Pair	6pm
		Music		6:15
The Sperry Serenaders	The Los Angeles Quartet	Louie's Hungry Five	Armour Orchestra	6:30
	Detectives Black and Blue	Music		6:45
Dance Orchestra	To the Ladies	Frank Watanabe and Honorable Archie	Paul Whiteman Orchestra	7pm
Alice in Toyland	Music	Penn and Cash, songs		7:15
Football Review	Laughing Gas	The Musical Candy Box	The RKO Theater	7:30
		The Bobrick Girls		7:45
Amos 'n' Andy	Chandu, the Magician	The Optimistic Do-Nuts	Doping the Game	8pm
The Stove Poker Philosopher	Pryor's Cremo Band		Brown-bilt Footlites	8:15
	The Camel Quarter Hour		The MJB Demi-Tasse Revue	8:30
	The Boswell Sisters, songs			8:45
	Beauties of History	Dixie Ensemble	The House of Color	9pm
Florsheim Frolics	Ben Bernie, the Old Maestro		Great Trials of History	9:15
	Harmony Highlights	News	The Dixie Symphony Quartet	9:30
Music		The Hollywood Legion Fight	The Prince Albert Quarter Hour	9:45
The Alabama Boys	The Ten o'Clock Wire		The Richfield Reporter	10pm
The Ranch Boys	Hotel Roosevelt Orchestra		Music	10:15
				10:30
News		The Arizona Wranglers		10:45

EVENING — FALL, 1931

Saturday

	BLUE	CBS	KNX	NBC
5pm	Music	Mark Hopkins Orchestra	Dance Orchestra	Danger Fighters
5:15		News		
5:30	Jack Baldwin, piano	Barn Dance Varieties		Council on Education
5:45			Timely Tips	
6pm	Music	Music	News	Music
6:15			Songs	
6:30		Felix Mills Orchestra	Louie's Hungry Five	The First Nighter Program
6:45		Detectives Black and Blue	Music	
7pm	Music	Hank Simmons' Show Boat	Frank Watanabe and Honorable Archie	Lucky Strike Dance Orchestra
7:15			The Arizona Wranglers	
7:30				
7:45	John Vale, songs			
8pm	Amos 'n' Andy	Chandu, the Magician	KNX Varieities	The Emporor of Crime
8:15	Patrol	Pryor's Cremo Band		The Gilmore Circus
8:30	Don Ricardo, songs	The Camel Quarter Hour		
8:45	The Sperry Smiles	The Signaleers		Doping the Game
9pm	The Ranch Boys	The Merrymakers	News	Music
9:15			Piano and Cello Recital	
9:30	Music	Harmony Highlights	The Question and Answer Lady	The Associated Spotlight Review
9:45		Ann Leaf at the Organ		
10pm	Songs	The Ten o'Clock Wire	The Embassy Club	
10:15	The Canfield Beach Boys	Hotel Roosevelt Orchestra		
10:30				
10:45				

DAYTIME — FALL, 1931

Sunday

	BLUE	CBS	KNX	NBC
8am	(Off the Air)	The Times Comics Pages	The Sharples Breakfast Club (7:00AM)	(Off the Air)
8:15				
8:30		The Voice of St. Louis		
8:45		Dog Talk		
9am		Home, Sweet Home		The Breakfast Frolic
9:15				
9:30				The KFI Trio
9:45				
10am	NBC Artists' Service		Judge Rutherford, legal talk	
10:15				Jean Cowan, songs
10:30	Sentinels of the Republic		Joseph Diskay, songs	The Lyric Trio
10:45	Music		Third Church of Christian Scientist	
11am	NBC Program	First Methodist Church of Los Angeles		The Canfield Beach Boys
11:15	Sunday Bright Spots			
11:30	Yeast Foamers Orchestra			
11:45				
12pm		New York Philharmonic Orchestra		Organ Recital
12:15				
12:30			Louise Johnson, astrology	Helen Guest, songs
12:45				
1pm			The IBSA Watchtower	Poetry
1:15				
1:30				Art Lecture
1:45				

DAYTIME — FALL, 1931

Monday-Friday

BLUE	CBS	KNX	NBC	
(Off the Air)	Hallelujah	The Sharples Breakfast Club	The Shell Happy Time Hour	8am
				8:15
				8:30
				8:45
	Don Bigelow Orchestra	Air Clinic	G. E. Circle	9am
	Music		Beautiful Thoughts	9:15
	Talk and Music / Betty Crocker, cooking	News and Views	Music / Helen Guest, songs	9:30
	The Columbia Revue			9:45
	Music / Pabstette / Tillie the Toiler	Be Young and Happy, Eddie Albright	Talk and Music	10am
Exercises	The Columbia Farm Hour			10:15
Roy Leffingwell Orchestra			Talk and Music / Woman's Magazine of the Air	10:30
	Music	The Domestics		10:45
Talk and Music	Ann Leaf at the Organ / The Columbia Recital	Talk and Music	Talk and Music / The Standard School Broadcast	11am
				11:15
Music / California Federation of Women's Clubs	Talk and Music / American School of the Air	Talk and Music / Jack Carter's Birthday Party		11:30
				11:45
Luncheon Concert	Biltmore Concert Orchestra	News	US Agricultural Talk	12pm
The National Farm and Home Hour		Music		12:15
	News	Dr. Matthews' Radio Church	Songs	12:30
	Talk and Music			12:45
Talk and Music		Paris Inn Frolic		1pm
Music / Gems of Melody			Music / Siesta Melodies	1:15
Music				1:30
			Bunny's Family	1:45

DAYTIME — FALL, 1931

Sunday

	BLUE	CBS	KNX	NBC
2pm	NBC Special	Pastorale	The Park Board Program	
2:15				
2:30	The Twilight Hour	Firelight Pictures		The Ascot Auto Races
2:45				
3pm	The Catholic Hour			
3:15				
3:30		Professor Lindsley, readings		
3:45				
4pm	The Vagabond's Quartet	Dr. Klein, economics	Advanced Thought	The Willys-Overland Special
4:15		Columbia Special	The Lubovsiki Trio	The Jelly Revue
4:30				The Three Bakers
4:45			Christian Business Men	

DAYTIME — FALL, 1931

Monday-Friday

BLUE	CBS	KNX	NBC	
Music / Mouth Health	The Happy Go Lucky Hour	The Bookworm	The NBC Matinee	2pm
				2:15
Talk and Music		Talk and Music		2:30
				2:45
Music / The Italian Language	Feminine Fancies		Talk and Music / Seeing Southern California	3pm
			Music	3:15
Talk and Music				3:30
				3:45
	Presenting Bing Crosby	Travelogue	Wild Jack's Cowboys	4pm
News	Music			4:15
Baron Keyes, stories			Talk and Music	4:30
				4:45

DAYTIME — FALL, 1931

Saturday

	BLUE	CBS	KNX	NBC
8am	(Off the Air)	Hallelujah	(Off the Air)	The Shell Happy Time Hour
8:15				
8:30				
8:45			The Sharples Breakfast Club	
9am		Don Bigelow Orchestra		Piano Recital
9:15				Beautiful Thoughts
9:30				The National Farm and Home Hour
9:45			Shopping Service	
10am		Hotel Taft Orchestra	Be Young and Happy, Eddie Albright	
10:15	Exercises			
10:30			Music	Woman's Magazine of the Air
10:45	Sports	Sports		
11am			Sports	
11:15				
11:30				French Lesson
11:45				Songs
12pm			News and Views	US Agricultural Talk
12:15				Organ Recital
12:30			Dr. Matthews' Radio Church	
12:45				
1pm			Paris Inn Frolic	
1:15		News		The Canfield Beach Boys
1:30		Sports		
1:45				Bunny's Family

DAYTIME — FALL, 1931

			Saturday	
	BLUE	CBS	KNX	NBC
2pm			Sports	Sports
2:15	Organ Recital			
2:30				
2:45				
3pm	Siesta Melodies			
3:15				
3:30				
3:45				
4pm	Spanish Lesson			
4:15	Songs			
4:30	Music			
4:45				

LISTINGS FOR 1932

EVENING — WINTER, 1932

Sunday

	BLUE	CBS	KNX	NBC
5pm	The Sunday Concert	Devil, Drugs, and Doctor	Dr. Matthews' Radio Church	Enna Jettick Melodies
5:15		The Vesper Hour		The Collier Hour
5:30				
5:45		Your Child		
6pm	Manley Hall, songs	The Roxy Symphony Concert	Music	
6:15	Music			The American Album of Familiar Music
6:30		Adventuring with Count Von Luckner	Ernest Holmes: Theodore C. Abel	
6:45	The Alabama Boys			The Buick Revelers
7pm	Raising Junior	Hedda Hopper's Hollywood	The Lubovsiki Trio	
7:15	The Lyric Trio			The Old Singing Master
7:30		Raymond Paige Orchestra	Music	
7:45	Sunday Evenings at Seth Parker	Ernest Hutcheson, piano		Music
8pm		The Edison String Choir	The First Presbyterian Church of Hollywood	
8:15	Sacred Songs			
8:30	Richard Davis Orchestra	California Melodies		The Carnation Contented Hour
8:45				
9pm	The Abas String Quartet	The Chevrolet Chronicles	A Night in Paris	The Chase and Sanborn Hour, Eddie Cantor
9:15			The Arizona Wranglers	
9:30		Sunday Sweets		
9:45		Musical Forget-Me-Nots		
10pm		The Ten o'Clock Wire	BPOE No 99 High Jinks	The Richfield Reporter
10:15		The KFRC Concert		Organ Recital
10:30				
10:45				

EVENING — WINTER, 1932

Monday

BLUE	CBS	KNX	NBC	
Big Brother	Leonard Joy Orchestra	The Arizona Wranglers	Fine Arts String Quartet	5pm
	News			5:15
	Kerry Conway's Chats on Words	The Crazy Water Rangers	Death Valley Days	5:30
California Medical Association Talks	The Gloom Chasers			5:45
Records	Music	News	Maytag Orchestra	6pm
Memories		The Texas Rangers		6:15
	The KFRC Song Recital	Lil' Joe Warner's Jolly Journal	The General Motors Concert	6:30
Cecil and Sally		Anson Weeks Orchestra		6:45
The National Radio Forum	Guy Lombardo Orchestra	Frank Watanabe and Honorable Archie	Music	7pm
		Music		7:15
Organ Recital	Music That Satisfies		The MJB Demi-Tasse Revue	7:30
Music	The Story of Myrt and Marge	Centreville Sketches		7:45
	The Blue Monday Jamboree	The Serenaders	Amos 'n' Andy	8pm
The Prince Albert Quarter Hour			The Lumberjacks Quartet	8:15
Songs		The Georgia Fifeld Players	The Voice of Firestone	8:30
Music				8:45
		News	Music	9pm
		Music	Sherlock Holmes	9:15
Earl Burtnett Orchestra		The Question and Answer Lady		9:30
			The Stebbins Boys	9:45
	The Ten o'Clock Wire	Jane Jone's Night Club	The Richfield Reporter	10pm
	Harold Roberts Orchestra		Jimmy Greer Orchestra	10:15
News and Views				10:30
				10:45

EVENING — WINTER, 1932

Tuesday

	BLUE	CBS	KNX	NBC
5pm	Voter's Service	Leonard Joy Orchestra	The Arizona Wranglers	Coffee Matinee
5:15		News		
5:30		Music		Heel Hugger Harmonies
5:45	The Nurseryman		Timely Tips	Vintage Melodies
6pm	Records	Ben Bernie, the Old Maestro	News	Musical Magazine
6:15			Bad Men and Bandits	
6:30		Salonesque	Lil' Joe Warner's Jolly Journal	The Fuller Brush Man
6:45	Cecil and Sally		Music	
7pm	Raising Junior	To the Ladies	Frank Watanabe and Honorable Archie	Lucky Strike Dance Orchestra
7:15	The Lyric Trio	Detectives Black and Blue	Rev. Shuler, religion	
7:30		The KFRC Concert	The KFRC Concert	
7:45	Music	The Story of Myrt and Marge	Spanish Music	
8pm		Bing Crosby, the Cremo Singer	The Lubovsiki Trio	Amos 'n' Andy
8:15	The Prince Albert Quarter Hour	Chandu, the Magician		Memory Lane
8:30	Music	The Camel Quarter Hour		
8:45		The Inglewood Park Concert		The Sperry Smiles
9pm			News	The Caswell Concert
9:15	Jean Cowan, songs	Songs	Music	Packard Orchestra
9:30	Earl Burtnett Orchestra	Old Friends	Lal Chand Mehra, india talk	
9:45		Music	Music	The Stebbins Boys
10pm		The Ten o'Clock Wire	Jane Jone's Night Club	The Richfield Reporter
10:15		Gene Quaw Orchestra		Jimmy Greer Orchestra
10:30	News and Views			
10:45				

EVENING — WINTER, 1932

Wednesday

BLUE	CBS	KNX	NBC	
Big Brother	Leonard Joy Orchestra	The Arizona Wranglers	Traffic Talk	5pm
	News		California Medical Association Talks	5:15
The Los Angeles Fire Deparment Orchestra	Songs		The Goodyear Program	5:30
	The Columbia Special	The Town Crier		5:45
Records	Music	News	The Halsey Stuart Concert	6pm
		The Crazy Waters Rangers		6:15
	The Week's Best Bets	Lil' Joe Warner's Jolly Journal	The Mobil Oil Concert	6:30
Cecil and Sally	Bringing Up Father	Music		6:45
Raising Junior	Vitality Personalities	Frank Watanabe and Honorable Archie	The Coca-Cola Program	7pm
Organ Recital	Detectives Black and Blue	The Rosicrucian String Ensemble		7:15
The Hof Brau Cafe'	Music That Satisfies		Follies and Quartet	7:30
	The Story of Myrt and Marge	The Bobrick Girls		7:45
Sports	Bing Crosby, the Cremo Singer	Idylls	Amos 'n' Andy	8pm
The Prince Albert Quarter Hour	Chandu, the Magician		The Lumberjacks Quartet	8:15
The Lyric Trio	The Camel Quarter Hour	The Serenaders	Team Mates	8:30
	Vignettes			8:45
		News	Rin-Tin-Tin Thriller	9pm
The Alabama Boys	Music	Songs	Carl Omeron, songs	9:15
Earl Burtnett Orchestra	The Isle of Golden Dreams	The Question and Answer Lady		9:30
			The Stebbins Boys	9:45
	The Ten o'Clock Wire	Jane Jone's Night Club	The Richfield Reporter	10pm
	Anson Weeks Orchestra		Jimmy Greer Orchestra	10:15
News and Views				10:30
				10:45

EVENING — WINTER, 1932

Thursday

	BLUE	CBS	KNX	NBC
5pm	Big Brother	Leonard Joy Orchestra	The Arizona Wranglers	The Fleischman Yeast Hour, Rudy Vallee
5:15		News News		
5:30	Records	Kerry Conway's Chats on Words		
5:45		Your Child	Timely Tips	
6pm		J. Warde Hutton Orchestra	News	Music of All Countries
6:15	The Lyric Trio		Bad Men and Bandits	
6:30		Leonard Joy Orchestra	Lil' Joe Warner's Jolly Journal	The Maxwell House Concerts
6:45	Cecil and Sally		Rev. Schuler, religion	
7pm	Raising Junior	Concert Miniature	Frank Watanabe and Honorable Archie	Lucky Strike Dance Orchestra
7:15	Organ Recital	Detectives Black and Blue	Smilin' Ed McConnell, songs	
7:30	Music	Music That Satisfies	Music	
7:45		The Story of Myrt and Marge	Centreville Sketches	
8pm		Bing Crosby, the Cremo Singer	Oh Yeah	Amos 'n' Andy
8:15	The Prince Albert Quarter Hour	Chandu, the Magician		The Standard Symphony Hour
8:30	The Gilmore Circus	The Camel Quarter Hour	The Arizona Wranglers	
8:45		The Medley of Error		
9pm	Music	The KFRC Surprise Program	News	
9:15			Dance Orchestra	The Sperry Smiles
9:30	Earl Burtnett Orchestra	Laughing Gas	The Question and Answer Lady	Royal Palm Orchestra
9:45				The Stebbins Boys
10pm		The Ten o'Clock Wire	Jane Jone's Night Club	The Richfield Reporter
10:15		The Singers' Club		Jimmy Greer Orchestra
10:30	News and Views	Anson Weeks Orchestra		
10:45				

EVENING — WINTER, 1932

Friday

BLUE	CBS	KNX	NBC	
The Cities Service Concerts	Leonard Joy Orchestra	Shopping Service (4:30PM)	The Lyric Trio	5pm
	News	Rabbi Winkler, religion		5:15
	The March of Time		Nick Harris	5:30
		The Town Crier	Songs	5:45
Nick Harris	Vera Vans' Vanities	News	Friendship Town	6pm
	Mona Content, piano	Songs		6:15
	Lovely Lady	Lil' Joe Warner's Jolly Journal	Armour Orchestra	6:30
Cecil and Sally	Gene Quaw Orchestra	The Adventures of Louis and Adolph		6:45
Raising Junior	To the Ladies	Frank Watanabe and Honorable Archie	Paul Whiteman Orchestra	7pm
The Scrapbook	Detectives Black and Blue	The Lubovsiki Trio		7:15
	Music That Satisfies		The RKO Theater	7:30
Records	The Story of Myrt and Marge	The Bobrick Girls		7:45
James Anderson, songs	Bing Crosby, the Cremo Singer	The Optimistic Do-Nuts	Amos 'n' Andy	8pm
The Prince Albert Quarter Hour	Chandu, the Magician		Brown-bilt Footlites	8:15
Music	The Camel Quarter Hour		The MJB Demi-Tasse	8:30
	Raymond Paige Orchestra		Revue	8:45
Earl Burtnett Orchestra		News	The Disturbers of the Air	9pm
	Anita Stewart, songs	Music		9:15
	Melody Speedway	Lal Chand Mehra, India talk		9:30
	Isham Jones Orchestra	The Hollywood Legion Fight	The Stebbins Boys	9:45
	The Ten o'Clock Wire		The Richfield Reporter	10pm
	Anson Weeks Orchestra		Jimmy Greer Orchestra	10:15
News and Views				10:30
		The Arizona Wranglers		10:45

EVENING — WINTER, 1932

Saturday

	BLUE	CBS	KNX	NBC
5pm	Big Brother	The Gloom Chasers	Dr. Matthews' Radio Church	Danger Fighters
5:15		News		
5:30		Music		Council on Education
5:45	Raine Bennett Orchestra	Vaughn de Leath, songs	Timely Tips	
6pm		Barn Dance Varieties	News	The Goodyear Program
6:15			Songs	
6:30		Gene Quaw Orchestra	Lil' Joe Warner's Jolly Journal	The First Nighter Program
6:45	Cecil and Sally		The Adventures of Louis and Adolph	
7pm	Raising Junior	Raymond Paige Orchestra	Frank Watanabe and Honorable Archie	Lucky Strike Dance Orchestra
7:15	Music	Detectives Black and Blue	The Arizona Wranglers	
7:30		Music That Satisfies		
7:45		Jack Miiller Orchestra	Music	
8pm	Children's Play	Bing Crosby, the Cremo Singer	Sky Dwellers	Amos 'n' Andy
8:15	The Prince Albert Quarter Hour	Chandu, the Magician		The Gilmore Circus
8:30	Music	The Camel Quarter Hour		
8:45	The Lyric Silhouettes	The Signaleers		Freshmen
9pm		The Merrymakers	News	Jimmy Greer Orchestra
9:15			William Hatch Orchestra	
9:30	Earl Burtnett Orchestra		The Question and Answer Lady	The Associated Spotlight Review
9:45				
10pm		The Ten o'Clock Wire	Jane Jone's Night Club	
10:15		Gene Quaw Orchestra		
10:30				
10:45				

DAYTIME — WINTER, 1932

Sunday

	BLUE	CBS	KNX	NBC
8am	(Off the Air)	The Times Comics Pages	The Sharples Breakfast Club (7:00AM)	(Off the Air)
8:15				
8:30		The Voice of St. Louis		
8:45				
9am		Home, Sweet Home	Michael Kelly, songs	Piano Moods
9:15				
9:30				Songland
9:45				
10am	Records		Judge Rutherford, legal talk	Helen Guest, songs
10:15				The Symphonic Hour
10:30			Joseph Diskay, songs	
10:45				
11am	Temple Baptist Church	Talk and Music	Third Church of Christian Scientist	
11:15				Sunday Bright Spots
11:30		The CBS Church of the Air		Yeast Foamer Orchestra
11:45				
12pm	Music	New York Philharmonic Orchestra		Organ Recital
12:15				
12:30			Louise Johnson, astrology	
12:45				
1pm	Gunnar Johansen, piano		The IBSA Watchtower	American Colony Life in Berlin
1:15				
1:30	Organ Recital			The Lyric Trio
1:45				

DAYTIME — WINTER, 1931

Monday-Friday

BLUE	CBS	KNX	NBC	
(Off the Air)	The Shell Happy Time Hour	The Sharples Breakfast Club	Your Child / Stock Market Reports	8am
			Music	8:15
	Hallelujah			8:30
				8:45
	Don Bigelow Orchestra	Air Clinic	G. E. Circle	9am
			Beautiful Thoughts	9:15
	Music / Betty Crocker, cooking	News and Views	Music / Helen Guest, songs	9:30
	The Columbia Revue			9:45
News	Talk and Music / Pabstette / Tillie the Toiler	Be Young and Happy, Eddie Albright	Talk and Music	10am
Exercises	The Columbia Farm Hour			10:15
Roy Leffingwell Orchestra		Economics Talk	Talk and Music / Woman's Magazine of the Air	10:30
				10:45
Talk and Music	Music	Records	Talk and Music	11am
		Records / Jack Carter's Birthday Party		11:15
	Music / American School of the Air			11:30
			Stock Market Reports	11:45
Biltmore Concert Orchestra	Music / Ann Leaf at the Organ	News	US Agricultural Talk	12pm
		Music / Doria Ballli, songs	The National Farm and HomeHour	12:15
	News			12:30
Talk and Music	Music / Columbia Salon Orchestra			12:45
	Music	Paris Inn Frolic	News	1pm
			Music	1:15
	The Times Forum			1:30
Bunny's Family				1:45

DAYTIME — WINTER, 1932

Sunday

	BLUE	CBS	KNX	NBC
2pm		Bob Bradford, songs	The Park Board Program	
2:15		Lavender and Old Lace		
2:30	The Twilight Hour	The Legion of the Lost		The Ascot Auto Races
2:45				
3pm	Records	Chicago Knights		
3:15				
3:30	Our American Schools	Professor Lindsley, readings		
3:45				
4pm			Advanced Thought	The Willys-Overland Special
4:15			Rev. Barnhouse, religion	Judge Yankwich, legal talk
4:30	The Musical Merry-Go-Round	Rabbi Magnin, religion		The Three Bakers
4:45			Radio Skit	

DAYTIME — WINTER, 1932

Monday-Friday

BLUE	CBS	KNX	NBC	
Music	The Happy Go Lucky Hour	The Bookworm	The NBC Matinee	2pm
Music / Mouth Health				2:15
Talk and Music		Talk and Music		2:30
				2:45
Music / The Italian Language	Feminine Fancies		Music / Seeing Southern California	3pm
				3:15
Talk and Music			Music / The Old Topper	3:30
			Music	3:45
	Originalities	Travelogue		4pm
News	Talk and Music			4:15
Talk / Big Brother			News	4:30
	Music / Seeing Southern California		Music	4:45

DAYTIME — WINTER, 1932

Saturday

	BLUE	CBS	KNX	NBC
8am	(Off the Air)	The Shell Happy Time Hour	(Off the Air)	Celebrated Sayings
8:15				
8:30		New York World Salon Orchestra		The Keys to Happiness
8:45			The Sharples Breakfast Club	
9am		Don Bigelow Orchestra		Piano Recital
9:15				Beautiful Thoughts
9:30			News and Views	The National Farm and Home Hour
9:45		Public Affairs		
10am	News	Records	Be Young and Happy, Eddie Albright	
10:15	Exercises	The Farm Network		
10:30	Roy Leffingwell Orchestra			Woman's Magazine of the Air
10:45				
11am	Records	The Funnyboners		
11:15		Saturday Syncopators		
11:30	Music	Columbia Salon Orchestra		French Lesson
11:45	Spanish Lesson			Piano Recital
12pm	The Metropolitan Opera	The Four Clubmen	News and Views	US Agricultural Talk
12:15				The Cosmpolitans
12:30		The Rhythm Kings		
12:45				
1pm		Ann Leaf at the Organ	Paris Inn Frolic	News
1:15				The String Wood Ensemble
1:30		The Times Forum		
1:45				The Stamp Man

DAYTIME — WINTER, 1932

Saturday

	BLUE	CBS	KNX	NBC
2pm	Records	Eddy Duchin Orchestra	The Bookworm	The Hill Billies
2:15				
2:30		Music	Records	The Rembrandt Trio
2:45				
3pm				
3:15		Freddy Martin Orchestra		
3:30		George Hall Orchestra		The Old Topper
3:45		Connee Boswell, songs		Tea Time Dance
4pm		Frederick William Wile, comment	Travelogue	
4:15		Tea Dasant		
4:30	News and Views			
4:45				News

EVENING — SPRING, 1932

Sunday

	BLUE	CBS	KNX	NBC
5pm	Our American Schools (3:30PM)	The Ziegfeld Follies of the Air	Dr. Matthews' Radio Church	Enna Jettick Melodies
5:15				The Collier Hour
5:30	Campus Comedians	Rabbi Magnin, religion		
5:45		Your Child		
6pm	Masterpieces of Music	Ever-Ready Radio Gaities	News	
6:15			Swami Dhirananda, religion	The American Album of Familiar Music
6:30	The Samiloff Trio	The Edison String Choir	Ernest Holmes: Theodore C. Abel	
6:45				The Buick Revelers
7pm	Raising Junior	Hedda Hopper's Hollywood	Rev. Duncan, religion	
7:15	The Palace Hotel Grand Concert			The Old Singing Master
7:30		Seeing Southern California		
7:45	Sunday Evenings at Seth Parkers		Jeanne and Joan, songs	Lights and Shadows
8pm		The Gauchos	The First Presbyterian Church of Hollywood	Music
8:15	Sacred Songs	The Greyhound Traveler		
8:30	Rudy Sieger Orchestra	The Parade of Melodies		The Carnation Contented Hour
8:45				
9pm	The Imperial Male Quartet	Melody Speedway	A Night in Paris	The Chase and Sanborn Hour, Eddie Cantor
9:15		Musical Cameos	The Lubovsiki Trio	
9:30	The Abas String Quartet	California Melodies		
9:45				
10pm	Book Review	The Ten o'Clock Wire		The Richfield Reporter
10:15		The KFRC Concert		Organ Recital
10:30	News and Views			
10:45				

EVENING — SPRING, 1932

Monday

BLUE	CBS	KNX	NBC	
Big Brother	Aunt Jemima	Shopping Service (4:15 PM)	The Lyric Trio	5pm
	News	The Arizona Wranglers		5:15
	Skippy		Death Valley Days	5:30
Little Orphan Annie	Idyllio	Chandu, the Magician		5:45
Yarley and Yenna	J. Warde Hutton Orchestra	News	Maytag Orchestra	6pm
The Wilshire Women's Choral Club		Anson Weeks Orchestra		6:15
	An Evening in Paris	The Canadian Grenadiers	The General Motors Concert	6:30
Cecil and Sally		Vivian Duncer and Lew Cody, songs		6:45
The National Radio Forum	Guy Lombardo Orchestra	Frank Watanabe and Honorable Archie	Sam Coslow Orchestra	7pm
		Rajput, Hindu Secret Service		7:15
Walter Tourtellette, organ	Music That Satisfies	Phil Spitalny Orchestra	The MJB Demi-Tasse Revue	7:30
Alice Gentle, songs	The Story of Myrt and Marge	Centreville Sketches		7:45
Coquettes	The Blue Monday Jamboree	The Serenaders	Amos 'n' Andy	8pm
The Prince Albert Quarter Hour			Memories	8:15
Music		The Georgia Fifeld Players	The Voice of Firestone	8:30
				8:45
		News	Rudyard Kipling's Stories	9pm
		Music		9:15
Earl Burtnett Orchestra		The Question and Answer Lady	The Interwoven Pair	9:30
			Royal Palm Orchestra	9:45
	The Ten o'Clock Wire	Bohemian Club Orchestra	The Richfield Reporter	10pm
	Anson Weeks Orchestra		Jimmy Greer Orchestra	10:15
News and Views				10:30
				10:45

EVENING — SPRING, 1932

Tuesday

	BLUE	CBS	KNX	NBC
5pm	Council on Education	The Hobby Hunter	Travelogue (4:00PM)	The Lyric Trio
5:15		News	The Arizona Wranglers	
5:30	The Nurseryman	Skippy		Heel Hugger Harmonies
5:45	Little Orphan Annie	Organ Recital	Chandu, the Magician	The Roamers Male Quartet
6pm	Yarley and Yenna	Ben Bernie, the Old Maestro	News	Musical Magazine
6:15	Music		Bad Men and Bandits	
6:30		Bert Lown Orchestra	Music	Hits and Bits
6:45	Cecil and Sally	The Foreign Lands Concert		
7pm	Raising Junior	The Voice of 1000 Shades, Jack Kerr	Frank Watanabe and Honorable Archie	Lucky Strike Dance Orchestra
7:15	Music	Detectives Black and Blue	Rev. Shuler, religion	
7:30		The KFRC Concert	The KFRC Concert	
7:45		The Story of Myrt and Marge	Just Willie	
8pm	Stonewall Jackson, songs	Joe Palooka	The Carefree Hour	Amos 'n' Andy
8:15	The Prince Albert Quarter Hour	Chandu, the Magician	The Lubovsiki Trio	Memory Lane
8:30	The Dinglebenders	The Camel Quarter Hour		
8:45	Music	The Olympiads		The Sperry Smiles
9pm			News	The Caswell Concert
9:15		Hollywood Nights	Music	Public Affairs
9:30	Earl Burtnett Orchestra	The Chevrolet Special		The Interwoven Pair
9:45		Isham Jones Orchestra		Royal Palm Orchestra
10pm		The Ten o'Clock Wire	Bohemian Club Orchestra	The Richfield Reporter
10:15		Gene Quaw Orchestra		Jimmy Greer Orchestra
10:30	News and Views			
10:45				

EVENING — SPRING, 1932

Wednesday

BLUE	CBS	KNX	NBC	
Big Brother	Aunt Jemima	Travelogue (4:00 PM)	Traffic Talk	5pm
	News	The Arizona Wranglers	The Silver Streaks	5:15
	Skippy		The Garden of Melodies	5:30
Little Orphan Annie	Serenade	Chandu, the Magician		5:45
Yarley and Yenna		News	The Goodyear Program	6pm
Music	The Columbians	Andy Santella Orchestra		6:15
	The Week's Best Bets	The Canadian Grenadiers	The Mobil Oil Concert	6:30
Cecil and Sally	Bringing Up Father	Vivian Duncan and Lew Cody, songs		6:45
Raising Junior	Music That Satisfies	Frank Watanabe and Honorable Archie	The Coca-Cola Program	7pm
Jean Cowan, songs	Detectives Black and Blue	Rajput, Hindu Secret Service		7:15
Marching Through	The Society's Playboy Hour	Phil Spitalny Orchestra	Verne Gray, songs	7:30
	The Story of Myrt and Marge	Jeanne and Joan, songs	Lights and Shadows	7:45
Stonewall Jackson, songs	Music	The Serenaders	Amos 'n' Andy	8pm
The Prince Albert Quarter Hour	Chandu, the Magician		Music	8:15
Music	The Camel Quarter Hour	The Lubovsiki Trio	Team Mates	8:30
	Broadcast Rehearsals			8:45
	To the Ladies	News	Eva Gruninger Atkinson, songs	9pm
	Eddy Duchin Orchestra	Music	The Frigidairians	9:15
Earl Burtnett Orchestra	The Isle of Golden Dreams	The Question and Answer Lady	The Interwovan Pair	9:30
			Music	9:45
	The Ten o'Clock Wire	Bohemian Club Orchestra	The Richfield Reporter	10pm
	Anson Weeks Orchestra		Jimmy Greer Orchestra	10:15
News and Views				10:30
				10:45

EVENING — SPRING, 1932

Thursday

	BLUE	CBS	KNX	NBC
5pm	Big Brother	The Hobby Hunter	Travelogue (4:00 PM)	The Fleischman Yeast Hour, Rudy Vallee
5:15		News	The Arizona Wranglers	
5:30		Skippy		
5:45	Little Orphan Annie	Your Child	Chandu, the Magician	
6pm	Yarley and Yenna	J. Warde Hutton Orchestra	News	The Big Six of the Air
6:15	Music		Bad Men and Bandits	
6:30		Seeing Southern California	The Canadian Grenadiers	Thompkins Corners
6:45	Cecil and Sally		Bringing Up Vivian	
7pm	Raising Junior		Frank Watanabe and Honorable Archie	Lucky Strike Dance Orchestra
7:15	The Lyric Trio	Detectives Black and Blue	Rev. Shuler religion	
7:30	Organ Recital	Music That Satisfies	Vincent Lopez Orchestra	
7:45	Music	The Story of Myrt and Marge		
8pm		Joe Palooka	Musical Memories	Amos 'n' Andy
8:15	The Prince Albert Quarter Hour	Chandu, the Magician		The Standard Symphony Hour
8:30	The Dinglebenders	The Camel Quarter Hour	The Lubovsiki Trio	
8:45	Robert Hurd Orchestra	The Inglewood Park Concert		
9pm			News	
9:15		Jose Aria Orchestra	Wild Jack's Cowboys	The Sperry Smiles
9:30	Earl Burtnett Orchestra	Today and Yesterday		The Interwovan Pair
9:45				Royal Palm Orchestra
10pm		The Ten o'Clock Wire	Bohemian Club Orchestra	The Richfield Reporter
10:15		The Singer's Club		Jimmy Greer Orchestra
10:30	News and Views	Anson Weeks Orchestra		
10:45				

EVENING — SPRING, 1932

Friday

BLUE	CBS	KNX	NBC	
Big Brother	Aunt Jemima	Shopping Service (4:15PM)	National Concert Orchestra	5pm
	News	Rabbi Winkler, religion		5:15
	Skippy			5:30
Little Orphan Annie	The Old Refrain	Chandu, the Magician		5:45
Yarley and Yenna	Vera Van's Vanities	News	Friendship Town	6pm
Ranse Valentine, rhymes	Mona Content, piano	Andy Santella Orchestra		6:15
	Lovely Lady	The Canadian Grenadiers	Armour Orchestra	6:30
Cecil and Sally	Gene Quaw Orchestra	Vivian Duncan and Lew Cody, songs		6:45
Raising Junior	Beau Bachelor	Frank Watanabe and Honorable Archie	Paul Whiteman Orchestra	7pm
Music	Detectives Black and Blue	Rajput, Hindu Secret Service		7:15
The Scrapbook	Music That Satisfies	Centreville Sketches	The Golden Melodies Concert	7:30
	The Story of Myrt and Marge	Jeanne and Joan, songs		7:45
Stonewall Jackson, songs	La Petite Cafe' Orchestra	The Optimistic Do-Nuts	Amos 'n' Andy	8pm
The Prince Albert Quarter Hour	Chandu, the Magician		The Frigidairians	8:15
Fred Forrest and Emma Hirst, songs	The Camel Quarter Hour		The MJB Demi-Tasse Revue	8:30
	Memories			8:45
	To the Ladies	News	The Voice of '76	9pm
	Vignettes	Music		9:15
Earl Burtnett Orchestra		Lal Chand Mehra, india talk	The Interwoven Pair	9:30
		The Hollywood Legion Fight	The Callifornians	9:45
	The Ten o'Clock Wire		The Richfield Reporter	10pm
	Anson Weeks Orchestra		Jimmy Greer Orchestra	10:15
News and Views				10:30
		The Arizona Wranglers		10:45

EVENING — SPRING, 1932

Saturday

	BLUE	CBS	KNX	NBC
5pm	Big Brother	Electric Eyes	The Town Crier	Danger Fighters
5:15		News	Dr. Matthews' Radio Church	
5:30		Skippy		Council on Education
5:45	Little Orphan Annie	Vaughn de Leath, songs	Chandu, the Magician	
6pm	Raine Bennett Orchestra	The Fisk University Singers	News	The Goodyear Program
6:15			Songs	
6:30		Fray and Braggiotti, songs	Lil' Joe Warner's Jolly Journal	The First Nighter Program
6:45	Cecil and Sally	Isham Jones Orchestra	Songs	
7pm	Raising Junior	Music That Satisfies	Frank Watanabe and Honorable Archie	Lucky Strike Dance Orchestra
7:15	Blythe Burns, songs	Detectives Black and Blue	The Arizona Wranglers	
7:30		Raymond Paige Orchestra		
7:45		The Street Singer	Jeanne and Joan, songs	
8pm		Don Redman Orchestra	The Laugh Parade	Amos 'n' Andy
8:15	The Prince Albert Quarter Hour	Chandu, the Magician		Good Times
8:30	The Dinglebenders	The Camel Quarter Hour		
8:45	Johnny Hamp Orchestra	Enric Madriquerra Orchestra		Beale Street Nights
9pm	Robert Hurd Orchestra	The Merrymakers	News	Jimmy Greer Orchestra
9:15			Music	
9:30	Earl Burtnett Orchestra		The Question and Answer Lady	The Associated Spotlight Review
9:45		Waves of Melody		
10pm		The Ten o'Clock Wire	Bohemian Club Orchestra	
10:15		Gene Quaw Orchestra		
10:30				
10:45				

DAYTIME — SPRING, 1932

Sunday

	BLUE	CBS	KNX	NBC
8am	(Off the Air)	The Times Comics Pages	The Sharples Breakfast Club (7:00AM)	(Off the Air)
8:15				
8:30		Uncle John		
8:45				
9am		Home, Sweet Home	The Avocado Man	Lilyan Ariel, piano
9:15				
9:30				Songland
9:45				Helen Guest, songs
10am	Nick Harris		Judge Rutherford, legal talk	The Symphonic Hour
10:15				
10:30			The Singing Cowboys	
10:45			Third Church of Christian Scientist	
11am	Records	The Pacific Islanders		The Alabama Boys
11:15				Viennese Ensemble
11:30		The CBS Church of the Air		Yeast Foamers Orchestra
11:45				
12pm		New York Philharmonic Orchestra		Organ Recital
12:15				
12:30	Music		Louise Johnson, astrology	
12:45				
1pm			The IBSA Watchtower	The Iodent Program, Jane Froman
1:15				Paul Taylor Quartet
1:30	Organ Recital			The Lifetime Revue
1:45				

DAYTIME — SPRING, 1932

Monday-Friday

BLUE	CBS	KNX	NBC	
(Off the Air)	The Shell Happy Time Hour	The Sharples Breakfast Club (6:45AM)	Your Child / Brighten Up / Stock Market	8am
			Music / Brighten Up	8:15
	Hallelujah		Music / Romance Exchange	8:30
				8:45
Exercises		Air Clinic	G. E. Circle	9am
			Beautiful Thoughts	9:15
	Music / Betty Crocker, cooking	News and Views	Music / Helen Guest, songs	9:30
	The Columbia Revue		Talk and Music	9:45
News and Views	Music / The Columbia Farm Hour	Be Young and Happy, Eddie Albright		10am
	Almanac of the Air			10:15
	Talk and Music / The Farm Network	Economics Talk	Talk and Music / Woman's Magazine of the Air	10:30
				10:45
German Lesson / News and Views	Music / Ann Leaf at the Organ	Talk and Music / Jack Carter's Birthday Party	Talk and Music / The Standard School Broadcast	11am
				11:15
	Columbia Salon Orchestra / American School of the Air			11:30
			Stock Market Reports	11:45
Biltmore Concert Orchestra	Music / Ann Leaf at the Organ	News	US Agricultural Talk	12pm
		Talk	The National Farm and HomeHour	12:15
	News	Noonday Revels / Dr. Matthews' Radio Church		12:30
Talk and Music	Talk			12:45
		Paris Inn Frolic	News	1pm
			Ann Warner Chats	1:15
	Forum			1:30
Bunny's Family			Music	1:45

DAYTIME — SPRING, 1932

Sunday

	BLUE	CBS	KNX	NBC
2pm		Professor Lindsley, readings	The Westlake Park Concert	Poetry and Music
2:15				
2:30	Records	Chicago Knights		The Twilight Hour
2:45		Song Stories		
3pm		The Legion of the Lost		Home, Sweet Home
3:15				
3:30	Our American Schools	Lavender and Old Lace		Judge Yankwich, legal talk
3:45				Day Dreams
4pm		Dr. Klein, economics	Advanced Thought	Sing a New Song
4:15		The Vesper Hour	Rev. Barnhouse, religion	The Rexall Radio Party
4:30				The Three Bakers
4:45				

DAYTIME — SPRING, 1932

Monday-Friday

BLUE	CBS	KNX	NBC	
Music	The Happy Go Lucky Hour	The Bookworm	The NBC Matinee	2pm
				2:15
		Los Angeles Fire Department Orchestra		2:30
				2:45
	Feminine Fancies	The Matinee Mirthmakers	Music	3pm
				3:15
		Talk and Music	Music / The Old Topper	3:30
			Talk and Music	3:45
California Medical Association Talks / Language Lessons	Originalities	Talk and Music /		4pm
News and Views	Talk and Music	Shopping Service /		4:15
		Travelogue		4:30
	Music / Chats on English		News	4:45

DAYTIME — SPRING, 1932

Saturday

	BLUE	CBS	KNX	NBC
8am	(Off the Air)	The Shell Happy Time Hour	(Off the Air)	Celebrated Sayings
8:15				
8:30		Hallelujah		The Keys to Happiness
8:45			The Sharples Breakfast Club	
9am	Exercises	Ted Brewer Orchestra		
9:15				Beautiful Thoughts
9:30			News and Views	The National Farm and Home Hour
9:45				
10am	News and Views	The Farm Network	Be Young and Happy, Eddie Albright	
10:15				
10:30			Weekend Preludes	Woman's Magazine of the Air
10:45	P. E. in City Schools			
11am		Saturday Syncopators		
11:15				
11:30		Columbia Salon Orchestra		French Lesson
11:45	Spanish Lesson			Stock Market Reports
12pm	Biltmore Concert Orchestra	The Four Clubmen	News and Views	US Agricultural Talk
12:15				The Cosmpolitans
12:30		News	Los Angeles Junior College Cappella Choir	
12:45		Midnight Sons Orchestra		
1pm		Ann Leaf at the Organ	Paris Inn Frolic	News
1:15				The String Wood Ensemble
1:30		Spanish Serenade		
1:45	Bunny's Family			The Stamp Man

DAYTIME — SPRING, 1932

Saturday

	BLUE	CBS	KNX	NBC
2pm	Records	Eddy Duchin Orchestra	The Bookworm	The Old Firehouse
2:15				
2:30		George Hall Orchestra	Records	The Nomads
2:45		Connee Boswell, songs		
3pm		Freddy Martin Orchestra	The Matinee Mirthquakers	On Parade
3:15				
3:30		Jack Miller Orchestra		
3:45		Don Belasco Orchestra		Tea Time Dance
4pm		Frederick William Wile, comment		
4:15	News and Views	Tea Dasant	Travelogue	
4:30			Weekend Preludes	
4:45				News

EVENING — SUMMER, 1932

Sunday

	BLUE	CBS	KNX	NBC
5pm	Records	The Lewisohn Stadium Concerts (4:30PM)	Dr. Matthews' Radio Church	Enna Jettick Melodies
5:15				The American Album of Familiar Music
5:30		Rabbi Magnin, religion		
5:45				The Classic Hour
6pm	The Bingville Weekly Bugle	The Crinoline Lady	Andy Santella Orchestra	
6:15	Neil Russell, songs		Swami Dhirananda, religion	The Old Singing Master
6:30	The Story of India	The Columbia Drama Laboratory	Ernest Holmes: Theodore C. Abel	
6:45	Sunday Evenings at Seth Parkers			Music
7pm	Paul Taylor's Quartet	Musical Cameos	Music	
7:15		The Gauchos		
7:30	Memories	The Parade of Melodies		Jay Whidden Orchestra
7:45			Rev. Duncan, religion	
8pm	The Sameloff Trio	The Edison String Choir	The First Presbyterian Church of Hollywood	Rudolpho Hoyos Orchestra
8:15				
8:30	Jay Whidden Orchestra	California Melodies		The Carnation Contented Hour
8:45				
9pm	Organ Recital	Music	News	Radio Play
9:15			Music	
9:30	The Abas String Quartet	The Laudisti Choir		Immortal Melodies
9:45				
10pm	Records	The Ten o'Clock Wire		The Richfield Reporter
10:15		J. Eslick Orchestra		Organ Recital
10:30	News and Views	Nile's Crazy Quilt		
10:45				

EVENING — SUMMER, 1932

Monday

BLUE	CBS	KNX	NBC	
Big Brother	Aunt Jemima	Cherio (4:45 PM)	The Skippers Male Quartet	5pm
	News	The Arizona Wranglers		5:15
The Singing Story Lady	Skippy		The Parade of the States	5:30
Al, Mack and Tommy, songs	Modern Male Chorus	Songs		5:45
The Wilshire Women's Choral Club	The Boswell Sisters, songs	News	The National Radio Forum	6pm
	Surprise Package	Anson Weeks Orchestra		6:15
	Guy Lombardo Orchestra	Si and Elmer	The MJB Demi-Tasse Revue	6:30
The Adventures of Ito		Songs		6:45
Music	Charles Carlile, songs	Frank Watanabe and Honorable Archie	Amos 'n' Andy	7pm
Lil' Joe Warner's Jolly Journal	Freddy Martin Orchestra	Music	Maxwell House Tune Blenders	7:15
Walter Tourtellette, organ	Howard Barlow Orchestra	The Life of Jim Powers	The Voice of Firestone	7:30
Pachmari		Music		7:45
Songs	The Blue Monday Jamboree	Music	George Washington Concert Orchestra	8pm
				8:15
The Composer's Series		The Georgia Fifeld Players	The Interwoven Pair	8:30
			The Lion Tamer	8:45
Hemlock Corners		News	The Californians	9pm
Organ Recital		The Lubovsiki Trio	Golden Melodies	9:15
				9:30
Close Partners			The Imperial Male Quartet	9:45
Ramona, songs	The Ten o'Clock Wire	Bohemian Club Orchestra	The Richfield Reporter	10pm
Records	Music		Phil Harris Orchestra	10:15
				10:30
				10:45

EVENING — SUMMER, 1932

Tuesday

	BLUE	CBS	KNX	NBC
5pm	Council on Education	Dave Martin and Nell Larson, songs	Cheerio (4:45 PM)	Music
5:15		News	The Arizona Wranglers	
5:30	The Singing Story Lady	Skippy		The Texaco Star Theater, Ed Wynn
5:45	Al, Mac and Tommy, songs	Detectives Black and Blue		
6pm	Records	Nathanial Shilkret Orchesta	News	Lucky Strike Dance Orchestra
6:15		J. Warde Hutton Orchestra	Music	
6:30		Lorna Ladd Interviews	Si and Elmer	
6:45	The Adventures of Ito	To the Lades	Songs	
7pm	Music		Frank Watanabe and Honorable Archie	Amos 'n' Andy
7:15	Lil' Joe Warner's Jolly Journal	Joe Palooka	Rev. Shuler, religion	Memory Lane
7:30	The Lyric Trio	Chandu, the Magician		
7:45	Pachmari	Howard Barlow Orchestra	Music	The Famous Food Parade
8pm	Songs	Little Jack Little Orchestra	Hoopi's Hawaiians	Jay Whidden Orchestra
8:15		Harold Stern Orchestra		
8:30	Music	Seeing Southern California	The American Legion Special	Blackstone Plantation
8:45				
9pm	Charles Craver's One-Man Show	The Bachelors Quartet	News	The Fun Factory
9:15	Organ Recital	Eb and Zeb	Dreamin' Time	
9:30		Ben Bernie, the Old Maestro	Idylls	
9:45	Close Partners			
10pm	Lakeside Dance Orchestra	The Ten o'Clock Wire	Bohemian Club Orchestra	The Richfield Reporter
10:15		Gene Quaw Orchestra		Phil Harris Orchestra
10:30	News and Views			
10:45				

EVENING — SUMMER, 1932

Wednesday

BLUE	CBS	KNX	NBC	
Big Brother	Songs	Cheerio (4:45pm)	Novelties	*5pm*
	News	The Arizona Wranglers		*5:15*
The Singing Story Lady	Skippy		The Mobil Oil Concert	*5:30*
Al, Mac and Tommy, songs	Detectives Black and Blue			*5:45*
The Lyric Trio	Music That Satisfies	News	The Corn Cob Pipe Program	*6pm*
	Mona Content, piano	Music		*6:15*
Music	Isham Jones Orchestra	Si and Elmer	The Lyric Trio	*6:30*
The Adventures of Ito		Songs	Tallani Tubbs	*6:45*
Songs	Charles Carlile, songs	Frank Watanabe and Honorable Archie	Amos 'n' Andy	*7pm*
Lil' Joe Warner's Jolly Journal	Ozzie Nelson Orchestra	Gertrude Ridenour, songs	Maxwell House Tune Blenders	*7:15*
The Lyric Trio	Chandu, the Magician	The Life of Jim Powers	Team Mates	*7:30*
Pachmari	Don Lee Symphony Orchestra	Music		*7:45*
Songs	Eddy Duchin Orchesta	Music	Organ Recital	*8pm*
			Helene Handin, Truthful Trooper	*8:15*
Jay Whidden Orchestra	The Eno Crime Club		The Interwovan Pair	*8:30*
			Music	*8:45*
Hemlock Corners	Memories	News	A Few Years Back	*9pm*
Organ Recital	Eb and Zeb	Music	The Goodyear Program	*9:15*
	The Isle of Golden Dreams	Idylls		*9:30*
Close Partners			The Pacemakers	*9:45*
Lakeside Dance Orchestra	The Ten o'Clock Wire	Bohemian Club Orchestra	The Richfield Reporter	*10pm*
	Dance Orchestra		Phil Harris Orchestra	*10:15*
News and Views				*10:30*
				10:45

EVENING — SUMMER, 1932

Thursday

	BLUE	CBS	KNX	NBC
5pm	Big Brother	Freddie Rich Orchestra	Cheerio (4:45PM)	The Lyric Trio
5:15		News	The Arizona Wranglers	
5:30	The Singing Story Lady	Skippy		Thompkins Corners
5:45	Al, Mac and Tommy, songs	Detectives Black and Blue		
6pm		Music That Satisfies	News	Lucky Strike Dance Orchestra
6:15	Charles Craver's One-Man Show	J. Warde Hutton Orchestra	Music	
6:30		Isham Jones Orchestra	Si and Elmer	
6:45	The Adventures of Ito		Songs	
7pm	Music	Irene Beasley, the Old Dutch Girl	Frank Watanabe and Honorable Archie	Amos 'n' Andy
7:15	Lil' Joe Warner's Jolly Journal	Joe Palooka	Rev. Shuler religion	The Coffee Concert
7:30	Organ Recital	Chandu, the Magician		The Grayeolians
7:45	Pachmari	The Inglewood Park Concert	Cello Recital	The Famous Food Parade
8pm	Songs		KNX Varieities	Music
8:15		Dance Orchestra		The Standard Symphony Hour
8:30	Music	The Eno Crime Club		
8:45				
9pm		The Bachelors Quartet	News	
9:15		Eb and Zeb	Dreamin' Time	Organ Recital
9:30		Dance Orchestra		
9:45	Close Partners		Music	Music
10pm	Records	The Ten o'Clock Wire	Bohemian Club Orchestra	The Richfield Reporter
10:15		Dance Orchestra		Phil Harris Orchestra
10:30	News and Views			
10:45				

EVENING — SUMMER, 1932

Friday

BLUE	CBS	KNX	NBC	
Big Brother	Music	Shopping Service (4:15PM)	The Lyric Trio	5pm
	News	Rabbi Winkler, religion		5:15
The Singing Story Lady	Skippy		Armour Orchestra	5:30
Al, Mac and Tommy, songs	Detectives Black and Blue	He Knew Women		5:45
	Music That Satisfies	News	Friendship Town	6pm
	The Pasadena Community Players	Music		6:15
Music	Guy Lombardo Orchestra	Si and Elmer		6:30
The Adventures of Ito		Songs		6:45
The Rhythm Girls	Charles Carille, songs	Frank Watanabe and Honorable Archie	Amos 'n' Andy	7pm
Lil' Joe Warner's Jolly Journal	Dancing by the Sea	Music	Maxwell House Tune Blenders	7:15
Country Jane, songs	Chandu, the Magician		The Gilmore Circus	7:30
Pachmari	Howard Barlow Orchestra	Public Affairs		7:45
Songs	Raymond Paige Orchestra	The Optimistic Do-Nuts		8pm
	Dance Orchestra			8:15
Jay Whidden Orchestra	Seeing Southern Calfornia		The Interwovan Pair	8:30
			Music	8:45
Hemlock Corners	The Bachelors Quartet	News	Hollywood Nights	9pm
Organ Recital	Eb and Zeb	Dance Orchestra		9:15
	The Kodak Weekend Hour		Thirty Minutes from Broadway	9:30
Close Partners		The Hollywood Legion Fight		9:45
Lakeside Dance Orchestra	The Ten o'Clock Wire		The Richfield Reporter	10pm
	Dance Orchestra		Phil Harris Orchestra	10:15
News and Views				10:30
		Andy Santella Orchestra		10:45

EVENING — SUMMER, 1932

Saturday

	BLUE	CBS	KNX	NBC
5pm	Big Brother	The Lewisohn Stadium Concerts (4:30 PM)	The Town Crier	The Cuckoo Hour
5:15		News	Dr. Matthews' Radio Church	
5:30	Dr. Snape's Question Hour	Skippy		The First Nighter Program
5:45		Detectives Black and Blue		
6pm	Records	Music That Satisfies	News	Lucky Strike Dance Orchestra
6:15		Public Affairs	Music	
6:30			Si and Elmer	
6:45		Isham Jones Orchestra	Songs	
7pm	Music	Dancing by the Sea	Frank Watanabe and Honorable Archie	Amos 'n' Andy
7:15			Gertrude Ridenour, songs	Good Times
7:30		Chandu, the Magician	The Life of Jim Powers	
7:45	Jay Whidden Orchestra	Harold Stern Orchestra	The Lubovsiki Trio	The Choraleers Quartet
8pm	The Hollywood Bowl Concert	Guy Lombardo Orchestra		The Hollywood Hillbillies
8:15				
8:30		Music		The Associated Spotlight Review
8:45			Songs	
9pm		The Merrymakers	News	
9:15			Dreamin' Time	
9:30			William Hatch Orchestra	
9:45	Records			
10pm		The Ten o'Clock Wire	Bohemian Club Orchestra	Phil Harris Orchestra
10:15		Gene Quaw Orchestra		
10:30				
10:45				

DAYTIME — SUMMER, 1932

Sunday

	BLUE	CBS	KNX	NBC
8am	(Off the Air)	The Times Comics Pages	The Sharples Breakfast Club (7:00AM)	(Off the Air)
8:15				
8:30		The Street Singer		
8:45		Emery Deutsch Orchestra		
9am	Nick Harris			The Arion Trio
9:15		The Four Clubmen		
9:30		Home, Sweet Home		The Great Composers Series
9:45				
10am			Judge Rutherford, legal talk	
10:15				
10:30		Organ Recital		Yeast Foamers Orchestra
10:45	Temple Baptist Church		Third Church of Christian Scientist	
11am		The Symphonic Hour		Wayne King Orchestra
11:15				
11:30				Piano Favorites
11:45				
12pm		The Cathedral Hour		The Iodent Program, Jane Froman
12:15				The Kremlin Art Quintet
12:30			Louise Johnson, astrology	The Optimistic Hour
12:45	Organ Recital			
1pm		The Mennen Program, Irene Beasley	Jehoviah's Witnesses	Julie Kelller, harp
1:15				Paul Taylor's Quartet
1:30		Poet's Gold		Organ Recital
1:45		Little Jack Little Orchestra		

DAYTIME — SUMMER, 1932

Monday-Friday

BLUE	CBS	KNX	NBC	
(Off the Air)	The Shell Happy Time Hour	The Sharples Breakfast Club (6:45AM)	G. E. Circle	8am
			Little Orphan Annie	8:15
	The Columbia Revue		Talk and Music	8:30
	Music			8:45
Exercises		Air Clinic		9am
				9:15
	Music / Betty Crocker, cooking	News		9:30
	Music	Maxine's Shopping Service		9:45
News and Views	Music / Gene Wolf, organ	Be Young and Happy, Eddie Albright		10am
	Milady's Notebook			10:15
	Music	Economics Talk	Talk and Music / Woman's Magazine of the Air	10:30
				10:45
	Music / Columbia Salon Orchestra	Talk and Music / Jack Carter's Birthday Party	Talk and Music	11am
				11:15
	Music			11:30
			Stock Market Reports	11:45
Talk and Music		News and Views	US Agricultural Talk	12pm
			The National Farm and HomeHour	12:15
	News	Music / Dr. Matthews' Radio Church		12:30
	Talk and Music			12:45
	The Times Forum	Paris Inn Frolic	News	1pm
			Ann Warner Chats	1:15
	Music			1:30
Bunny's Family			Music	1:45

DAYTIME — SUMMER, 1932

Sunday

	BLUE	CBS	KNX	NBC
2pm	Records	The Ballad Hour	The Westlake Park Concert	Conventionalities
2:15				
2:30		Professor Lindsley, readings		
2:45				
3pm		Dr. Klein, economics		The Greatest Stories Ever Told
3:15		Chicago Knights		
3:30				Music
3:45		Theodore Karle, songs		
4pm		George Hall Orchestra	Advanced Thought	The Chase and Sanborn Hour, Eddie Cantor
4:15			Music	
4:30		The Lewisohn Stadium Concerts	The Independent Merchants Program	
4:45			Martin L. Thomas, comment	

DAYTIME — SUMMER, 1932

Monday-Friday

BLUE	CBS	KNX	NBC	
Music	The Happy Go Lucky Hour	The Bookworm	Talk and Music	2pm
				2:15
				2:30
Music / Donald Novis, songs			Back of the News in Washington	2:45
Muisc	Feminine Fancies	The Matinee Mirthmakers	Music	3pm
				3:15
Music / The Italian Lamguage				3:30
				3:45
News and Views	Talk and Music	Travelogue	Music / The Fleischmann Yeast Hour, Rudy Vallee	4pm
		Shopping Service		4:15
			Music / Death Valley Days	4:30
	Music / Chats on Words	Cheerio		4:45

DAYTIME — SUMMER, 1932

Saturday

	BLUE	CBS	KNX	NBC
8am	(Off the Air)	The Shell Happy Time Hour	(Off the Air)	On Wings of Song
8:15				Little Orphan Annie
8:30				On Wings of Song
8:45			The Sharples Breakfast Club	
9am	Exercises	George Hall Orchestra		Harold Stokes Orchestra
9:15				
9:30		The Madison String Ensemble	News	The National Farm and Home Hour
9:45			Maxine's Shopping Service	
10am	News	Saturday Syncopators	Be Young and Happy, Eddie Albright	
10:15	Hollywood Bowl Talk			
10:30	The Farm Forum		Weekend Preludes	Woman's Magazine of the Air
10:45		Milady's Notebook		
11am	Physical Education	The Boston Pop Revue		
11:15				
11:30		The Round Towners	Maxine's Shopping Service	French Lesson
11:45	Spanish Lesson			Stock Market Reports
12pm	Biltmore Concert Orchestra	Organ Recital	News and Views	US Agricultural Talk
12:15				
12:30		News		
12:45		Tommy Christian Orchestra		
1pm		Dancing by the Sea	Paris Inn Frolic	News
1:15				Ann Warner Chats
1:30		Between the Bookends		
1:45	Bunny's Family	George Hall Orchestra		Music

DAYTIME — SUMMER, 1932

Saturday

	BLUE	CBS	KNX	NBC
2pm	Records	Freddy Martin Orchestra	The Bookworm	The Hollywood Hillbillies
2:15				
2:30			Records	The Nomads
2:45		Ozzie Nelson Orchestra		
3pm			The Matinee Mirthquakers	Footlight Fantasies
3:15		George Hall Orchestra		
3:30		Do-Re-Me		The Rhythm Girls
3:45		The Street Singer		News
4pm	News and Views	Edwin C. Hill, news		Music
4:15		Vaughn de Leath, songs		
4:30		The Lewisohn Stadium Concerts		Secret Service Spy Stories
4:45				

EVENING — FALL, 1932

Sunday

	BLUE	CBS	KNX	NBC
5pm	Rendezvous	George Hall Orchestra	Dr. Matthews' Radio Church	The Chase and Sanborn Hour, Eddie Cantor
5:15				
5:30	The Sunday Concert	The Roxy Concertiers		
5:45				
6pm		The Linut Bath Club Revue, Fred Allen	Ernest Holmes: Theodore C. Abel	Enna Jettick Melodies
6:15				The American Album of Familiar Music
6:30	Kenneth Spencer, songs	The Edison String Choir	Music	
6:45	Gunnar Johnson, piano		The Serenaders	Lifetime Revue
7pm		Musical Cameos	Music	
7:15	Tom and Dud, songs	Ernest Hutchinson, piano		K-7 Secret Service Spy Stories
7:30	The Silhouettes	National Sports Relief	Golden Memories	
7:45	Sunday Evenings at Seth Parkers		The Mantel Lamp	The Serenaders
8pm		The Gauchos	The First Presbyterian Church of Hollywood	The KFI Fun Factor
8:15	Paul Taylor's Quartet	Your Child		
8:30	Rudy Sieger Orchestra	The Parade of Melodies		
8:45				
9pm	The Reader's Guide	The Merrymakers	News	The Domino Club
9:15			The Lubovsiki Trio	
9:30	Music			
9:45				
10pm	Denver Musician's Program	The Ten o'Clock Wire		The Richfield Reporter
10:15		Ted Fiorito Orchestra		Hotel Miramar Orchestra
10:30	On Wings of Music			
10:45				

EVENING — FALL, 1932

Monday

BLUE	CBS	KNX	NBC	
Big Brother	The H-Bar-O Rangers	Cecil and Sally	The Lyric Trio	5pm
	News	Music	Wheatenaville Sketches	5:15
The Singing Story Lady	Skippy		Public Affairs	5:30
Al, Mack and Tommy, songs	Glen Gray Orchestra	Songs		5:45
The Music Doctors		News	Helene Handin, songs	6pm
	Hal Smith Orchestra	Jimmy, Mac and Bill, songs	Public Affairs	6:15
Maury Leaf Orchestra	An Evening in Paris	Si and Elmer	Paul Whiteman Orchestra	6:30
Lucy and Octavius		The Serenaders		6:45
The National Radio Forum	Music That Satisfies	Frank Watanabe and Honorable Archie	Sam Coslow Orchestra	7pm
	Easy Aces	Pieces of Eight		7:15
Walter Tourtellette, organ	Juanita Tennyson, songs	The Newlyweds	The MJB Demi-Tasse Revue	7:30
Alice Gentle, songs	The Story of Myrt and Marge	Tarzan of the Apes		7:45
The Hollywood Hillbillies	Don Barlow Orchestra	Music	Amos 'n' Andy	8pm
	Public Affairs	Public Affairs	The Tastyeast Jesters	8:15
Musical Hi-Lites	The Blue Monday Jamboree	California Real Estate Association	Public Affairs	8:30
		Rummy and Dummy	Music	8:45
The Commisioner's Daughter		News	Tallent Tubbs, comment	9pm
		The Lubovsiki Trio	Music	9:15
The NBC Road Show				9:30
				9:45
	The Ten o'Clock Wire	Bal Tamborin Orchestra	The Richfield Reporter	10pm
	Etude Ethiopians		Pacific on Parade	10:15
				10:30
	Music			10:45

EVENING — FALL, 1932

Tuesday

	BLUE	CBS	KNX	NBC
5pm	Council on Education	Public Affairs	Cecil and Sally	Balladettes
5:15		News	Music	
5:30	The Singing Story Lady	Skippy		Dog Talk
5:45	Al, Mac and Tommy, songs	The Buccaneers	Chandu, the Magician	Wheatenaville Sketches
6pm	Music	Music That Satisfies	News	Music
6:15		Threads of Happiness	Jimmy, Mac and Bill, songs	
6:30	Mathematics	Glen Gray Orchestra	Si and Elmer	The Texaco StarTheater, Ed Wynn
6:45	Lucy and Octavius	Public Affairs	The Serenaders	
7pm	Nick Harris	Jay C. Flippen-cies	Frank Watanabe and Honorable Archie	The Lucky Strike Hour, Walter O'Keefe
7:15		Public Affairs	Rev. Shuler, religion	
7:30	Waltz Time	Chandu, the Magician		
7:45		The Story of Myrt and Marge	Tarzan, the Ape Man	
8pm	Western Artists	Public Affairs	The American Legion	Amos 'n' Andy
8:15	Music	Tallent Tubbs, comment	Public Affairs	Memory Lane
8:30		To the Ladies	Jimmy Grier Orchestra	
8:45			Golden Memories	Tapestries of Life
9pm		Music	News	
9:15		Eb and Zeb	Public Affairs	
9:30	Hotel Miramar Orchestra	Mid-Week Jubilee	Patches	Ben Bernie, the Old Maestro
9:45				
10pm	Niesley and Mosher, songs	The Ten o'Clock Wire		The Richfield Reporter
10:15	The Music Garden	Ted Fiorito Orchestra		Pacific on Parade
10:30				
10:45	Synco Thots			

EVENING — FALL, 1932

Wednesday

BLUE	CBS	KNX	NBC	
Big Brother	The H-Bar-O Rangers	Cecil and Sally	The Lyric Trio	5pm
	News	The KNX String Ensemble		5:15
The Singing Story Lady	Skippy		Instrumental Group	5:30
Al, Mac and Tommy, songs	The Don Lee Players	Chandu, the Magician	Wheatenaville Sketches	5:45
The Sunset Serenaders	Rev. Shuler, religion	News	The Goodyear Program	6pm
	Moods Moderne	Jimmy, Mac and Bill, songs		6:15
Maury Leaf Orchestra		Si and Elmer	Music	6:30
Lucy and Octavius	Public Affairs	The Serenaders		6:45
The Hollywood Hillbillies	Music That Satisfies	Frank Watanabe and Honorable Archie	The Corn Cob Pipe Club	7pm
	Easy Aces	Pieces of Eight		7:15
Records	Chandu, the Magician	The Newlyweds	Music	7:30
	The Story of Myrt and Marge	Tarzan, the Ape Man	Organ Recital	7:45
Public Affairs	Columbia Symphony Orchestra	Dance Orchestra	Amos 'n' Andy	8pm
	Your Child		The Tastyeast Jesters	8:15
Silver Strains	The Eno Crime Club	The Rosicrucian Ensemble	Team Mates	8:30
		Rummy and Dummy		8:45
Helen Guest, songs	Realty Values Protective League	News	The Serenaders	9pm
	Eb and Zeb	Public Affairs	Sherlock Holmes	9:15
Hotel Miramar Orchestra	The Isle of Golden Dreams	Music		9:30
			Music	9:45
The Doric Quartet	The Ten o'Clock Wire	Bal Tabarin Orchestra	The Richfield Reporter	10pm
One Man's Family	Ted Fiorito Orchestra		Pacific on Parade	10:15
				10:30
				10:45

EVENING — FALL, 1932

Thursday

	BLUE	CBS	KNX	NBC
5pm	Big Brother	Henry Busse Orchestra	Cecil and Sally	The Fleischman Yeast Hour, Rudy Vallee
5:15		News	The KNX Ensemble	
5:30	The Singing Story Lady	Skippy		
5:45	Al, Mac and Tommy, songs	Three Shades of Blue	Chandu, the Magician	
6pm	Memories	Music That Satisfies	News	The Maxwell House Showboat
6:15	Lorna Ladd's Oral Longnettes	Public Affairs	Jimmy, Mac and Bill, songs	
6:30		Omar Khayyam	Si and Elmer	
6:45	Lucy and Octavius		The Serenaders	
7pm	The Hollywood Hillbillies	Public Affairs	Frank Watanabe and Honorable Archie	The Lucky Strike Hour, Jack Pearl
7:15	Organ Recital	Realty Values Protective League	Rev. Shuler, religion	
7:30		Chandu, the Magician		
7:45	Rudolpho Hoyos Orchestra	The Story of Myrt and Marge	Tarzan, the Ape Man	
8pm		The Inglewood Park Concert	Public Affairs	Amos 'n' Andy
8:15			Dr. Breiglieb, health	The Standard Symphony Hour
8:30	Cesare Sedaro Concert	The Eno Crime Club	Golden Memories	
8:45	Synco Thots			
9pm	Hotel Miramar Orchestra	Don Clark Orchestra	News	
9:15		Eb and Zeb	Music	Football Rally
9:30	Pigskin Romances	Emil Coleman Orchestra	The Lubovsiki Trio	Public Affairs
9:45				Songs
10pm	Ship of Dreams	The Ten o'Clock Wire		The Richfield Reporter
10:15		Ted Fiorito Orchestra		Pacific on Parade
10:30				
10:45	The Coquettes			

EVENING — FALL, 1932

Friday

BLUE	CBS	KNX	NBC	
Big Brother	The H-Bar-O Rangers	Cecil and Sally	Organ Recital	*5pm*
	Skippy	Rabbi Winkler, religion		*5:15*
The Singing Story Lady	The March of Time			*5:30*
Al, Mac and Tommy, songs		Chandu, the Magician	Wheatenaville Sketches	*5:45*
Music	The All-American Football Show	News	The First Nighter Program	*6pm*
		Jimmy, Mac and Bill, songs		*6:15*
Maury Leaf Orchestra	The Pasadena Community Players	Si and Elmer	Armour Orchestra	*6:30*
Lucy and Octavius	Public Affairs	The Serenaders		*6:45*
The Hollywood Hillbillies	Music That Satisfies	Frank Watanabe and Honorable Archie	The Makers of History	*7pm*
	Easy Aces	Pieces of Eight		*7:15*
The Abas String Quartet	Chandu, the Magician	The Newlyweds	The Elgin Adventurer's Club	*7:30*
	The Story of Myrt and Marge	Tarzan, the Ape Man		*7:45*
Football Rally	Don Barlow Orchestra	The Optimistic Do-Nuts	Amos 'n' Andy	*8pm*
	Keynotes		The Tastyeast Jesters	*8:15*
Cesare Sodero Concert	Guy Lombardo Orchestra		The Gilmore Circus	*8:30*
	Realty Values Protective League			*8:45*
The Kingdom Builders Play	The Don Lee Players	News		*9pm*
	Eb and Zeb	Public Affairs		*9:15*
Hotel Miramar Orchestra	Between the Goal Posts	Miniature Revue	Public Affairs	*9:30*
		The Hollywood Legion Fight	The Serenaders	*9:45*
Star Books	The Ten o'Clock Wire		The Richfield Reporter	*10pm*
	Ted Fiorito Orchestra		Pacific on Parade	*10:15*
				10:30
		The KNX Ensemble		*10:45*

EVENING — FALL, 1932

Saturday

	BLUE	CBS	KNX	NBC
5pm	Big Brother	Glen Gray Orchestra	Cecil and Sally	News
5:15		News	Dr. Matthews' Radio Church	The Arion Trio
5:30	Dr. Snape's Question Hour	Skippy		
5:45	Little Orphan Annie	Henry Busse Orchestra	Chandu, the Magician	Wheatenaville Sketches
6pm	Musical Echoes	Music That Satisfies	News	Erno Rapee Orchestra
6:15		Do-Re-Mi	Jimmy, Mac and Bill, songs	
6:30	The Argentine Trio	Ann Leaf at the Organ	Si and Elmer	
6:45	Julie Kellar, harp	The Syracuse Variety Hour	The Serenaders	
7pm	The Hollywood Hillbillies		Frank Watanabe and Honorable Archie	Lucky Strike Dance Orchestra
7:15		Patrick Marsh Orchestra	Marion Mansfield, songs	
7:30		Chandu, the Magician	The Georgia Fifeld Players	
7:45	National Concert Orchestra	Guy Lombardo Orchestra		
8pm			In Case	Amos 'n' Andy
8:15	Football Resume'			The Coffee Concert
8:30	Night Song	Harold Stern Orchestra		Family Robinson
8:45			Music	
9pm	Hotel Pennsylvania Orchestra	California Melodies	News	Hotel Miramar Orchestra
9:15			Dance Orchestra	
9:30	Dance Orchestra	Ted Fiorito Orchestra	Violin Recital	The Associated Spotlight Review
9:45				
10pm	Jay Whidden Orchestra	The Ten o'Clock Wire	Dance Orchestra	
10:15		Ted Fiorito Orchestra		
10:30	Bal Tabarin Orchestra	Dancing with the Stars	Organ Recital	
10:45				

DAYTIME — FALL, 1932

Sunday

	BLUE	CBS	KNX	NBC
8am	Impressions of Italy	The Times Comics Pages	The Sharples Breakfast Club (7:00AM)	(Off the Air)
8:15				
8:30	Major Bowe's Capitol Family	The Melody Makers		
8:45		News		
9am		The Salt Lake Tabernacle Choir	Richard Cannon, songs	Nick Harris
9:15			Swami Dhirananda, religion	
9:30	The Russian Symphonic Choir	Home, Sweet Home		
9:45				
10am	Song Album		Judge Rutherford, legal talk	The Symphonic Hour
10:15				
10:30	Morning Moods	The CBS Church of the Air		
10:45			Third Church of Christian Scientist	
11am	Bible Stories	Ann Leaf at the Organ		
11:15		Albert Hay, organ		
11:30		Francisco del Campo,,songs		Yeast Foamers Orchestra
11:45		The Hoosier Editor		
12pm	The Romancers	New York Philharmonic Orchestra		Lady Esther Serenade
12:15				
12:30			Louise Johnson, astrology	Edna Brady, songs
12:45				
1pm	Songland		Jehoviah's Witnesses	The Iodent Program, Jane Froman
1:15				Wildroot Chat
1:30	Quartet Time			Julie Kellar, harp
1:45				Organ Recital

DAYTIME — FALL, 1932

Monday-Friday

BLUE	CBS	KNX	NBC	
Exercises	The Shell Happy Time Hour	The Sharples Breakfast Club (6:45 AM)	John and Ned, songs	8am
Music			Little Orphan Annie	8:15
	Music		Economics Talk	8:30
			Cross Cuts of the Day	8:45
Edna Fischer, piano	Music / The Columbia Revue	Air Clinic	Lil' Joe Warner's Jolly Journal	9am
Music / Dixie Memories			Fashion Tour	9:15
Music	Music / Betty Crocker, cooking	News	Music	9:30
	Music	Maxine's Shopping Service		9:45
Mardi Gras		Be Young and Happy, Eddie Albright		10am
				10:15
News		Economics Talk	Talk and Music / Woman's Magazine of the Air	10:30
Language Lesson				10:45
Words and Music	Music	Talk and Music / Jack Carter's Birthday Party	Talk and Music / The Standard School Broadcast	11am
				11:15
Talk and Music	Columbia Salon Orchestra / American School of the Air			11:30
			Stock Market Reports	11:45
	Music	News	US Agricultural Talk	12pm
		Talk	The National Farm and Home Hour	12:15
	News	Music / Dr. Matthews' Radio Church		12:30
	Music			12:45
Music / The Radio Guild		Paris Inn Frolic	News	1pm
			The Lyric Trio / Ann Warner Chats	1:15
				1:30
				1:45

DAYTIME — FALL, 1932

Sunday

	BLUE	CBS	KNX	NBC
2pm	Conventionalities	Professor Lindsley, readings	The Westlake Park Concert	
2:15		Rabbi Magnin, religion		
2:30		The Legion of the Lost		Big Ben Dream Dramas
2:45				The Kremlin Art Quintet
3pm	Organ Recital	The Ascot Auto Races		The Atwater-Kent Auditions
3:15				
3:30	Our American Schools			Highlights of the Bible
3:45				
4pm			Advanced Thought	The Classic Hour
4:15			Oriental Orchestra	
4:30	The Abas String Quartet	Musical Memories		Great Moments in History
4:45		The Canta Nina Girls	Martin L. Thomas, comment	

DAYTIME — FALL, 1932

Monday-Friday

BLUE	CBS	KNX	NBC	
Music / The Music Masters	The Happy Go Lucky Hour	The Bookworm	Mid-Day Musicale	*2pm*
			Music / Dramedary Caravan	*2:15*
		Los Angeles Fire Department Orchestra		*2:30*
				2:45
Music / The Buccaneers	Feminine Fancies	The Matinee Mirthmakers	Music	*3pm*
				3:15
Music / The Italian Language				*3:30*
			Talk and Music	*3:45*
Talk and Music	Talk and Music	Travelogue	G. E. Circle	*4pm*
News			The Royal Vagabonds	*4:15*
Music			The Stebbins Boys	*4:30*
			Talk	*4:45*

DAYTIME — FALL, 1932

Saturday

	BLUE	CBS	KNX	NBC
8am	(Off the Air)	The Shell Happy Time Hour	(Off the Air)	John and Ned, songs
8:15	Bainbridge Colby			Little Orphan Annie
8:30	Night Song	The Columbia Revue		Piano Recital
8:45			The Sharples Breakfast Club	Bits of Melody
9am	Edna Fisher, piano	Buddy Herrod Orchestra		Economics Talk
9:15	Dixie Memories			Lil' Joe Warner's Jolly Journal
9:30	Music		News	The National Farm and Home Hour
9:45			Maxine's Shopping Service	
10am	Exercises	George Hall Orchestra	Be Young and Happy, Eddie Albright	
10:15				
10:30		Football Souvenirs		Woman's Magazine of the Air
10:45	Sports	Sports		
11am				
11:15				
11:30				Dr. Dick, health
11:45				Stock Market Reports
12pm			News and Views	US Agricultural Talk
12:15				
12:30				
12:45				
1pm		News	Paris Inn Frolic	News
1:15		Spanish Serenaders		Piano Recital
1:30		Sports		Airplane Contact
1:45				Sports

DAYTIME — FALL, 1932

Saturday

	BLUE	CBS	KNX	NBC
2pm	Spanish Serenaders		Sports	
2:15				
2:30				
2:45	Concert Echoes			
3pm	Waldorf-Astoria Orchestra			
3:15				
3:30	Willliam S. Hard, news			
3:45	Tom and Dud, songs			
4pm				
4:15	News			
4:30	The Cuckoo Hour, Ray Knight			
4:45				The Hollywood Hillbillies

LISTINGS FOR 1933

EVENING — WINTER, 1933

Sunday

	BLUE	CBS	KNX	NBC
5pm	Rendezvous	John Henry, Black River Giant	Dr. Matthews' Radio Church	The Chase and Sanborn Hour, Eddie Cantor
5:15		Andre Kostelanetz Orchestra		
5:30	Mystery Drama			
5:45		John Henry, Black River Giant		
6pm	The Sunday Concert	The Linut Bath Club Revue, Fred Allen	Ernest Holmes: Theodore C. Abel	The General Electric Concert
6:15				
6:30	Gunnar Johnson, piano	The Melody Hour	Organ Recital	The American Album of Familiar Music
6:45			The Serenaders	
7pm	John and Ned, songs	Ernest Hutchinson, piano	Music	Secret Service Spy Stories
7:15				Music
7:30	Nick Harris	The Gauchos	Reveries	
7:45	Sunday Evenings at Seth Parkers		Music	
8pm		Isham Jones Orchestra	The First Presbyterian Church of Hollywood	
8:15	The Pierce Brothers Quartet	Your Child		Walter Winchell's Jergens Journal
8:30	Rudy Sieger Orchestra	The Parade of Melodies		Melodic Serenade
8:45				
9pm	The Reader's Guide	The Merrymakers	News	Tapestries of Life
9:15			The Lubovsiki Trio	
9:30	Netherland Plaza Orchestra			Music
9:45				
10pm	Denver Musician's Program	The Ten o'Clock Wire		The Richfield Reporter
10:15		Ted Fiorito Orchestra		Gus Arnheim Orchestra
10:30	On Wings of Music			
10:45				

EVENING — WINTER, 1933

Monday

BLUE	CBS	KNX	NBC	
Chamber of Commerce	Bobby Benson	Organ Recital	The Lyric Trio	5pm
Synco Thots	News		Helene Handin, songs	5:15
Culbertson on Bridge	Skippy	Detectives Black and Blue	Little Orphan Annie	5:30
Al, Mack and Tommy, songs	The Paradise Islanders	Songs	Wheatenaville Sketches	5:45
The Music Doctors	Music That Satisfies	News	The A&P Gypsies	6pm
	Howard Ely, songs	Cecil and Sally		6:15
Safety First	Dancing at the Bellevue	Si and Elmer	The Buick Program	6:30
Lorna Ladd's Oral Lornettes		The Serenaders		6:45
The Hollywood Hillbillies	Morton Downey, songs	Frank Watanabe and Honorable Archie	The Makers of History	7pm
	Juanita Tennyson, songs	Pieces of Eight		7:15
Walter Tourtellette, organ	The Columbia Revue	Hollywood Hams	The MJB Demi-Tasse Revue	7:30
USC Symphony Orchestra	The Story of Myrt and Marge	The Guardsmen		7:45
	The Blue Monday Jamboree	Frost Warnings	Amos 'n' Andy	8pm
Dr. Einstein, comment		California Real Estate Association	The Seal of Doom	8:15
		The Happy Chappies	The Voice of Firestone	8:30
				8:45
The Rise of the Goldbergs		News	The KFI Fun Factory	9pm
The Nomads		Crockett's Mountaineers		9:15
The NBC Road Show		The Lubovsiki Trio		9:30
				9:45
	The Ten o'Clock Wire	Organ Recital	The Richfield Reporter	10pm
	Etude Ethiopians		Phil Harris Orchestra	10:15
	Biltmore Concert Orchestra	The Arizona Wranglers		10:30
				10:45

EVENING — WINTER, 1933

Tuesday

	BLUE	CBS	KNX	NBC
5pm	Hotel Congress Orchestra	Fray and Braggioti, Travelogue songs	Memories (4:00PM)	State Teacher's
5:15		News		
5:30	Jack and Jimmy, songs	Skippy	Detectives Black and Blue	Little Orphan Annie
5:45	Al, Mac and Tommy, songs	Kay Kyser Orchestra	Chandu, the Magician	Wheatenaville Sketches
6pm	Recollections	Music That Satisfies	News	Thirty Minutes from Broadway
6:15		Threads of Happiness	Cecil and Sally	Captain Don Wilkie, comment
6:30		California Melodies	Si and Elmer	The Texaco Star Theater, Ed Wynn
6:45	Mathematics		The Serenaders	
7pm	John and Ned, songs	Those McCarthy Girls	Frank Watanabe and Honorable Archie	The Lucky Strike Hour, Walter O'Keefe
7:15	Helen Guest, songs	Keyboard Varieties	The Singing Strings	
7:30	Rainbow Harmonies	Chandu, the Magician	Hollywood Hams	
7:45	Virginia Fiohri, songs	The Story of Myrt and Marge	The Laf-O-Graf Theater	
8pm		The Globe Headlines	The American Legion	Amos 'n' Andy
8:15	Pacific Coast Advertising Agency Association	Howard Barlow Orchestra		Memory Lane
8:30	The Unknown Songwriter	Dick Aurandt, organ	The Happy Chappies	
8:45	Gus Arnheim Orchestra	Don Clark Orchestra	Golden Memories	Adventures in Health
9pm	The Rise of the Goldbergs	Joe Hayne Orchestra	News	Tapestries of Life
9:15	Hotel Lexington Orchestra	The Unknown Hands	Crockett's Mountaineers	
9:30	The Storyteller	Harold Stern Orchestra	Music	Ben Bernie, the Old Maestro
9:45				
10pm	Niesley and Mosher, songs	The Ten o'Clock Wire	Organ Recital	The Richfield Reporter
10:15	Chiffon Jazz	Eb and Zeb		Phil Harris Orchestra
10:30		Tom Coakley Orchestra	The Arizona Wranglers	
10:45	Kenneth Spencer, songs			

EVENING — WINTER, 1933

Wednesday

BLUE	CBS	KNX	NBC	
State Teacher's College	Bobby Benson	Welegan (4:45 PM)	The Lyric Trio	*5pm*
	News			*5:15*
Jack and Jimmy, songs	Skippy	Detectives Black and Blue	Little Orphan Annie	*5:30*
Al, Mac and Tommy, songs	The Institute of World Affairs	Chandu, the Magician	Wheatenaville Sketches	*5:45*
The Sunset Serenaders	Music That Satisfies	News	Charles Wellman, songs	*6pm*
	The Romantic Bachelor	Cecil and Sally		*6:15*
	Jimmy Bittick Orchestra	Si and Elmer	Morton Downey, songs	*6:30*
John Henry Lyon, music talk		The Serenaders		*6:45*
Dance Pageant	The Boswell Sisters, songs	Frank Watanabe and Honorable Archie	The Corn Cob Pipe Club	*7pm*
	The Buccaneers	Pieces of Eight		*7:15*
Bal Tabarin Orchestra	Chandu, the Magician	Josephy Diskay Orchestra	The Singing Service Men	*7:30*
	The Story of Myrt and Marge	The Happy Chappies	Golden Memories	*7:45*
The Marshall Mavericks	The Globe Headlines	The KNX Parade	Amos 'n' Andy	*8pm*
	Robert Burns the Poet		The Seal of the Don	*8:15*
Gus Arnheim Orchestra			One Man's Family	*8:30*
	Isham Jones Orchestra			*8:45*
The Rise of the Goldbergs	Attrocities of 1933	News	Melody Time	*9pm*
Kenneth Spencer, songs		Crockett's Mountaineers	Sherlock Holmes	*9:15*
Meredith Wilson Orchestra	The Isle of Golden Dreams	Patches		*9:30*
			Songs	*9:45*
Music	The Ten o'Clock Wire	Dance Orchestra	The Richfield Reporter	*10pm*
	Eb and Zeb		Phil Harris Orchestra	*10:15*
The Doric Quartet	Tom Coakley Orchestra	The Arizona Wranglers		*10:30*
The Slumber Hour				*10:45*

EVENING — WINTER, 1933

Thursday

	BLUE	CBS	KNX	NBC
5pm	Nathan Abas, violin	Mel Snyder Orchestra	Welegan (4:45 PM)	The Fleischman Yeast Hour, Rudy Vallee
5:15		News		
5:30	Jack and Jimmy, songs	Skippy	Detectives Black and Blue	
5:45	Al, Mac and Tommy, songs	The Swiss Yodelers	Chandu, the Magician	
6pm	The Rhythm Ramblers	Music That Satisfies	News	The Maxwell House Showboat
6:15		Larry Funk Orchestra	Cecil and Sally	
6:30	Memories	Stoopnagle and Budd	Si and Elmer	
6:45			The Serenaders	
7pm	Charles Wellman, songs	The Inglewood Park Concert	Frank Watanabe and Honorable Archie	The Lucky Strike Hour, Jack Pearl
7:15			The Singing Strings	
7:30	Organ Recital	Chandu, the Magician	Hollywood Hams	
7:45		The Story of Myrt and Marge	The Guardsmen	
8pm	Myron Niesley, songs	The Globe Headlines	Organ Recital	Amos 'n' Andy
8:15	Organ Recital	Howard Barlow Orchestra	Francis White, songs	The Standard Symphony Hour
8:30	Guy Arnheim Orchestra	Richard Durant, songs		
8:45		I. Zingari, songs	Golden Memories	
9pm	The Rise of the Goldbergs	Eddy Duchin Orchestra	News	
9:15	Synco Thots		Crockett's Mountaineers	Thurston, the Magician
9:30	Hotel Congress Orchestra	The Zoellner String Quartet	The Lubovsiki Trio	Music
9:45				
10pm	Mystery Serial	The Ten o'Clock Wire	Idylls	The Richfield Reporter
10:15		Eb and Zeb		Phil Harris Orchestra
10:30	Ship of Dreams	Tom Coakley Orchestra	The Arizona Wranglers	
10:45				

EVENING — WINTER, 1933

Friday

BLUE	CBS	KNX	NBC	
Bouquet of Melodies	Bobby Benson	Marion Mansfield, songs	Organ Recital	5pm
	Skippy	The Universal Song Service		5:15
Jack and Jimmy, songs	The March of Time	Detectives Black and Blue	Little Orphan Annie	5:30
Al, Mac and Tommy, songs		Chandu, the Magician	Wheatenaville Sketches	5:45
Robert Hurd Orchestra	Music That Satisfies	News	The First Nighter Program	6pm
	The Pasadena Community Players	Cecil and Sally		6:15
The Manhattan Seranaders		Si and Elmer	Armour Orchestra	6:30
Dr. Eames, children	Edwin C. Hill, news	The Serenaders		6:45
John and Ned, songs	The Columbia Revue	Frank Watanabe and Honorable Archie	The Big Six of the Air	7pm
		Pieces of Eight		7:15
Musical Hi-LItes	Chandu, the Magician	Hollywood Hams	The Seal of the Don	7:30
	The Story of Myrt and Marge	The Guardsmen	Music	7:45
Fantasy	The Globe Headlines	The Optimistic Do-Nuts	Amos 'n' Andy	8pm
Songs	Columbia Symphony Orchestra		The Gilmore Circus	8:15
Guy Arnheim Orchestra	Abe Lyman Orchestra			8:30
	The Voice of Romance			8:45
The Rise of the Goldbergs	The Buccaneers	News		9pm
Oriental Musicale	The Unknown Hands	Crockett's Mountaineers	Thurston, the Magician	9:15
Hollywood on the Air	Clyde McCoy Orchestra	The Happy Chappies	Music	9:30
	Hal Kemp Orchestra	The Hollywood Legion Fight		9:45
The NBC Talent Parade	The Ten o'Clock Wire		The Richfield Reporter	10pm
	Eb and Zeb		Phil Harris Orchestra	10:15
	Tom Coakley Orchestra			10:30
		The Arizona Wranglers		10:45

EVENING — WINTER, 1933

Saturday

	BLUE	CBS	KNX	NBC
5pm	The American Taxpayers League	Cafe Terrnee Orchestra	Welegan (4:45pm)	The Arion Trio
5:15	Echoes of the Palisades	News	Dr. Matthews' Radio Church'	Poet of the Air
5:30	Dr. Snape's Question Hour	Skippy		Little Orphan Annie
5:45		Gypsy Orchestra	Chandu, the Magician	Wheatenaville Sketches
6pm	Rhythm Shadows	Music That Satisfies	News	Cleveland High School Orchestra
6:15		Edwin C. Hill, news	Cecil and Sally	
6:30	Education at the Crossroads	Jimmy Bittick Orchestra	Si and Elmer	The Oldsmobile Program
6:45	Julie Kellar, harp		The Serenaders	
7pm	The Medicine Show	The Boswell Sisters, songs	Frank Watanabe and Honorable Archie	Lucky Strike Dance Orchestra
7:15		The Islanders and Cavaliers	Songs	
7:30	National Concert Orchestra	Chandu, the Magician	The Singing Strings	
7:45		Gertrude Niesen, songs	Hollywood Hams	
8pm	Music	Guy Lombardo Orchestra	Frost Warning	The Caswell Concert
8:15			Varieties	Family Robinson
8:30	Gus Arnheim Orchestra	Raymond Paige Orchestra		
8:45				Captain Don Wilkie, comment
9pm	Hotel Pennsylvania Orchestra	Duke Ellington Orchestra	News	The Associated Spotlight Review
9:15			Crockett's Mountaineers	
9:30	Hotel Edgewater Beach Orchestra	Tom Coakley Orchestra	The Georgia Fifeld Players	
9:45				
10pm	Cole McElroy Orchestra	The Ten o'Clock Wire	Dance Orchestra	
10:15		Tom Coakley Orchestra		
10:30	Bal Tabarin Orchestra		The Arizona Wranglers	Dance Orchestra
10:45				

DAYTIME — WINTER, 1933

Sunday

	BLUE	CBS	KNX	NBC
8am	Radio Rubes	The Times Comics Pages	The Sharples Breakfast Club (7:00AM)	(Off the Air)
8:15	Major Bowes' Capitol Family			
8:30		The Melody Makers		
8:45		News		
9am		The Salt Lake Tabernacle Choir	The Avocado Man	Jose Arlas Orchestra
9:15	Roxy and His Gang			
9:30		Home, Sweet Home	Organ Recital	Song Album
9:45				
10am			Judge Rutherford, legal talk	Piano PIctures
10:15	Organ Recital		Organ Recital	
10:30	The Cecilians	The CBS Church of the Air		The Pilgrims
10:45			Third Church of Christian Scientist	
11am	Bible Stories	Smiin' Ed McConnell, songs		The Monarch Mystery Tenor
11:15		Fred Lane's Book Review		Saxophone Octette
11:30		Francisco del Campo, songs		Yeast Foamers Orchestra
11:45		Poet's Gold		
12pm	Pastels	New York Philharmonic Orchestra		Lady Esther Serenade
12:15			Lal Chand Mehra, india talk	
12:30	Melody Mixers		Louise Johnson, astrology	The Hour of Worship
12:45				
1pm			Jehoviah's Witnesses	The Iodent Program, Jane Froman
1:15				Wildroot Chat
1:30	Music			Julie Kellar, harp
1:45				Wesley Tourtellette, organ

DAYTIME — WINTER, 1933

Monday-Friday

BLUE	CBS	KNX	NBC	
Exercises	The Shell Happy Time Hour	The Sharples Breakfast Club (6:45 AM)	Talk and Music	8am
Music			Household Hints	8:15
	Music		Cross Cuts of the Day	8:30
				8:45
	Bobby Harrod Orchestra	Air Clinic	Langendorf Pictorial	9am
Music / Dixie Memories			Lil' Joe Warner's Jolly Journal	9:15
Musc	Music / Betty Crocker, cooking	News	Fashion Tour	9:30
	Talk and Music	Maxine's Shopping Service		9:45
Mardi Gras		Be Young and Happy, Eddie Albright	The Arion Trio	10am
				10:15
News		Economics Talk	Talk and Music / Woman's Magazine of the Air	10:30
Language Lesson			.	10:45
Words and Music	Music	Talk and Music / Jack Carter's Birthday Party	Talk and Music / The Standard School Broadcast	11am
				11:15
Talk and Music	The American School of the Air			11:30
			Stock Market Reports	11:45
	Talk and Music	News	US Agricultural Talk	12pm
		Talk	The National Farm and HomeHour	12:15
	News			12:30
	Music			12:45
Music / The Radio Guild		Paris Inn Frolic	News	1pm
			Ann Warner Chats	1:15
				1:30
			Music	1:45

DAYTIME — WINTER, 1933

Sunday

	BLUE	CBS	KNX	NBC
2pm	John Smallman's a'Cappella Choir	Professor Lindsley, readings	The Westlake Park Concert	
2:15		Rabbi Magnin, religion		
2:30	The Bohemians	The Legion of the Lost		Joseph Koestner Orchestra
2:45				
3pm	The Catholic Hour	Current Events		Judge Yankwich, legal talk
3:15		Little Jack Little Orchestra		Songland
3:30	Our American Schools	The Cathedral Hour		The Melodians
3:45				
4pm	The Golden Choristeers	Dr. Klein, economics	Organ Recital	The Lyric Trio
4:15		Walter Smith Orchestra	Redbook Dramas	
4:30	The Abas String Quartet		Oriental Orchestra	Great Moments in History
4:45		The Canta Nina Girls		

DAYTIME — WINTER, 1933

Monday-Friday

BLUE	CBS	KNX	NBC	
Music	The Happy Go Lucky Hour	The Bookworm	News	*2pm*
			Music	*2:15*
		Los Angeles Fire Department Orchestra		*2:30*
				2:45
Music / The Italian Language	Feminine Fancies	The Matinee Mirthmakers		*3pm*
Music				*3:15*
				3:30
				3:45
Talk and Music	Talk and Music	Travelogue		*4pm*
News				*4:15*
Music			News	*4:30*
	Between the Bookends	Welegan	Noren Gammel Character Sketches	*4:45*

DAYTIME — WINTER, 1933

Saturday

	BLUE	CBS	KNX	NBC
8am	Exercises	The Shell Happy Time Hour	(Off the Air)	Melodies of the South
8:15	Bits of Melody			Household Hints
8:30	Swen Svenson	Concert Miniature		The Arion Trio
8:45			The Sharples Breakfast Club	
9am	Thomas Mitchell, comment	Buddy Herrod Orchestra		Johnny Marvin, songs
9:15	Dixie Memories			Piano Recital
9:30	Music	Happy Felton Orchestra	News	The National Farm and Home Hour
9:45	Physical Education		Be Young and Happy, Eddie Albright	
10am		George Hall Orchestra		
10:15				
10:30	The Farm Forum	Madison Ensemble		Woman's Magazine of the Air
10:45				
11am	The Metropolitan Opera	Saturday Syncopators	Organ Recital	
11:15				
11:30		Columbia Salon Orchestra		Rue Tyler's Rhythm Kids
11:45				Stock Market Reports
12pm		The Round Towners	News and Views	US Agricultural Talk
12:15				
12:30		News	Dr. Matthews' Radio Church	
12:45		Ted Husing, sports		
1pm		Bob Holman Orchestra	Paris Inn Frolic	News
1:15				Music
1:30		Leon Balasco Orchestra		
1:45	Concert Favorites			

DAYTIME — WINTER, 1933

		Saturday		
	BLUE	CBS	KNX	NBC
2pm	Hotel Sherman Orchestra	Eddy Duchin Orchestra	The Bookworm	The Cosmpolitans
2:15				
2:30	Beau Balladeer	Between the Bookends	Opera Recording	The Bluettes
2:45	Concert Echoes	Tiny Newland, songs		Johnny O'Brien, songs
3pm	Waldorf-Astoria Orchestra	America's Grub Street		Organ Recital
3:15		Do-Re-Mi		
3:30	Laws for Society	Willie Butts, songs		
3:45		The Funnyboners		
4pm	News	Ted Fiorito Orchestra		The Ambassador Tea Dance
4:15	Maria Thorpe, talk			
4:30	Twenty Fingers	Mayor Davis Orchestra		
4:45	Barbard Dale, songs		Welegan	News

EVENING — SPRING, 1933

Sunday

	BLUE	CBS	KNX	NBC
5pm	The Colonial Hour (3:30PM)	John Henry, Black River Giant	Ethel Hubler, talk	The Chase and Sanborn Hour, Eddie Cantor
5:15		Andre Kostelanetz Orchestra		
5:30	The National Guild Players		Dr. Matthews' Radio Church	
5:45		John Henry, Black River Giant		
6pm	Records	The Gauchos		The Manhattan Merry-Go-Round
6:15				
6:30		The Melody Hour	Ernest Holmes: Theodore C. Abel	The American Album of Familiar Music
6:45				
7pm	David Lawrence, songs	The Columbia Revue	Captain Don Wilkie, comment	The Singing Servicemen
7:15	Confessions of a Racketeer		The Lubovsiki Trio	The Real Silk Program
7:30	Richard Garrick, songs	Quiet Harmonies		
7:45	Sunday Evenings at Seth Parkers			Golden Memories
8pm		Mellow'd Memories	The First Presbyterian Church of Hollywood	Music
8:15	The Pierce Brothers Quartet	Your Child		Walter Winchell's Jergens Journal
8:30	Echoes of the Palisades	Abe Lyman Orchestra		Robert Hurd Orchestra
8:45				
9pm	The Reader's Guide	The Merrymakers	News	Tapestries of Life
9:15			Judge Rutherford, legal talk	
9:30	USC Symphony Orchestra		The Arizona Wranglers	Eno Crime Clues
9:45				
10pm		The Ten o'Clock Wire	The Back Home Hour, Paul Rader	The Richfield Reporter
10:15	Bridge to Dreamland	Ted Fiorito Orchestra		Gus Arnheim Orchestra
10:30				
10:45				

EVENING — SPRING, 1933

Monday

BLUE	CBS	KNX	NBC	
The Oahu Seranaders	Songsmiths	The All-American Girls	Growin' Up	5pm
	News		Round the World Club	5:15
Uncle Jimmy	Skippy	Crockett's Mountaineers	Little Orphan Annie	5:30
Al, Mac and Tommy, songs	Maude and Cousin Bill	Songs	Wheatenaville Sketches	5:45
Broadway Bits	Grand Opera Miniatures	News	The Makers of History	6pm
		The Arizona Wranglers		6:15
Safety First	Kay Thompson and Frank Jenks, songs	Lawrence King Orchestra	Charles Wellman, songs	6:30
Sports	W. H. Anderson, comment	Growin' Up		6:45
Songs	The Norsemen	Frank Watanabe and Honorable Archie	Keller, Sergeant and Ross, songs	7pm
	Ben Pollack Orchestra	Detectives Black and Blue	Days of the Don	7:15
Etude Ethopians	Dog Catchers	Fifty Famous	The MJB Demi-Tasse Revue	7:30
	The Story of Myrt and Marge			7:45
	The Blue Monday Jamboree	Dance Orchestra	Amos 'n' Andy	8pm
Molly Muddles the News		California Real Estate Association	Octavius Cohen's Mystery Story	8:15
Lorna Ladd's Oral Lornettes			Don Carney's Dog Chats	8:30
John and Ned, songs		Drury Lane, songs	Betty Lou and Vonnie, songs	8:45
The Doric Quartet		News and Views	Thirty Minutes from Broadway	9pm
				9:15
Hollywood on the Air		Jay Whidden Orchestra	Eno Crime Clues	9:30
				9:45
	The Ten o'Clock Wire	Paris Inn Frolic	The Richfield Reporter	10pm
Mark Hopkins Orchestra	Canfield's Islanders		Phil Harris Orchestra	10:15
	Biltmore Concert Orchestra			10:30
				10:45

EVENING — SPRING, 1933

Tuesday

	BLUE	CBS	KNX	NBC
5pm	Coquettes	Musical Album	Travelogue (4:00PM)	Growin' Up
5:15		News	Crockett's Mountaineers	Round the World Club
5:30	Uncle Jimmy	Skippy		Little Orphan Annie
5:45	Al, Mac and Tommy, songs	Maude and Cousin Bill	Chandu, the Magician	Wheatenaville Sketches
6pm	Deadline	Those McCarthy Girls	News	The Balladettes
6:15		Threads of Happiness	The Arizona Wranglers	The Pierce Brothers Quartet
6:30	The Pasadena Major Athletic Association	California Melodies	Lawrence King Orchestra	The Texaco Star Theater, Ed Wynn
6:45	News		Growin' Up	
7pm	Homer Canfield, songs	Barn Dance Varieties	Frank Watanabe and Honorable Archie	Lives at Stake
7:15			Miles of Melody	
7:30	The Hollywood Bowl Hour	Chandu, the Magician		Loyce Whiteman, songs
7:45		The Story of Myrt and Marge	Helene Handin Interview	
8pm		The Globe Headlines	The Lubovsiki Trio	Amos 'n' Andy
8:15	Molly Muddles the News	Columbia Symphony Orchestra		Memory Lane
8:30	Gus Arnheim Orchestra	The Hodge Podge Lodge		
8:45			Golden Memories	Eb and Zeb
9pm	Waltz Time	Band of Distinction	News	Tapestries of Life
9:15		The Buccaneers	Marion Mansfield, songs	
9:30		USC Symphony Orchestra	Jay Whidden Orchestra	Ben Bernie, the Old Maestro
9:45				
10pm		The Ten o'Clock Wire	The Back Home Hour, Paul Rader	The Richfield Reporter
10:15	Mark Hopkin Orchestra	Ted Fiorito Orchstra		Phil Harris Orchestra
10:30				
10:45				

EVENING — SPRING, 1933

Wednesday

BLUE	CBS	KNX	NBC	
Harry Stanton Orchestra	Pastel Harmonies	The All-American Girl	Growin' Up	5pm
	News	Organ Recital	Round the World Club	5:15
Uncle Jimmy	Skippy		Little Orphan Annie	5:30
Al, Mac and Tommy, songs	Maude and Cousin Bill	Chandu, the Magician	Wheatenaville Sketches	5:45
Harvey Peterson, songs	Dr. Kleinsmid, health	News	Music	6pm
Memories	The Romantic Bachelor	The Arizona Wranglers		6:15
John Henry Lyon, music talk	Raymond Paige Orchestra	Lawrence King Orchestra		6:30
Sports	Evansong	Growin' Up		6:45
Al Pearce and His Gang	Fred Waring Orchestra	Frank Watanabe and Honorable Archie	The Corn Cob Pipe Club	7pm
		Detectives Black and Blue		7:15
	Chandu, the Magician	The Auto Club Program	Eddie Peabody, songs	7:30
	The Story of Myrt and Marge	The Eddie Bush Trio		7:45
	The Globe Headlines	The Lubovsiki Trio	Amos 'n' Andy	8pm
	Mellow'd Melodies		Octavius Cohen's Mystery Story	8:15
Gus Arnheim Orchestra	Cafe de Paris	Martin Luther Thomas, comment	One Man's Family	8:30
		Marion Mansfield, songs		8:45
Meredith Wilson Orchestra	Eddy Duchin Orchestra	News	Dave Marshall Orchestra	9pm
		Rance Valentine, rhymes	Sherlock Holmes	9:15
	Ozzie Nelson Orchestra	Jay Whidden Orchestra		9:30
Hotel Edgewater Beach Orchestra			Dramatic Skit	9:45
	The Ten o'Clock Wire	Paris Inn Frolic	The Richfield Reporter	10pm
Mark Hopkins Orchestra	Ted Fiorito Orchestra		Phil Harris Orchestra	10:15
				10:30
				10:45

EVENING — SPRING, 1933

Thursday

	BLUE	CBS	KNX	NBC
5pm	Merle Thorpe, songs (4:45PM)	Do-Re-Mi	Dog Talk	The Fleischman Yeast Hour, Rudy Vallee
5:15		News	Organ Recital	
5:30	Uncle Jimmy	Skippy		
5:45	Al, Mac and Tommy, songs	Institute of World Affairs	Chandu, the Magician	
6pm	Songs	Songsmiths	News	The Maxwell House Showboat
6:15		The Pasadena Community Players	The Arizona Wranglers	
6:30		Stoopnagle and Budd	Lawrence King Orchestra	
6:45	Sports		Growin' Up	
7pm	Records	The Inglewood Park Concert	Frank Watanabe and Honorable Archie	The Lucky Strike Hour, Jack Pearl
7:15			Miles of Melody	
7:30			Chandu, the Magician	
7:45	Nick Harris	The Story of Myrt and Marge	The Midweek Parade	
8pm		The Globe Headlines		Amos 'n' Andy
8:15	Molly Muddles the News	The Laff Clinic	Rev. Shuler, religion	The Standard Symphony Hour
8:30	Guy Arnheim Orchestra		The Happy Chappies	
8:45			Golden Memories	
9pm	The Pasadena Major Athletic Association	Band of Distinction	News	
9:15		Dance Orchestra	Marion Mansfield, songs	Thurston, the Magician
9:30	Concert in Rhythm		Music	The KFI Fun Factory
9:45				
10pm		The Ten o'Clock Wire	The Back Home Hour, Paul Rader	The Richfield Reporter
10:15	Mark Hopkins Orchestra	Ted Fiorito Orchestra		Phil Harris Orchestra
10:30	Ship of Dreams			
10:45				

EVENING — SPRING, 1933

Friday

BLUE	CBS	KNX	NBC	
Charles Hart, songs	News	Music	Growin' Up	5pm
	Skippy		The Lyric Trio	5:15
Uncle Jimmy	Music		Little Orphan Annie	5:30
Al, Mac and Tommy, songs		Chandu, the Magician	Wheatenaville Sketches	5:45
Los Angeles Fire Department Orchestra	Freddie Rich Orchestra	News	The First Nighter Program	6pm
		The Arizona Wranglers		6:15
Homer Canfield, songs	Edwin C. Hill, news	Lawrence King Orchestra	The Armour Star Jester, Phil Baker	6:30
Sports	Music	Growin' Up		6:45
Paul Roberts, songs	The Columbia Revue	Frank Watanabe and Honorable Archie	The Big Six of the Air	7pm
		Detectives Black and Blue		7:15
The Tune Detectives	Chandu, the Magician	The Auto Club Program	Stardust	7:30
Sarah and Sassafras	The Story of Myrt and Marge	The Eddie Bush Trio	Music	7:45
Helen Guest, songs	The Globe Headlines	The Optimistic Do-Nuts	Amos 'n' Andy	8pm
Molly Muddles the News	Mellow'd Melodies		The Gilmore Circus	8:15
Guy Arnheim Orchestra	Reminiscing			8:30
	Abe Lyman Orchestra			8:45
The Edward Lynn Players		News and Views		9pm
	Dance Orchestra		Thurston, the Magician	9:15
		Jay Whidden Orchestra	The Musical Grocery Store	9:30
		The Hollywood Legion Fight		9:45
	The Ten o'Clock Wire		The Richfield Reporter	10pm
Mark Hopkins Orchestra	Ted Fiorito Orchestra		Phil Harris Orchestra	10:15
				10:30
		Paris Inn Frolic		10:45

EVENING — SPRING, 1933

Saturday

	BLUE	CBS	KNX	NBC
5pm	Talk and Music	Fray and Braggiotti, songs	Organ Recital (4:45PM)	Talk
5:15		News	Dr. Matthews' Radio Church	Round the World Club
5:30	Dr. Snape's Question Hour	Skippy		Little Orphan Annie
5:45		Music	Chandu, the Magician	Wheatenaville Sketches
6pm	Boston Symphony Orchestra		News	Los Angeles Philharmonic Orchestra
6:15		The Boswell Sisters, songs	Music	
6:30				
6:45		Saturday Frivolities	Uncle Don Wilkie, comment	
7pm	Harp Recital		Frank Watanabe and Honorable Archie	Lucky Strike Dance Orchestra
7:15		Music	Miles of Melody	
7:30		Chandu, the Magician		
7:45		Gertrude Niesen, songs	Music	
8pm		School Orchestra	Varieties	The Caswell Concert
8:15	Molly Muddles the News			Octavis Cohen's Mystery Story
8:30	Gus Arnheim Orchestra			Family Robinson
8:45				
9pm	Records	Band of Distinction	News	The Associated Spotlight Review
9:15		Dance Orchestra	The Happy Chappies	
9:30		Joseph Kamokan's Hawaiians	Jay Whidden Orchestra	
9:45				
10pm		The Ten o'Clock Wire	Paris Inn Frolic	
10:15		Ted Fiorito Orchestra		
10:30	Musical Echoes			Phil Harris Orchestra
10:45				

DAYTIME — SPRING, 1933

Sunday

	BLUE	CBS	KNX	NBC
8am	Radio Rubes	The Times Comics Pages	The Sharples Breakfast Club (6:45AM)	(Off the Air)
8:15	Major Bowes' Capitol Family			
8:30		The Salt Lake Tabernacle Choir		
8:45				
9am			Rev. Shuler, religion	The Church Quarter-Hour
9:15				Radio City Music Hall
9:30		Emery Deutsch Orchestra		
9:45		The Street Singer	H. B. Drollinger, economics	
10am	Dr. Wunder, health	Home, Sweet Home		
10:15			Organ Recital	Dr. Casselbury, health
10:30	Moonshine and Honeysuckle			Shakesphere Program
10:45			Third Church of Christian Scientist	
11am	Paul Kellar, piano	Hazel Warner, songs		The Monarch Mystery Tenor
11:15		Francisco del Campo,,songs		The International Radio Forum
11:30		The KFRC Little Concert		Yeast Foamers Orchestra
11:45		Fred Lane's Book Review		
12pm		New York Philharmonic Orchestra		Lady Esther Serenade
12:15			Lal Chand Mehra, india talk	
12:30			Louise Johnson, astrology	The Hour of Worship
12:45				
1pm			Jehoviah's Witnesses	The Well Spring of Music
1:15				Wildroot Chat

DAYTIME — SPRING, 1933

Monday-Friday

BLUE	CBS	KNX	NBC	
Exercises	Morning Moods	The Sharples Breakfast Club (6:45AM)	Talk / The Old Memory Box	*8am*
Jack and Patsy, songs	Music		Piano Recital	*8:15*
Petey Knox, songs			Cross Cuts of the Day	*8:30*
				8:45
Johnny Marvin, songs	Bobby Herrod Orchestra	Air Clinic	Lil' Joe Warner's Jolly Journal	*9am*
The Buckaroos			Talk and Music	*9:15*
County Medical Association Talks	Music / Betty Crocker, cooking	News		*9:30*
	Talk and Music	Maxine's Shopping Service		*9:45*
Music / The Arion Trio	Music / Marie, the Little French Princess	Be Young and Happy, Eddie Albright		*10am*
	Music			*10:15*
News		Economics Talk	Talk and Music / Woman's Magazine of the Air	*10:30*
Language Lesson				*10:45*
		Music	Talk and Music / The Standard School Broadcast	*11am*
				11:15
	The American School of the Air	H. B. Drollinger, economics		*11:30*
Sisters of the Skillet			Stock Market Reports	*11:45*
Edna Fischer, piano	Talk and Music	News	US Agricultural Talk	*12pm*
Charlie Wellman and Company		Talk and Music	The National Farm and HomeHour	*12:15*
Music	News			*12:30*
	Music			*12:45*
Music / The Radio Guild		Paris Inn Frolic	News	*1pm*
			Ann Warner Chats	*1:15*

DAYTIME — SPRING, 1933

Sunday

	BLUE	CBS	KNX	NBC
1:30	The National Youth Conference			Wesley Tourtellette, organ
1:45				
2pm	John Smallman's a'Cappella Choir	Professor Lindsley, readings	The Westlake Park Concert	
2:15		Rabbi Magnin, religion		Julie Kellar, harp
2:30		Wiliam Knight, songs		Pages of Romance
2:45		Chicago Knights		
3pm	The Catholic Hour	Public Affairs		Judge Yankwich, legal talk
3:15				Barbara Jamieson, piano
3:30	The Colonial Hour			USC Symphony Orchestra
3:45				
4pm			Organ Recital	The Classic Hour
4:15				
4:30		Fray and Braggiotti, songs	Rev. Shuler, religion	Great Moments in History
4:45		Between the Bookends		

DAYTIME — SPRING, 1933

Monday-Friday

BLUE	CBS	KNX	NBC	
				1:30
			Music	1:45
Music	The Happy Go Lucky Hour	The Bookworm	Al Pearce and His Gang	2pm
				2:15
		Los Angeles Fire Department Orchestra		2:30
				2:45
Music / The Italian Language	Feminine Fancies	The Matinee Mirthmakers	Music	3pm
Music				3:15
				3:30
				3:45
Grand Terrace Orchestra	Talk and Music	Travelogue		4pm
Talk and Music				4:15
		Travelogue / Dr. Matthews' Radio Church	News	4:30
			Baron Keyes, stories	4:45

DAYTIME — SPRING, 1933

Saturday

	BLUE	CBS	KNX	NBC
8am	Exercises	The Adventures of Helen and Mary	(Off the Air)	The Morning Parade
8:15	Jack and Patsy, songs			Piano Recital
8:30	Petey Knox, songs	Music		Cross-Cuts of the Day
8:45	Al, Mac and Tommy, songs		The Sharples Breakfast Club	
9am	Johnny Marvin, songs	Harold Knight Orchestra		Lil' Joe Warner's Jolly Journal
9:15				Rue Tyler's Rhythm Kids
9:30	Physical Education	Bobby Herrod Orchestra	News and Views	The National Farm and Home Hour
9:45				
10am		George Hall Orchestra	Be Young and Happy, Eddie Albright	
10:15				
10:30		Madison Ensemble		Woman's Magazine of the Air
10:45				
11am		Dancing Echoes	Organ Recital	
11:15		The Five Octaves		
11:30	Synco Thots	The Beasley Singers		Character Sketches
11:45	Sisters of the Skillet			Stock Market Reports
12pm	Edna Fisher, piano	The Round Towners	News and Views	US Agricultural Talk
12:15		Spanish Seranade		
12:30		News	Dr. Matthews' Radio Church	
12:45		Dance Orchestra		
1pm	Dance Masters		Paris Inn Frolic	Music
1:15				
1:30		J. Mansfield Orchestra		
1:45				

DAYTIME — SPRING, 1933

Saturday

	BLUE	CBS	KNX	NBC
2pm		Eddy Duchin Orchestra	The Bookworm	The Cosmpolitans
2:15				
2:30	Melody Bouquet	Between the Bookends		Poet of the Air
2:45		Tiny Newland, songs		
3pm	Waldorf-Astoria Orchestra	America's Grub Street	Music	Organ Recital
3:15		Paul Tremaine Orchestra		
3:30	Laws for Society	Nell Larson, songs		
3:45	Songs	Freddy Martin Orchestra		
4pm	News	News		The Ambassador Tea Dance
4:15	Music	Ted Fiorito Orchestra		
4:30	The American Choir			
4:45	Barbard Dale, songs	The Street Singer	Organ Recital	News

EVENING — SUMMER, 1933

Sunday

	BLUE	CBS	KNX	NBC
5pm	Christian Science Program	Philadelphia Symphony Orchestra (4:30PM)	Ethel Hubler, talk	The Manhattan Merry-Go-Round
5:15	Madame Rose, songs			
5:30			Dr. Matthews' Radio Church	The American Album of Familiar Music
5:45	Meglin Melodies			
6pm				Colonel Louis McHenry Howe, comment
6:15				Impressions of Italy
6:30		Rhythm Rhapsody	Ernest Holmes: Theodore C. Abel	
6:45	Sunday Evenings at Seth Parkers			Swashbucklers
7pm		Guy Lombardo Orchestra	Captain Don Wilkie, comment	
7:15	The Pierce Brothers Quartet		Music	Songs
7:30	Orchestral Gems	Salon Moderne		Organ Recital
7:45				
8pm	Richelieu	Isham Jones Orchestra	The First Presbyterian Church of Hollywood	Standard on Parade
8:15		Mellow'd Memories		
8:30		Ted Lewis Orchestra		
8:45				
9pm	The Reader's Guide	The Merrymakers	News	Gayeties of 1933
9:15			Judge Rutherford, legal talk	
9:30	USC Symphony Orchestra		The Lubovsiki Trio	
9:45				
10pm		The Ten o'Clock Wire		The Richfield Reporter
10:15		Gus Arnheim Orchestra		Bridge to Dreamland
10:30				
10:45				

EVENING — SUMMER, 1933

Monday

BLUE	CBS	KNX	NBC	
Piano Duo (4:45 PM)	The Manhattan Serenaders	The Story Town Express	Human Behavior	5pm
	The Street Singer		Lal Chand Mehra, india talk	5:15
The Academy of Teachers of Singing	Kay Thompson, songs	Organ Recital	Counselor	5:30
	Dick Aurandt, songs	The Rhythm Boys	Edwin Franco Goldman Band	5:45
The Hour Glass	Andre Kostelanetz Orchestra	News	Raine Bennett, poetry	6pm
Organ Recital		Jay Rubinoff Orchestra	The Hour Glass	6:15
The Paramount Supper Show	Little Jack Little Orchestra	Lawrence King Orchestra	The Parade of Melody	6:30
	Howard Barlow Orchestra	Growin' Up		6:45
	Columbia Symphony Orchestra	Frank Watanabe and Honorable Archie	Amos 'n' Andy	7pm
Rudy Weidoff, songs	The Inglewood Park Concert	Detectives Black and Blue	Douglas Steade, songs	7:15
Music		The Hawk	The MJB Demi-Tasse Revue	7:30
Eb and Zeb	The Four-Star Fun Frolic	The Count of Monte Cristo		7:45
Hollywood on the Air	The Blue Monday Jamboree	The Lubovsiki Trio	The Makers of History	8pm
				8:15
Lorna Ladd's Oral Lornettes			Stars of the West	8:30
				8:45
The Drama Hour		News	The Singing Service Men	9pm
		Music	Music	9:15
Musicale		Opera in Miniature		9:30
		Marion Mansfield, songs		9:45
Records	The Ten o'Clock Wire	Paris Inn Frolic	The Richfield Reporter	10pm
	Cafe de Paris		The Melody Mixers	10:15
				10:30
				10:45

EVENING — SUMMER, 1933

Tuesday

	BLUE	CBS	KNX	NBC
5pm	Arnold and Amber, songs (4:45 PM)	The Children's Radio Theater	The Story Town Express	The Balladettes
5:15	The Balladettes	Frank Westphal Orchestra	Sheriff Underwood Presents	Douglas Steade, songs
5:30		Nino Martini, songs		The Texaco Star Theater, Ed Wynn
5:45			Ted Reed, songs	
6pm		California Melodies	News	Lives at Stake
6:15	Organ Recital		King's Cowboy Revue	
6:30			Lawrence King Orchestra	The Pierce Brothers Quartet
6:45	The Paramount Supper Show	Light Opera	Growin' Up	Music
7pm			Frank Watanabe and Honorable Archie	Amos 'n' Andy
7:15	Music	Chandu, the Magician	The Singing Guardsmen	Memory Lane
7:30		Military Band	Julie Kellar, harp	
7:45	Eb and Zeb	The Four-Star Fun Frolic	The Count of Monte Cristo	Adventures in Health
8pm	Records	The Globe Headlines		The Rhythm Rascals
8:15		Freddy Martin Orchestra	Tax Reduction	The Phillistines
8:30		Conqueror of the Skies		Ben Bernie, the Old Maestro
8:45			Golden Memories	
9pm	Carefree Carnival	Gus Arnheim Orchestra	News	Tapestries of Life
9:15			Miles of Melody	
9:30		The Hodge Podge Lodge		Eno Crime Clues
9:45			Marion Mansfield, songs	
10pm		The Ten o'Clock Wire	Paris Inn Frolic	The Richfield Reporter
10:15		Ray West Orchestra		Mark Hopkins Orchestra
10:30				
10:45		Golden Sands		

EVENING — SUMMER, 1933

Wednesday

BLUE	CBS	KNX	NBC	
The Associated Glee Clubs	Nora Shiller, songs	The Story Town Express	News	5pm
	The Street Singer		Raymond Robbins, talk	5:15
Myron Neisley, songs	Kay Thompson, songs	Organ Recital	Julie Kellar, harp	5:30
The Argentine Trio	Charle Lung, songs	The All-American Girls	Nick Harris	5:45
	Fred Waring Orchestra	News	The Corn Cob Pipe Club	6pm
Organ Recital		Jay Rubinoff Orchestra		6:15
	Dancing Cubes	Lawrence King Orchestral	Captain Dobbsie's Ship of Joy	6:30
The Paramount Supper Show	Edwin C. Hill, news	Growin' Up		6:45
	Howard Barlow Orchestra	Frank Watanabe and Honorable Archie	Amos 'n' Andy	7pm
	Chandu, the Magician	Detectives Black and Blue	June King, songs	7:15
	Tom Green Orchestra	The Hawk	Eddie Peabody, songs	7:30
Eb and Zeb	The Four-Star Fun Frolic	The Count of Monte Cristo		7:45
	The Globe Headlines	Basket of Fun	The Phillistines	8pm
Hotel Roosevelt Orchestra	Mellow'd Melodies		Thirty Minutes from Broadway	8:15
Deadline	Guy Lombardo Orchestra			8:30
			Hotel Edgewater Beach Orchestra	8:45
	Ray West Orchestra	News	One Man's Family	9pm
	Gus Arnheim Orchestra	Music		9:15
Waltz Time	Catherine the Great	Organ Recital	Eno Crime Clues	9:30
				9:45
Records	The Ten o'Clock Wire	Paris Inn Frolic	The Richfield Reporter	10pm
	Ray West Orchestra		Mark Hopkins Orchestra	10:15
	The Isle of Golden Dreams			10:30
				10:45

EVENING — SUMMER, 1933

Thursday

	BLUE	CBS	KNX	NBC
5pm	Dance Journal	The Los Angeles Fire Department	The Story Town Express	Music
5:15		Town Topics	Sheriff Underwood Presents	
5:30	Memory's Melodys	Mark Warnow Orchestra		The Counselor
5:45		The Pasadena Community Players	Bouquet of Memories	Douglas Stead, songs
6pm		Deep River	News	Drama
6:15	Organ Recital		King's Cowboy Revue	
6:30		Songs	Lawrence King Orchestra	
6:45	Charlie Wellman and Company	Columbia Symphony Orchestra	Growin' Up	
7pm			Frank Watanabe and Honorable Archie	Amos 'n' Andy
7:15	The Rhythm Rascals	Chandu, the Magician	Light Opera	Packard Orchesrra
7:30		The Vagabonds Quartet		Death Valley Days
7:45	Eb and Zeb	The Four-Star Fun Frolic	The Count of Monte Cristo	
8pm	Music	The Globe Headlines	The Midweek Parade	The Standard Symphony Hour
8:15		The Laff Clinic		
8:30				
8:45			Golden Memories	
9pm		Gus Arnheim Orchestra	News	The Maxwell House Showboat
9:15			Miles of Melody	
9:30		The Buccaneers		
9:45		Kay Thompson, songs	Sheriff Underwood Presents	
10pm		The Ten o'Clock Wire	Paris Inn Frolic	The Richfield Reporter
10:15	Mark Hopkins Orchestra	Ray West Orchestra		Sid Lippman Orchestra
10:30				
10:45		Berceuse		

EVENING — SUMMER, 1933

Friday

BLUE	CBS	KNX	NBC	
Southern Harmony (4:45PM)	Dick Aurandt, songs	The Story Town Express	Let's Listen to Harris	5pm
	The Street Singer	Sheriff Underwood Presents		5:15
Out of the East	The Melody Mardi Gras	Organ Recital	California Teachers Association	5:30
	In the Gloaming	The All-American Girls	Paul Roberts, songs	5:45
Helen Guest, songs	The Chesterfield Program	News	The First Nighter Program	6pm
Organ Recital		Jay Rubinoff Orchestra		6:15
	Dancing Cubes	Lawrence King Orchestra	The Phantom Strings	6:30
Abe Lyman Orchestra	Edwin C. Hill, news	Growin' Up	Hillbilly Heart Throbs	6:45
	Howard Barlow Orchestra	Frank Watanabe and Honorable Archie	Amos 'n' Andy	7pm
Henry Selby Orchestra	Chandu, the Magician	Detectives Black and Blue	Drama	7:15
	Military Band	The Hawk	The Musical Grocery Store	7:30
Eb and Zeb	The Four-Star Fun Frolic	The Count of Monte Cristo		7:45
Music	The Globe Headlines	The Optimistic Do-Nuts	The Outdoor Gazette	8pm
	Mellow'd Melodies		The Gilmore Circus	8:15
	Tapestries of Life			8:30
				8:45
Records	Gus Arnheim Orchestra	News and Views		9pm
			The Armour Star Jester, Phil Baler	9:15
	Music	Marion Mansfield, songs		9:30
		The Hollywood Legion Fight	Music	9:45
	The Ten o'Clock Wire		The Richfield Reporter	10pm
Mark Hopkins Orchestra	Ray West Orchestra		Sid Lippman Orchestra	10:15
				10:30
		Paris Inn Frolic		10:45

EVENING — SUMMER, 1933

Saturday

	BLUE	CBS	KNX	NBC
5pm	News and Views (4:30PM)	The Philadelphia Summer Concert (4:30PM)	The Story Town Express	New York Philharmonic Orchestra (4:30PM)
5:15			Dr. Matthews' Radio Church	
5:30	Dr. Snape's Question Hour	Ann Leaf at the Organ		
5:45		Fred Berren's Revue	Ted Reed, songs	
6pm	Records		News	Lucky Strike Dance Orchestra
6:15		Isham Jones Orchestra	King's Cowboy Revue	
6:30			Lawrence King Orchestra	
6:45		Gertrude Niesen, songs	Phillip Musgrave, cello	
7pm		Jerry Friedman Orchestra	Frank Watanabe and Honorable Archie	The Pacific Serenaders
7:15		Chandu, the Magician	Julie Kellar, harp	
7:30	Hotel Montclaire Orchestra	Charles Davis Orchestra	Music	Marvin Manzel, piano
7:45				
8pm	The Australian Sundowners	Barney Rapp Orchestra	Varieties	The Caswell Concert
8:15				The Hollywood Bowl Concert
8:30		Gus Arnheim Orchestral		
8:45				
9pm		Ray West Orchestra	News	
9:15			Miles of Melody	
9:30				
9:45			Music	
10pm		The Ten o'Clock Wire	Paris Inn Frolic	Bal Taborin Orchestra
10:15		Gus Arnheim Orchestra		
10:30	Blue Moonlight			Sid Lippman Orchestra
10:45				

DAYTIME — SUMMER, 1933

Sunday

	BLUE	CBS	KNX	NBC
8am	Major Bowes' Capitol Family	The Salt Lake Tabernacle Choir	The Sharples Breakfast Club (7:00AM)	(Off the Air)
8:15	The Radio City Music Hall			
8:30		The Times Comics Pages		
8:45				
9am		Ford Freibel, organ	Rev. Shuler, religion	The Church Quarter-Hour
9:15				Palmer House Orchestra
9:30		The Compinsky Trio	Organ Recital	Dr. Goodell, health
9:45				
10am		Home, Sweet Home	Music	Gene Arnold Orchestra
10:15				Piano Recital
10:30				Jan Garber Orchestra
10:45	Temple Baptist Church			
11am		The Weaver of Dreams		Lady Esther Serenade
11:15		Columbia Symphony Orchestra		
11:30				The National Radio Pulpit
11:45			Lal Chand Mehra, india talk	
12pm		The Cathedral Hour		Fiddlers Three
12:15			Lal Chand Mehra, india talk	Wildroot Chat
12:30	Music		Louise Johnson, astrology	Psychology
12:45				Barbara Jamieson, piano
1pm	The World of Religion	Willard Robison Orchestra	Opera Recordings	The Classic Hour
1:15		Vera Van, songs		
1:30	Organ Recital	Fantasies		The Eva Jesse Choir
1:45		Claude Sweeten Orchestra		

DAYTIME — SUMMER, 1933

Monday-Friday

BLUE	CBS	KNX	NBC	
Exercises	George Hall Orchestra	The Sharples Breakfast Club (6:45AM)	Johnny Marvin, songs	8am
			Music	8:15
	Music			8:30
				8:45
Vic and Sade		Air Clinic	Lil' Joe Warner's Jolly Journal	9am
The Buckaroos			The Buckaroos	9:15
Music	Music / Betty Crocker, cooking	News	Music	9:30
	Talk and Music	Maxine's Shopping Service		9:45
	Music / Marie, the Little French Princess	Be Young and Happy, Eddie Albright		10am
	Music			10:15
News and Views			Talk and Music / Woman's Magazine of the Air	10:30
				10:45
Language Lesson		Organ Recital		11am
				11:15
			Words and Music	11:30
Happy Jack Turner, songs			Stock Market Reports	11:45
Music	Talk and Music	News	US Agricultural Talk	12pm
		Jay Rubinoff Orchestra	The National Farm and Home Hour	12:15
Charlie Wellman and Company	News			12:30
	Talk and Music			12:45
Music / The Radio Guild		Paris Inn Frolic	News	1pm
			Ann Warner Chats	1:15
				1:30
			Music	1:45

DAYTIME — SUMMER, 1933

Sunday

	BLUE	CBS	KNX	NBC
2pm	The Catholic Hour	Eddy Duchin Orchestra	The Exposition Park Concert	Organ Recital
2:15				
2:30	Pollikoff Novelty Orchestra	Professor Lindsley, readings		USC Symphony Orchestra
2:45		Chicago Knights		
3pm		The Gauchos		The Harrmonic Rascals
3:15				Olga Albaul, songs
3:30		John Henry, Black River Giant		Wisdom of the Ages
3:45		Chicago Varieties		
4pm	The Congress Hall Band		Organ Recital	The Chase and Sanborn Hour, Bert Lahr
4:15		John Henry, Black River Giant		
4:30	The Cathedral on the Air	Philadelphia Symphony Orchestra	Rev. Shuler, religion	
4:45				

DAYTIME — SUMMER, 1933

Monday-Friday

BLUE	CBS	KNX	NBC	
Music	The Happy Go Lucky Hour	The Bookworm	Al Pearce and His Gang	2pm
				2:15
		Music		2:30
				2:45
Music / The Italian Language	Feminine Fancies	Music / Organ Recital	Pictorial	3pm
Music				3:15
			The Ranch Boys	3:30
				3:45
	Talk and Music	Travelogue	Music /	4pm
	The Hodge Podge Lodge	Music	The Fleischmann Yeart Hour, Rudy Vallee /	4:15
News		Music / Dr. Matthews' Radio Church		4:30
Music	Music		News	4:45

DAYTIME — SUMMER, 1933

Saturday

	BLUE	CBS	KNX	NBC
8am	Exercises	Vincent Travers Orchestra	(Off the Air)	Caroline Clement, songs
8:15				Piano Recital
8:30	Stock Market Reports	Frank La Marr Orchestra		The Syncopators
8:45			The Sharples Breakfast Club	
9am	Vic and Sade	George Hall Orchestra		Lil' Joe Warner's Jolly Journal
9:15	Palmer House Orchestra			Sarah Ellen Barnes, songs
9:30	Physical Education	Madison Ensemble	News and Views	The National Farm and Home Hour
9:45				
10am		Dancing Echoes	Be Young and Happy, Eddie Albright	
10:15		The Three Peppers		
10:30		Jan Savitt Orchestra		Woman's Magazine of the Air
10:45				
11am		Italian Idyll	Organ Recital	
11:15				
11:30	Marshall's Mavericks	Mark Warnow Orchestra		Character Sketches
11:45				Stock Market Reports
12pm	The Rhythm Rascals	Spanish Serenade	News	US Agricultural Talk
12:15	The Magic Kettle	Eli Dantzig Orchestra	Michael Kelly, songs	
12:30		Earl Craven, gossip	Dr. Matthews' Radio Church	
12:45		The Ambassador Trio		
1pm	Dance Orchestra	George Dolbier Orchestra	Paris Inn Frolic	News
1:15				Songs
1:30		Between the Bookends		
1:45		Tito Guizar, guitar		

DAYTIME — SUMMER, 1933

Saturday

	BLUE	CBS	KNX	NBC
2pm		Buddy Wagner Orchestra	The Bookworm	The Melody Mixers
2:15				
2:30		Francisco del Campo, songs	Organ Recital	
2:45		Irving Conn Orchestra		
3pm		The Four Eton Boys	Opera Recordings	Songs
3:15		Mildred Bailey songs		Annie, Judy and Zek, songs
3:30	Jack and Loretta Clemens, songs	Elder Michaux Congregation		News
3:45	The Optimistic Mrs. Jones			The Ambassador Tea Dance
4pm	Waldorf-Astoria Orchestral	Gus Arnheim Orchestra		
4:15				
4:30	News and Views	The Philadelphia Summer Concert		New York Philharmonic Orchestra
4:45				

EVENING — FALL, 1933

Sunday

	BLUE	CBS	KNX	NBC
5pm	Our American Schools (3:30 PM)	Freddie Rich Orchestra	Ethel Hubler, talk	The Chase and Sanborn Hour, Bert Lahr
5:15				
5:30			Dr. Matthews' Radio Church	
5:45				
6pm	Helen Lewyn, piano	The Seven Star Revue		The Manhattan Merry-Go-Round
6:15				
6:30			Ernest Holmes: Theodore C. Abel	The American Album of Familiar Music
6:45	Organ Recital			
7pm		Your Child	Julie Kellar, harp	The Chevrolet Program, Jack Benny
7:15			Jay Rubinoff Orchestra	
7:30		Quiet Harmonies	Charlie Hamp, organ	Colonel Louis Howe, comment
7:45	Mobilization for Human Needs			The Makers of History
8pm		Guy Lombardo Orchestra	The First Presbyterian Church of Hollywood	
8:15	The Pierce Brothers Quartet			Music
8:30		Dance Orchestra		Death Valley Days
8:45				
9pm		The Merrymakers	News	Ghost Stories
9:15			Judge Rutherford, legal talk	The Reader's Guild
9:30	USC Symphony Orchestra		The Lubovsiki Trio	The Mirth Parade
9:45				The Singing Servicemen
10pm		The Ten o'Clock Wire		The Richfield Reporter
10:15	Bridge to Dreamland	Gus Arnheim Orchestra		Richelieu
10:30		Ted Fiorito Orchestra		
10:45				

EVENING — FALL, 1933

Monday

BLUE	CBS	KNX	NBC	
Roy Leffingwell Orchestra	The Rhythm Kings	The Story Town Express	Human Behavior	5pm
	The Armchair Philosopher	College Daze and Knights	Two Men and a Maid	5:15
News	Bing Crosby Entertains		Billy Bachelor	5:30
Education		The Rhythm Boys	Little Orphan Annie	5:45
Songs	Bobby Benson	News	Elieen Piggott, songs	6pm
The Adventures of Klickety Klack	The Manhattan Serenaders	King's Cowboy Revue	Poetry	6:15
Twilight Reveries	The Ex-Lax Big Show	The Singing Guardsmen	Just Around the Corner	6:30
		Songs		6:45
Music	Lady Esther Serenade	Frank Watanabe and Honorable Archie	The Carnation Contented Hour	7pm
Douglas Stead, songs		Detectives Black and Blue		7:15
	O'Keefe and Merritt, songs	Red Davis	The MJB Demi-Tasse Revue	7:30
Music	The Story of Myrt and Marge	Smilin' Ed McConnell, songs		7:45
	The Shell Show	The Count of Monte Cristo	Amos 'n' Andy	8pm
Eb and Zeb		The Lubovsiki Trio	The Philistines	8:15
Music			Stars of the West	8:30
Lorna Ladd's Oral Lornettes				8:45
Music	The Blue Monday Jamboree	News	The Side Show	9pm
The Drama Hour		Charlie Hamp, organ		9:15
			The Mirth Parade	9:30
Hal Roberts Orchestra		Curt Hoeck Orchestra	Tim and Irene	9:45
	The Ten o'Clock Wire	Davey Mack Orchestra	The Richfield Reporter	10pm
The Melody Mixers	Dick Aurandt, songs		Frank Luther, songs	10:15
			The Melody Mixers	10:30
				10:45

EVENING — FALL, 1933

Tuesday

	BLUE	CBS	KNX	NBC
5pm	The Golden Sword	Songs	The Story Town Express	Music
5:15	Music	The Children's Radio Theater	Mark Kirk, songs	Rhyme and Rhythm
5:30	News	Charlie Lung, songs	Bouquet of Memories	Billy Bachelor
5:45	Music	Kate Smith and Her Swanee Music		Little Orphan Sketches
6pm	The Arion Trio	California Melodies	News	Duel de Kerekjarto, songs
6:15	The Adventures of Klickety Klack		Music	The Pierce Brothers Quartet
6:30	Twilight Reveries	Philadelphia Symphony Orchestra	King's Cowboy Revue	The Texaco Star Theater, Ed Wynn
6:45			Chandu, the Magician	
7pm	Music	Red Stanley Orchestra	Frank Watanabe and Honorable Archie	Lives at Stake
7:15		The Inglewood Park Concert	The Singing Guardsmen	
7:30			Elvia Allman, songs	The Ry-Krisp Program
7:45		The Story of Myrt and Marge	Lawrence King Orchestra	Music
8pm		The Globe Headlines	The Count of Monte Cristo	Amos 'n' Andy
8:15	Eb and Zeb	Elmer Everett Yess	Tax Reduction	Memory Lane
8:30	Music	Mellow'd Memories		
8:45		The Voice of Experience	Golden Memories	Adventures in Health
9pm	Hal Roberts Orchestra	Ted Fiorito Orchestra	News	Ben Bernie, the Old Maestro
9:15			Light Opera	
9:30	Magnolia Minstels	The Hodge Podge Lodge		Eno Crime Clues
9:45			Dance Orchestra	
10pm		The Ten o'Clock Wire	Davey Mack Orchestra	The Richfield Reporter
10:15	Mark Hopkins Orchestra	Marvelous Melodies		Comedy Stars of Hollywood
10:30		The Harlem Gentlemen		Sid Lippman Orchestra
10:45				

EVENING — FALL, 1933

Wednesday

BLUE	CBS	KNX	NBC	
Roy Leffingwell Orchestra	The All-Year Club	The Story Town Express	Music	5pm
Music	Stranger than Fiction	College Daze and Knights	Julie Kellar, harp	5:15
News and Views	Albert Spaulding, violin	Music	Billy Bachelor	5:30
		The Song Service	Little Orphan Annie	5:45
Business Principles	Bobby Benson	News	Music	6pm
The Adventures of Klickety Klack	Kate Smith and Her Swanee Music	Jose Obispo, songs		6:15
Twilight Reveries	Guy Lombardo Orchestra	King's Cowboy Revue		6:30
		Chandu, the Magician		6:45
Music	Fred Waring Orchestra	Frank Watanabe and Honorable Archie	The Corn Cob Pipe Club	7pm
Paul Roberts, songs		Detectives Black and Blue		7:15
The National Radio Forum	The Town Crier	Red Davis	Music	7:30
	The Story of Myrt and Marge	The Count of Monte Cristo		7:45
Silvio Lavatelli, songs	The Globe Headlines	Opera of the Air	Amos 'n' Andy	8pm
Eb and Zeb	Red Stanley Orchestra		Dog Stories	8:15
Duel de Kerekjarto, songs	Edwin C. Hill, news		One Man's Family	8:30
	Marvelous Melodies			8:45
Hal Roberts Orchestra	Three Old Favorites	News	The Old Memory Box	9pm
		Charlie Hamp, organ	Sports	9:15
Waltz Time	Catherine the Great		Eno Crime Clues	9:30
		Curt Houck Orchestra		9:45
	The Ten o'Clock Wire	Davey Mack Orchestra	The Richfield Reporter	10pm
Mark Hopkins Orchestra	The Harlem Gentlemen		Frank Luther, songs	10:15
			Sid Lippman Orchestra	10:30
				10:45

EVENING — FALL, 1933

Thursday

	BLUE	CBS	KNX	NBC
5pm	The Golden Sword	Songs	The Story Town Express	The Fleischman Yeast Hour, Rudy Vallee
5:15	News and Views	The Children's Radio Theater	Mark Kirk, songs	
5:30		Charlie Lung, songs		
5:45		The Harlem Serenade		
6pm		Andre Kostelanetz Orchestra	News	The Maxwell House Showboat
6:15	The Adventures of Klickety Klack		Jay Rubinoff Orchestra	
6:30	Twilight Reveries	The Columbia Dramatic Guild	King's Cowboy Revue	
6:45			Chandu, the Magician	
7pm	Songs	Willard Robison Orchestra	Frank Watanabe and Honorable Archie	The Kraft Music Hall
7:15	James Burroughs, songs		The Singing Guarsdmen	
7:30		Phil Regan, songs	Elvia Allman, songs	
7:45	The Lyric Trio	The Story of Myrt and Marge	Lawrence King Orchestra	
8pm		The Globe Headlines	The Count of Monte Cristo	Amos 'n' Andy
8:15	Ed and Zeb	Elmer Everett Yess	Varieties	The Standard Symphony Hour
8:30	Nick Harris	Singin' Sam, the Barbasol Man		
8:45		The All-Star Revue	Drury Lane, songs	
9pm	Hal Roberts Orchestra		News	
9:15		The Harlem Gentlemen	Treasure Chest	Ghost Stories
9:30		KSL Dance Orchestra		S. S. Harmony
9:45			Curt Houck Orchestra	
10pm		The Ten o'Clock Wire	Tabloid Opera	The Richfield Reporter
10:15	Mark Hopkins Orchestra	Dick Aurandt, songs		Comedy Stars of Broadway
10:30		Ted Fiorito Orchestra		Sid Lippman Orchestra
10:45				

EVENING — FALL, 1933

Friday

BLUE	CBS	KNX	NBC	
The Golden Sword	The Western Clock	The Story Town Express	Jimmie West Coast	5pm
The Balladettes	The Armchair Philosopher	College Daze and Knights	Barbara Burr, songs	5:15
	The March of Time		Billy Bachelor	5:30
Los Angeles Fire Department Orchestra		Jay Rubinoff Orchestra	Little Orphan Annie	5:45
	Bobby Benson	News	Let's Listen to Harris	6pm
The Adventures of Klickety Klack	Threads of Happiness	King's Cowboy Revue		6:15
Organ Recital	The All-American Show	Marion Mansfield, songs	The Armour Star Jester, Phil Baker	6:30
		Chandu, the Magician		6:45
Music	Olsen and Johnson	Frank Watanabe and Honorable Archie	The First Nighter Program	7pm
The King of Toy Mountain		Detectives Black and Blue		7:15
	The Town Crier	Red Davis	Eddie Peabody, songs	7:30
Music	The Story of Myrt and Marge	Lawrence King Orchestra		7:45
	The Globe Headlines	The Optimistic Do-Nuts	Amos 'n' Andy	8pm
Eb and Zeb	Mellow'd Melodies		The Gilmore Circus	8:15
Los Angeles Junior College Orchestra	Edwin C. Hill, news			8:30
Joseph Bjorndahl, songs	Marvelous Melodies			8:45
Hal Roberts Orchestra	Tapestries of LIfe	News		9pm
		Poetry, Prose and Melody	The Salad Bowl Revue, Fred Allen	9:15
Musical Cameos	Dance Orchestra			9:30
		The Hollywood Legion Fight	Tim and Irene	9:45
	The Ten o'Clock Wire		The Richfield Reporter	10pm
Mark Hopkins Orchestra	The Harlem Gentlemen		Frank Luther, songs	10:15
			Sid Lippman Orchestra	10:30
		Curt Houck Orchestra		10:45

EVENING — FALL, 1933

Saturday

	BLUE	CBS	KNX	NBC
5pm	Secret Service Spy Stories	Studio Program	Sports (2:00PM)	Rev. Fuller, religion
5:15		Songs	Dr. Matthews' Radio Church	
5:30	Dr. Snape's Question Hour	Triple Bar X Day and Nights		Billy Bachelor
5:45			Songs	Little Orphan Annie
6pm		Elder Michaux Congregation	News	The Lucky Strike Hour, Jack Pearl
6:15			Music	
6:30	Jamboree	Symphonic Strings	The Parade of 1933	Paul Roberts, songs
6:45			Chandu, the Magician	The Pickens Sisters, songs
7pm	Organ Recital	Public Affairs	Frank Watanabe and Honorable Archie	The Saturday Night Party
7:15		Ann Leaf at the Organ	Philip Musgrave, cello	
7:30		The George Jessel Show	Elvia Allman, songs	
7:45			Lawrence King Orchestra	
8pm		Isham Jones Orchestra	Curt Houck Orchestra	The Caswell Concert
8:15	Ranse Valentine, rhymes	Elmer Everett Yess		The Seven Seas
8:30	Hollywood on the Air	The Harlem Gentlemen		Frances Ingram, songs
8:45		Red Stanley Orchestra	News	Dave Marshall Orchestra
9pm	The NRA Radio Show	The NRA Radio Show	The NRA Radio Show	The NRA Radio Show
9:15				
9:30				
9:45				
10pm	Hal Robert Orchestra	The Ten o'Clock Wire	Davey Mack Orchestra	Charles Hart, songs
10:15		The Harlem Gentlemen		Comedy Stars of Broadway
10:30	Blue Moonlight			Sid Lippman Orchestra
10:45				

DAYTIME — FALL, 1933

Sunday

	BLUE	CBS	KNX	NBC
8am	Gruen and Hall, songs	Rhoda Arnold and Taylor Buckley, songs	The Sharples Breakfast Club (7:00AM)	(Off the Air)
8:15	Major Bowes' Capitol Family			
8:30		The Times Comics Pages		
8:45				
9am		The Salt Lake Tabernacle Choir	Rev. Shuler, religion	The Church Quarter-Hour
9:15				Seeing Other Americans
9:30		Madiison Ensemble		The Promenade Concert
9:45			Dr. King, health	
10am		Home, Sweet Home	Music	
10:15				
10:30				Highlights of the Bible
10:45	Temple Baptist Church			
11am		Helen Morgan, songs		Gene Arnold and the Commodores
11:15				
11:30		Roy Hendricks Orchestra		Yeast Foamers Orchestra
11:45		The Georgians	Lal Chand Mehra, india talk	
12pm		New York Philharmonic Orchestra		Lady Esther Serenade
12:15				
12:30	The National Radio Pulpit		Louise Johnson, astrology	Psychology
12:45				
1pm	Fiddlers Three			Lal Chand Mehra, india talk
1:15	Talk			Wildroot Chat
1:30	John Smallman's a'Cappella Choir			The Hoover Sentinels
1:45				

DAYTIME — FALL, 1933

Monday-Friday

BLUE	CBS	KNX	NBC	
Exercises (7:30AM)	Financial News	The Sharples Breakfast Club (6:45AM)	Talk / The Old Memory Box	8am
Cross Cuts of the Day	Music		Piano Recital	8:15
	Music / Tony Won's Scrapbook		Music	8:30
	Music			8:45
	The Voice of Experience		Lil' Joe Warner's Jolly Journal	9am
	Talk and Music		Music	9:15
Talk / The Arion Trio				9:30
		News	Melissa's Chats	9:45
Organ Recital	Music / Marie, the Little French Princess	Be Young and Happy, Eddie Albright	Charlie Wellman and Company	10am
	Talk and Music		Victor Lindlahr, health	10:15
News and Views	Music / Easy Aces		Woman's Magazine of the Air	10:30
				10:45
Language Lesson	Just Plain Bill	Music		11am
	Music		Music	11:15
Babes in Hollywood	Ann Leaf at the Organ	Organ Recital		11:30
Music	Music		Stock Market Reports	11:45
		News and Views	US Agricultural Talk	12pm
Charlie Wellman and Company			The National Farm and HomeHour	12:15
		Jay Rubinoff Orchestra		12:30
				12:45
Music / The Radio Guild		Davey Mack Orchestra	Betty and Bob	1pm
			Ann Warner Chats	1:15
				1:30
			Music	1:45

DAYTIME — FALL, 1933

Sunday

	BLUE	CBS	KNX	NBC
2pm		Salon Moderne	The Exposition Park Concert	The Friendly Hour
2:15				
2:30		Organ Recital		Grand Hotel
2:45		Music		
3pm	The Catholic Hour	Rabbi Magnin, religion		USC Symphony Orchestra
3:15		Professor Lindsley, readings		
3:30	Our American Schools	Smilin' Ed McConnell, songs		Drama
3:45		H. V. Kaltenborn, news		
4pm		Music	The Golden Quarter Hour	Vincent Lopez Orchestra
4:15		Ace Brigade Orchesra	English Lesson	
4:30		Marvelous Melodies	Rev. Shuler, religion	The Baker's Broadcast, Joe Penner
4:45				

DAYTIME — FALL, 1933

Monday-Friday

BLUE	CBS	KNX	NBC	
Music	The Happy Go Lucky Hour	The Bookworm	Al Pearce and His Gang	*2pm*
				2:15
				2:30
				2:45
Music / The Italian Language	Feminine Fancies	Music	Pictorial	*3pm*
Viennese Ensemble			Music	*3:15*
Music				*3:30*
				3:45
	Music / The Hodge Podge Lodge	Travelogue		*4pm*
				4:15
		Travelogue / Dr. Matthews' Radio Church		*4:30*
	Between the Bookends			*4:45*

DAYTIME — FALL, 1933

Saturday

	BLUE	CBS	KNX	NBC
8am	Exercises (7:30AM)	The Adventures of Helen and Mary	(Off the Air)	Jean George, piano
8:15				Cross-Cuts of the Day
8:30		Concert Miniature		
8:45			The Sharples Breakfast Club	
9am		Vincent Travers Orchestra		The Magic Hour
9:15	NRA Talk			Lil' Joe Warner's Jolly Journal
9:30	Physical Education	Enoch Light Orchestra		The National Farm and Home Hour
9:45			News	
10am		George Hall Orchestra	Be Young and Happy, Eddie Albright	
10:15				
10:30		Edison Ensemble		The Merry Men Quartet
10:45	Sports			Music
11am		Dancing Echoes	Saddle Pals	
11:15		Football Souvenir		
11:30		Sports	Organ Recital	Jean George, piano
11:45				Stock Market Reports
12pm			News and Views	US Agricultural Talk
12:15				Organ Recital
12:30				
12:45			Dr. Matthews' Radio Church	
1pm		Edison Ensemble	Davey Mack Orchestra	News
1:15				The Rhythm Kids
1:30		Stock Market Reports		Organ Recital
1:45		Saturday Syncopators		The Week-End Revue

DAYTIME — FALL, 1933

Saturday

	BLUE	CBS	KNX	NBC
2pm	The Lady Next Door	Sports	Sports	Sports
2:15				
2:30	The Three Scamps			
2:45	Songs			
3pm	Twenty Fingers of Harmony			
3:15	Hotel Paramount Orchestra			
3:30				
3:45	Grandmother's Trunk			
4pm	The Golden Sword			
4:15				
4:30	The Melody Mixers	Ted Fiorito Orchestra		
4:45	News			

LISTINGS FOR 1934

EVENING — WINTER, 1934

Sunday

	BLUE	CBS	KNX	NBC
5pm	The French Theater of the Air (3:30PM)	Music	Ethel Hubler, talk	The Chase and Sanborn Hour, Eddie Cantor
5:15				
5:30		An Evening in Paris	Dr. Matthews' Radio Church	
5:45				
6pm	Wesley Tourtellotte, organ	The Seven Star Revue		The Manhattan Merry-Go-Round
6:15				
6:30			Ernest Holmes: Theodore C. Abel	The American Album of Familiar Music
6:45				
7pm		Dramas of Childhood	Julie Kellar, harp	The Chevrolet Program, Jack Benny
7:15	Rangoon		Jay Rubinoff Orchestra	
7:30		The Merrymakers	Sol Hoopil's Hawaiians	Hind's Hall of Fame
7:45	The Pierce Brothers Quartet			
8pm			The First Presbyterian Church of Hollywood	John B. Kennedy, news
8:15	Helen Lewyn, piano			Walter Winchell's Jergens Journal
8:30		Eddy Duchin Orchestra		Death Valley Days
8:45				
9pm		Ted Fiorito Orchestra	News	The Reader's Guild
9:15			Judge Rutherford, legal talk	
9:30	USC Symphony Orchestra			Music
9:45			The Lubovsiki Trio	
10pm		The Ten o'Clock Wire		The Richfield Reporter
10:15	Bridge to Dreamland	Dance Orchestra		Richelieu
10:30				
10:45				

EVENING — WINTER, 1934

Monday

BLUE	CBS	KNX	NBC	
Human Behavior	Ruth Royale, songs	The Story Town Express	Piano Recital	5pm
The Golden Sword	Bobby Benson	College Daze and Knights	Health Talk	5:15
	Bing Crosby Entertains	The Noble Sisters, songs	Billy Bachelor	5:30
Bumota Kay, songs		Tom Wallace, songs	Little Orphan Annie	5:45
The Adventures of Klickety Klack	Philadelphia Symphony Orchestra	News	The Sinclair Wiener Minstrels	6pm
News	Buick Presents	Jay Rubinoff Orchestra		6:15
Twilight Reveries	The Ex-Lax Big Show		The Ship of Joy	6:30
		Bill, Mac and Jimmy, songs		6:45
The Hawaiians	Lady Esther Serenade	Frank Watanabe and Honorable Archie	The Carnation Contented Hour	7pm
Rangoon		Detectives Black and Blue		7:15
Los Angeles Junior College Orchestra	Songs	Red Davis	The MJB Demi-Tasse Revue	7:30
	The Story of Myrt and Marge	Songs		7:45
	The Shell Show	Frost Warnings	Amos 'n' Andy	8pm
Eb and Zeb			The Philistines	8:15
Music		So This is Radio	The Voice of Firestone	8:30
		Music		8:45
	Gallery of Favorites	News	The Side Show	9pm
		The Lubovsiki Trio		9:15
Waltz Time	Little Jack Little Orchestra		The Old Memory Box	9:30
Dance Orchestra				9:45
	The Ten o'Clock Wire	Pietro Pontrelli Orchestra	The Richfield Reporter	10pm
	Bill Fleck Orchestra		Herbert Kaye Orchestra	10:15
	Jack Ross' Round-Up			10:30
				10:45

EVENING — WINTER, 1934

Tuesday

	BLUE	CBS	KNX	NBC
5pm	The Golden Sword	The Children's Radio Theater	The Story Town Express	Leo Reisman Orchestra
5:15		Bobby Benson	Mark Kirk, songs	
5:30		Charlie Lung, songs	Urbin Hartman, songs	Billy Bachelor
5:45	NRA Talk	Fray and Braggiotti, piano		Little Orphan Annie
6pm	The Adventures of Klickety Klack	Philadelphia Symphony Orchestra	News	Songs
6:15	News	The Town Crier	Jay Rubinoff Orchestra	
6:30	Twilight Reveries	The George Jessel Show	King's Cowboy Revue	The Texaco Star Theater, Ed Wynn
6:45			Chandu, the Magician	
7pm	Paul Roberts, songs	The Camel Caravan	Frank Watanabe and Honorable Archie	Cruise of the Seth Parker
7:15	Rangoon		Old Coin Romances	
7:30	Romance at Fifty	Music	Elvia Allman, songs	Madame Sylvia, gossip
7:45	Dance Orchestra	The Story of Myrt and Marge	Lawrence King Orchestra	Tim and Irene
8pm		The Inglewood Park Concert	Frost Warnings	Amos 'n' Andy
8:15	Eb and Zeb		Music	Memory Lane
8:30	Music	Mellow'd Memories	So This is Radio	
8:45		The Voice of Experience	Drury Lane, songs	Adventures in Health
9pm	Music	Dance Orchestra	News	Ben Bernie, the Old Maestro
9:15			The Range Riders	
9:30		The Hodge Podge Lodge	Skit	Winning of the West
9:45				
10pm		The Ten o'Clock Wire	Pietro Pontrelli Orchestra	The Richfield Reporter
10:15		Ted Fiorito Orchestra		Herbert Kaye Orchestra
10:30		Bill Fleck Orchestra		
10:45				

EVENING — WINTER, 1934

Wednesday

BLUE	CBS	KNX	NBC	
The Golden Sword	The All-Year Club	The Story Town Express	Julie Kellar, harp	*5pm*
Canzonetta	Bobby Benson	College Daze and Knights	Health Talk	*5:15*
	Albert Spaulding, violin	The Noble Sisters, songs	Billy Bachelor	*5:30*
		The Song Service	Little Orphan Annie	*5:45*
The Adventures of Klickety Klack	Philadelphia Symphony Orchestra	News	The Ipana Troubadours	*6pm*
News	Stoopnagle and Budd	Jay Rubinoff Orchestra		*6:15*
Twilight Reveries	The White Owl Program, Burns and Allen	King's Cowboy Revue	Our Home on the Range, John McCormick	*6:30*
		Bill, Mac and Jimmy, songs		*6:45*
The Hawaiians	Fred Waring Orchestra	Frank Watanabe and Honorable Archie	The Corn Cob Pipe Club	*7pm*
Rangoon		Detectives Black and Blue		*7:15*
The National Radio Forum	Songs	Red Davis	The Makers of History	*7:30*
	The Story of Myrt and Marge	Lawrence King Orchestra		*7:45*
Music	Calling All Cars	Frost Warnings	Amos 'n' Andy	*8pm*
Eb and Zeb		Songs	Twenty Thousand Years in Sing Sing	*8:15*
Virginia Fiohri, songs	Edwin C. Hill, news	So This is Radio		*8:30*
	The Buccaneers	Drury Lane, songs	Stars of the West	*8:45*
Popular Science	Little Jack Little Orchestra	News		*9pm*
Music	Three Old Favorites	Realty Program	Dance Orchestra	*9:15*
			Eno Crime Clues	*9:30*
	Dance Orchestra	Jack Dale Orchestra		*9:45*
	The Ten o'Clock Wire	Pietro Pontrelli Orchestra	The Richfield Reporter	*10pm*
	Ted Fiorito Orchestra		Herbert Kaye Orchestra	*10:15*
	Bill Fleck Orchestra			*10:30*
				10:45

EVENING — WINTER, 1934

Thursday

	BLUE	CBS	KNX	NBC
5pm	The Golden Sword	The Children's Radio Theater	The Story Town Express	The Fleischman Yeast Hour, Rudy Vallee
5:15		Bobby Benson	USC Male Chorus	
5:30		Charlie Lung, songs	Urbin Hartman, songs	
5:45	Dr. Caldecott, health	Clark Dennis, songs	Professor Lataner, talk	
6pm	The Adventures of Klickety Klack	Philadelphia Symphony Orchestra		The Maxwell House Showboat
6:15	News	Buick Presents	Jay Rubinoff Orchestra	
6:30	Twilight Reveries	California Melodies	King's Cowboy Revue	
6:45			Chandu, the Magician	
7pm	Robert Hurd Orchestra	The Camel Caravan	Frank Watanabe and Honorable Archie	The Kraft Music Hall
7:15			Music	
7:30	The Bluettes	The Isle of Romance	Elvia Allman, songs	
7:45	Emil Farnlund Orchestra	The Story of Myrt and Marge	Lawrence King Orchestra	
8pm		Hermie King Orchestra	Frost Warnings	Amos 'n' Andy
8:15	Ed and Zeb		International Sextette	The Standard Symphony Hour
8:30	Nick Harris	Edwin C. Hill, news	So This is Radio	
8:45		Isham Jones Orchestra	The Range Riders	
9pm	World's Sporting Events	Henry Busse Orchestra	News	
9:15	Quartet Time	The Blue Monday Jamboree	Ranse Valentine, rhymes	Comedy Stars of Hollywood
9:30	Music		The Lubovsiki Trio	Enos Crime Clues
9:45				
10pm		The Ten o'Clock Wire	Pietro Pontrelli Orchestra	The Richfield Reporter
10:15		Ted Fiorito Orchestra		Herbert Kaye Orchestra
10:30		Bill Fleck Orchestra		
10:45				

EVENING — WINTER, 1934

Friday

BLUE	CBS	KNX	NBC	
The Golden Sword	Songs	The Story Town Express	Jimmie West Coast	5pm
	Bobby Benson	College Daze and Knights	The Melody Mixers	5:15
Los Angeles Fire Department Orchestra	The March of Time	The Noble Sisters, songs	Billy Bachelor	5:30
		Tom Wallace, songs	Little Orphan Annie	5:45
The Adventures of Klickety Klack	Philadelphia Symphony Orchestra	News	Let's Listen to Harris	6pm
News	The Town Crier	Jay Rubinoff Orchestra		6:15
Twilight Reveries	Canada Melody Strings	King's Cowboy Revue	The Armour Star Jester, Phil Baker	6:30
		Bill, Mac and Jimmy, songs		6:45
	Olsen and Johnson	Frank Watanabe and Honorable Archie	The First Nighter Program	7pm
		Detectives Black and Blue		7:15
The Armco Iron Master	Music	Red Davis	One Man's Family	7:30
	The Story of Myrt and Marge	Lawrence King Orchestra		7:45
Music	Songs	The Optimistic Do-Nuts	Amos 'n' Andy	8pm
Eb and Zeb	Mellow'd Melodies		The Gilmore Circus	8:15
Perry Selby, songs	Edwin C. Hill, news			8:30
	Isham Jones Orchestra			8:45
	Tapestries of Life	News		9pm
The Old Memory Box		Music	Homer B. Welborne, golf	9:15
Musical Cameos	Catherine the Great		The Old Memory Box	9:30
		The Hollywood Legion Fight	Harry Sosnik Orchestra	9:45
	The Ten o'Clock Wire		The Richfield Reporter	10pm
	Ted Fiorito Orchestra		Herbert Kaye Orchestra	10:15
	Gordon Henderson Orchestra			10:30
		Pietro Pontrelli Orchestra		10:45

EVENING — WINTER, 1934

Saturday

	BLUE	CBS	KNX	NBC
5pm	Economics in the New Deal	Music (4:45 PM)	Organ Recital	Rev. Fuller, religion
5:15		Elder Michaux Congregation	Dr. Matthews' Radio Church	
5:30	Temple Baptist Church			Billy Bachelor
5:45	News	Trade and Mark, songs	Ranse Valentine, rhymes	Little Orphan Annie
6pm	Boston Symphony Orchestra	Philadelphia Symphony Orchestra	News	Organ Recital
6:15		Stoopnagle and Budd	Music	
6:30		The Carborundum Hour	King's Cowboy Revue	Music
6:45			Chandu, the Magician	The Singing Service Men
7pm	Songs	The Adventures of Admiral Byrd	Frank Watanabe and Honorable Archie	The Saturday Night Party
7:15	Rangoon		Music	
7:30	Dr. Kingsley, organ	Songs	Elvia Allman, songs	
7:45		Leaders to Action	Lawrence King Orchestra	
8pm	Recreation	Guy Lombardo Orchestra	Jack Carter's Varieties	The Caswell Concert
8:15				The Hollywood Looking Glass
8:30	Music	Ted Fiorito Orchestra		
8:45				Robert Hurd, songs
9pm	Hollywood on the Air	Hermie King Orchestra	News	Carefree Carnival
9:15			Music	
9:30		Bill Fleck Orchestra	Marcello Ventura, songs	
9:45				
10pm	The Classic Hour	The Ten o'Clock Wire	Pietro Pontrelli Orchestra	Jules Buffano Orchestra
10:15		Ted Fiorito Orchestra		
10:30		Music		Blue Moonlight
10:45				

DAYTIME — WINTER, 1934

Sunday

	BLUE	CBS	KNX	NBC
8am	Gruen and Hall, songs	The Times Comics Pages	The Sharples Breakfast Club (7:00 AM)	(Off the Air)
8:15	Major Bowes' Capitol Family			
8:30		The CBS Church of the Air		
8:45				
9am		The Salt Lake Tabernacle Choir	Rev. Shuler, religion	The Church Quarter-Hour
9:15	The Gordon String Quartet			Dr. Casselberry, health
9:30	Maurice Zam, symphony talk	Madison Ensemble		The Radio City Music Hall
9:45			Dr. King, health	
10am		The CBS Church of the Air	Music	
10:15				
10:30	Lal Chand Mehra, india talk	Lazy Dan, the Minstrel Man		Young People's Conference
10:45	Temple Baptist Church			
11am		Helen Morgan, songs	Organ Recital	Gene Arnold and the Commodores
11:15				
11:30		The Islanders	H. B. Drollinger, economics	The Canadian Grenadiers
11:45			Lal Chand Merha, india talk	
12pm		New York Philharmonic Orchestra		Lady Esther Serenade
12:15			Organ Recital	
12:30			Louise Johnson, astrology	Yeast Foamers Orchestra
12:45				
1pm	Talk		Lance Ensemble	Submarine G-10
1:15				Wildroot Chat
1:30				The Hoover Sentinels
1:45				

DAYTIME — WINTER, 1934

Monday-Friday

BLUE	CBS	KNX	NBC	
Exercises (7:30AM)	Financial News	The Sharples Breakfast Club (6:45AM)	Talk	8am
	Morning Moods		Music / Cross Cuts of the Day	8:15
	Music / Tony Won's Scrapbook			8:30
Music / Cross Cuts of the Day	Music		Music	8:45
	The Voice of Experience		Charlie Wellman and Company	9am
	The Blue Ridge Colonel		Music / Betty Crocker, cooking	9:15
Music	Music		Talk and Music	9:30
			Melissa's Chats	9:45
	Music / Marie, the Little French Princess	Be Young and Happy, Eddie Albright	Music	10am
	Music		Victor Lindlahr, health	10:15
	Music / Easy Aces		Woman's Magazine of the Air	10:30
	Music			10:45
Talk / Language Lesson	Just Plain Bill	Music		11am
	The Romance of Helen Trent			11:15
SMacout	The American School of the Air		US Agricultural Talk	11:30
Music			Stock Market Reports	11:45
	Music	News		12pm
News	Talk / The Voice of Experience	Drury Lane, songs	The National Farm and HomeHour	12:15
Charlie Wellman and Company	Music	Jay Rubinoff Orchestra		12:30
				12:45
Music / The Radio Guild		Pietro Pontrelli Orchestra	Betty and Bob	1pm
			News	1:15
			Ma Perkins	1:30
			Music	1:45

DAYTIME — WINTER, 1934

Sunday

	BLUE	CBS	KNX	NBC
2pm	National Vespers	The Modern Bridge Builder	The Park Board Program	The Princess Pat Players
2:15		Salon Moderne		
2:30	Talk	Dick Aurandt, songs		Grand Hotel
2:45		Helen Nagin, songs		
3pm	The Catholic Hour	Rabbi Magnin, religion		USC Symphony Orchestra
3:15		Professor Lindsley, readings		
3:30	The French Theater of the Air	The Lyric Trio		Our American Schools
3:45		Charles Carille, songs		
4pm		Newspaper Adventures		Ted Weems' Midwinter Varieties
4:15		Ace Brigade Orchesra	English Lesson	
4:30		H. V. Kaltenborn, news	Rev. Shuler, religion	The Baker's Broadcast, Joe Penner
4:45		The Catholic Mission Hour		

DAYTIME — WINTER, 1934

Monday-Friday

BLUE	CBS	KNX	NBC	
Talk and Music	The Happy Go Lucky Hour	The Bookworm	Al Pearce and His Gang	2pm
				2:15
				2:30
				2:45
Music / The Italian Language	Feminine Fancies	Music	Pictorial	3pm
Music			Ann Warner Chats	3:15
	Beauty Talk			3:30
	Music		Music	3:45
Music / Twenty Fingers of Harmony	The Hodge Podge Lodge			4pm
Music / You and Your Government		Music / Dr. Matthews' Radio Church	Music / Nick Harris	4:15
Mary's Friendly Garden	Music	Talk and Music	Music	4:30
	Between the Bookends			4:45

DAYTIME — WINTER, 1934

Saturday

	BLUE	CBS	KNX	NBC
8am	Pietro Yon, organ (7:45PM)	The New York Philharmonic Children's Concert	The Sharples Breakfast Club (6:45AM)	Jean George, piano
8:15				Cross-Cuts of the Day
8:30				
8:45				
9am		Vincent Travers Orchestra	Organ Recital	
9:15				
9:30	Physical Education	Enoch Light Orchestra		The National Farm and Home Hour
9:45			News	
10am		Edison Ensemble	Be Young and Happy, Eddie Albright	
10:15				
10:30		Harold Knight Orchestra		Woman's Magazine of the Air
10:45	Sports			
11am		Ann Leaf at the Organ	Organ Recital	The Metropolitan Opera
11:15				
11:30		Public Affairs		
11:45				
12pm	News and Views	Dancing Echoes	News and Views	
12:15				
12:30		Talk		
12:45				
1pm		Saturday Syncopators	Pietro Pontrelli Orchestra	
1:15				
1:30		Madison Ensemble		
1:45				

DAYTIME — WINTER, 1934

Saturday

	BLUE	CBS	KNX	NBC
2pm		Dance Orchestra	The Bookworm	
2:15				Music
2:30		Songs		Public Affairs
2:45		Spanish Serenade		
3pm	Wesley Tourtellotte, organ	Meet the Artist		Al Pearce and His Gang
3:15		Songs		
3:30		Captain William Campbell, air talk		Music
3:45		Angelo Ferdinando Orchestra		Ted Black Orchestra
4pm	The Golden Sword	Frederick William Wile, news		
4:15		Tito Guizar, guitar		Religion in the News
4:30	Rue Tyler's Rhythm Kids	The American Mixed Quartet		The Arion Trio
4:45		Music		

EVENING — SPRING, 1934

Sunday

	BLUE	CBS	KNX	NBC
5pm	Judge Yankwich, legal talk	An Evening in Paris	Ethel Hubler, talk	The Chase and Sanborn Hour, Jimmy Durante
5:15				
5:30		Fred Waring Orchestra	Dr. Matthews' Radio Church	
5:45	Franz Hoffman, piano			
6pm	Wesley Tourtellotte, organ	Dramas of Childhood	Ernest Holmes: Theodore C. Abel	The Manhattan Merry-Go-Round
6:15				
6:30		Freddie Rich Orchestra	Heart to Heart	The American Album of Familiar Music
6:45				
7pm	The Marvicor Trio	Lady Esther Serenade	Music	Victor Young Orchestra
7:15			The Lubovsiki Trio	
7:30	The Burr McIntosh Show	The Merrymakers		Hind's Hall of Fame
7:45	The Pierce Brothers Quartet			
8pm	Baron Von Reichenberg, talk		The First Presbyterian Church of Hollywood	Wendell Hall, songs
8:15				Walter Winchell's Jergens Journal
8:30	The Tournament of Roses Band	The Music Festival		Death Valley Days
8:45				
9pm	The Reader's Guide	Charlie Davis Orchestra		Adventures in Health
9:15	Records		Judge Rutherford, legal talk	True Story
9:30		Henry Busse Orchestra	Crockett's Mountaineers	
9:45				
10pm	Famous Arabian Orchestra	The Ten o'Clock Wire		
10:15		Gus Arnheim Orchestra		
10:30	Bridge to Dreamland			
10:45				

EVENING — SPRING, 1934

Monday

BLUE	CBS	KNX	NBC	
Music	The Adventures of John Ridd	The Story Town Express	Music By Gershwin (4:30PM)	5pm
	Charlie Lung, songs	John Bruce, songs		5:15
	Bing Crosby Entertains	Marshall Grant, songs	Billy Bachelor	5:30
		Financial Counselor	Little Orphan Annie	5:45
	The Chesterfield Show		The Sinclair Wiener Minstrels	6pm
News		Borowsky Orchestra		6:15
Music	The Ex-Lax Big Show	Donald Novis, songs	The Ship of Joy	6:30
		Marion Mansfield, songs		6:45
	Lady Esther Serenade	Frank Watanabe and Honorable Archie	The Carnation Contented Hour	7pm
		Crazy Quilt		7:15
Los Angeles Junior College Orchestra	Military Band	The Voice Parade	The MJB Demi-Tasse Revue	7:30
	The Story of Myrt and Marge			7:45
Talk	The Shell Show	The In-Laws	Amos 'n' Andy	8pm
The Stove Poker Philosopher		The Rosicrucians	The Philistines	8:15
			The Voice of Firestone	8:30
				8:45
Hollywood on the Air	Leon Belasco Orchestra		The Makers of History	9pm
Fishing and Hunting Talk		Ranse Valentine, rhymes		9:15
	Pancho Diggs Orchestra	Crockett's Mountaineers	Music of All Countries	9:30
College Inn Orchestra				9:45
	The Ten o'Clock Wire	Pietro Pontrelli Orchestra	The Richfield Reporter	10pm
	Bill Fleck Orchestra		Jay Whidden Orchestra	10:15
Jay Whiden Orchestra	The Radio Players			10:30
				10:45

EVENING — SPRING, 1934

Tuesday

	BLUE	CBS	KNX	NBC
5pm	Mary's Friendly Garden (4:30PM)	Talk and Music	The Story Town Express	The Balladettes
5:15		Charlie Lung, songs		
5:30		California Melodies		Music
5:45	NRA Talk			Little Orphan Annie
6pm		Music		Music
6:15	News	Ruth Etting, songs	King's Cowboy Revue	
6:30	Twilight Reveries	Minneapolis Symphony Orchestra	Music	The Texaco Star Theater, Ed Wynn
6:45			Records	
7pm	Paul Roberts, songs	The Camel Caravan	Frank Watanabe and Honorable Archie	The Palmolive Beauty Box Theater
7:15	Records		The Avengers	
7:30	Romance at Fifty	Leaders of Tomorrow	The Lubovsiki Trio	
7:45	Violin Recital	The Story of Myrt and Marge		
8pm		The Inglewood Park Concert	The In-Laws	Amos 'n' Andy
8:15	Eb and Zeb		Homer Canfield Orchestra	Memory Lane
8:30	Dr. Liebling, health	Charles Bennett Orchestra	The Forge of Freedom	
8:45		The Voice of Experience		
9pm	Music	The Hodge Podge Lodge		Ben Bernie, the Old Maestro
9:15				
9:30	Carol Lofner Orchestra	Music	Crockett's Mountaineers	The Song of Araby
9:45				
10pm		The Ten o'Clock Wire		The Richfield Reporter
10:15	Jay Whidden Orchestra	Bill Fleck Orchestra		Jay Whidden Orchestra
10:30		Gus Arnheim Orchestra	Drury Lane, songs	
10:45			Paris Inn Frolic	

EVENING — SPRING, 1934

Wednesday

BLUE	CBS	KNX	NBC	
Mary's Friendly Garden (4:30PM)	Public Affairs	The Story Town Express	The Jack Pearl Show	5pm
	Charlie Lung, songs	Radio Harp		5:15
	Albert Spaulding, violin	Sunset Serenade	Songs	5:30
Albert Bergman, legal talk		The Song Service	Little Orphan Annie	5:45
Music	The Chesterfield Show		Music	6pm
News		King's Cowboy Revue		6:15
Twilight Reveries	The White Owl Program, Burns and Allen	Music	Our Home on the Range, John McCormick	6:30
				6:45
Opera Records	Ted Fiorito Orchestra	Frank Watanabe and Honorable Archie	The Corn Cob Pipe Club	7pm
		Mona Lowe, songs		7:15
	Leaders of Tomorrow		Music	7:30
	The Story of Myrt and Marge			7:45
	Calling All Cars	The In-Laws	Amos 'n' Andy	8pm
		Don Blanding, songs	The Cuckoo Hour, Ray Knight	8:15
The All-Americans	Crystal Dreams	Crime Clues		8:30
	Frank Dailey Orchestra		Marching Along	8:45
Popular Science	Claude Hopkins Orchestra		The Hour of Smiles, Fred Allen	9pm
				9:15
Carol Lofner Orchestra	George Hall Orchestra	Crockett's Mountaineers		9:30
				9:45
	The Ten o'Clock Wire		The Richfield Reporter	10pm
Jay Whidden Orchestra	Bill Fleck Orchestra		Jay Whidden Orchestra	10:15
	Gus Arnheim Orchestra	Paris Inn Frolic		10:30
				10:45

EVENING — SPRING, 1934

Thursday

	BLUE	CBS	KNX	NBC
5pm	Public Affairs (4:30PM)	Raffles, the Amateur Cracksman	Dr. Matthews' Radio Church (4:15PM)	The Fleischman Yeast Hour, Rudy Vallee
5:15				
5:30		Harry Sosnick Orchestra		
5:45	Dr. Ernest Caldecott, talk	Orchestra		House Showboat
6:15	News			
6:30	Organ Recital	Fred Waring Orchestra		
6:45				
7pm	Music	The Camel Caravan	Frank Watanabe and Honorable Archie	The Kraft Music Hall
7:15			The Avengers	
7:30		Jean Ellington, songs		
7:45		The Story of Myrt and Marge		
8pm		Music		Amos 'n' Andy
8:15				The Standard Symphony Hour
8:30	Nick Harris	Edwin C. Hill, news	Crime Clues	
8:45		Isham Jones Orchestra		
9pm	The Old Observer			
9:15		The Blue Monday Jamboree		Winning of the West
9:30	Carol Lofner Orchestra		Crockett's Mountaineers	
9:45				
10pm		The Ten o'Clock Wire		The Richfield Reporter
10:15		Bill Fleck Orchestra		Jay Whidden Orchestra
10:30	Jay Whidden Orchestra	Gus Arnheim Orchestra	Drury Lane, songs	
10:45				

EVENING — SPRING, 1934

Friday

BLUE	CBS	KNX	NBC	
Human Behavior	The Adventures of John Ridd	The Story Town Express	Music By Gershwin (4:30PM)	5pm
Canzonetta	Irving Aaronson Orchestra	Julie Kellar, harp		5:15
	The March of Time	Marshall Grant, organ	Billy Bachelor	5:30
	Braggioti, piano	Piano Recital	Little Orphan Annie to Harris	5:45 6pm
News	Ruth Etting, songs			6:15
Twilight Reveries	The Powder Box Revue		The Armour Star Jester, Phil Baker	6:30
				6:45
Music	The Program of the Week	Frank Watanabe and Honorable Archie	The First Nighter Program	7pm
		Music		7:15
The Crucifixion	Frederick Stark's Rocketeers		The General Tire Show, Jack Benny	7:30
The Hawaiians	The Story of Myrt and Marge			7:45
Charlie and Buddy, songs	Military Band	The In-Laws	Amos 'n' Andy	8pm
Eb and Zeb		Don Blanding, songs	One Man's Family	8:15
Ethopian Chorus	Isham Jones Orchestra			8:30
Public Affairs	Friday Frolics		Friday Frolics	8:45
				9pm
Jay Whidden Orchestra	Tapestries of Life			9:15
Carol Lofner Orchestra			The Old Memory Box	9:30
	Bill Fleck Orchestra			9:45
	The Ten o'Clock Wire		The Richfield Reporter	10pm
	Bill Fleck Orchestra		Jack Bain Orchestra	10:15
Jack Bain Orchestra	Gus Arnheim Orchestra	Drury Lane, songs		10:30
				10:45

EVENING — SPRING, 1934

Saturday

	BLUE	CBS	KNX	NBC
5pm	Art in America	Gus Arnheim Orchestra	Organ Recital (2:00PM)	Rev. Fuller, religion
5:15	The Bavarian Peasant Band		Dr. Matthews' Radio Church	
5:30	Temple Baptist Church	Morton Downey, songs		Billy Bachelor
5:45		Songs		Little Orphan Annie
6pm	Paul Roberts, songs	The Chesterfield Show		The Colgate House Party
6:15	News and Views		Music	
6:30		Looking at Life		Beatrice Fairfax, advice
6:45		Music		
7pm	Poet of the Air	The Adventures of Admiral Byrd	Frank Watanabe and Honorable Archie	The Saturday Night Party
7:15			Music	
7:30	Dr. Kingsley, organ	The Rhythm Revue	USC Talk	The National Barn Dance
7:45				
8pm	Recreation	Ted Fiorito Orchestra		
8:15				
8:30	Music	Peter the Great		
8:45				
9pm	Records	Gus Arnheim Orchestra		Carefree Carnival
9:15				
9:30		Jackie Souder Orchestra		
9:45				
10pm	Blue Moonlight	The Ten o'Clock Wire		Dance Orchestra
10:15		Bill Fleck Orchestra		
10:30	Dance Time in Denver	Dance Orchestra		
10:45				

DAYTIME — SPRING, 1934

Sunday

	BLUE	CBS	KNX	NBC
8am	Gruen and Hall, songs	The Times Comics Pages	The Sharples Breakfast Club (6:45 AM)	(Off the Air)
8:15	Major Bowes' Capitol Family			Major Bowes' Capitol Family
8:30		The Salt Lake Tabernacle Choir		
8:45				
9am		The Whispering Strings	Rev. Shuler, religion	
9:15	The Gordon String Quartet	Public Affairs		
9:30				The Radio City Music Hall
9:45	The Hollywood Conservatory of Music		Dr. King, health	
10am	Maurice Zam, symphony talk	The CBS Church of the Air	Music	
10:15				
10:30		Lazy Dan, the Minstrel Man		Young People's Conference
10:45	Temple Baptist Church			
11am		Broadway Varieties	Organ Recital	Gene Arnold and the Commodores
11:15				
11:30		Tussy Dreams of Beauty	H. B. Drollinger, economics	Rings of Melody
11:45		Jean Leonard, songs	Lal Chand Merha, india talk	
12pm		New York Philharmonic Orchestra		Quartet Time
12:15			Barmani Concert Orchestra	
12:30			Louise Johnson, astrology	Yeast Foamers Orchestra
12:45				
1pm	Dr. Bernard, health			A. P. Terhune's Dog Dramas
1:15				John B. Kennedy, news

DAYTIME — SPRING, 1934

Monday-Friday

BLUE	CBS	KNX	NBC	
Exercises (7:45AM)	The Rolling Stones	The Sharples Breakfast Club (6:45AM)	Music	*8am*
	Frivolettes		Music / Your Child	*8:15*
	Music / Tony Wons' Scrapbook		Music	*8:30*
Music				*8:45*
	The Voice of Experience			*9am*
	Music		Music / Betty Crocker, cooking	*9:15*
			Music	*9:30*
				9:45
	Music / Marie, the Little French Princess	Be Young and Happy, Eddie Albright	Talk and Music	*10am*
	Music			*10:15*
	Music / Easy Aces		Woman's Magazine of the Air	*10:30*
	Music			*10:45*
Talk	Just Plain Bill	Organ Recital		*11am*
	The Romance of Helen Trent			*11:15*
Talk / Smackout	The American School of the Air			*11:30*
Music				*11:45*
	Music	Music		*12pm*
News and Views			The National Farm and HomeHour	*12:15*
				12:30
		Drury Lane, songs		*12:45*
		Pietro Pontrelli Orchestra	Betty and Bob	*1pm*
			News	*1:15*

DAYTIME — SPRING, 1934

Sunday

	BLUE	CBS	KNX	NBC
1:30			Hal Roberts Orchestra	Music
1:45				
2pm	National Vespers	Rabbi Magnin, religion	The Exposition Park Concert	
2:15		Drama		
2:30	Swami Yoganda, religion			Grand Hotel
2:45		Salon Moderne		
3pm	The Catholic Hour			USC College of Music
3:15		Professor Lindsley, readings		
3:30	Music	Smilin' Ed McConnell, songs		The Romance of Science
3:45	Easter Drama	The Randall Trio		Pages from the Book of Life
4pm		Newspaper Adventures		Charlie Previn Orchestra
4:15	Scientfic Research	The Welch Madrigal Choir		
4:30	Mother Gray	Clarence Wheeler Orchestra	Rev. Shuler, religion	The Baker's Broadcast, Joe Penner
4:45		The Catholic Mission Hour		

DAYTIME — SPRING, 1934

Monday-Friday

BLUE	CBS	KNX	NBC	
Talk and Music			Ma Perkins	1:30
Music / The Lady Next Door			Music	1:45
Talk and Music	The Happy Go Lucky Hour	Talk and Music	Al Pearce and His Gang	2pm
				2:15
				2:30
				2:45
	Feminine Fancies	The Bookworm	Pictorial	3pm
			Ann Warner Chats	3:15
	Music	Music		3:30
USC Symphony Orchestra			Organ Recital	3:45
Talk and Music	Music / Better English	Talk and Music	Music	4pm
	Music / The Texas Rangers	Talk and Music / Dr. Matthews' Radio Church		4:15
Public Affairs / Mary's Friendly Garden	Talk and Music		Music / Music By Gershwin	4:30
				4:45

DAYTIME — SPRING, 1934

Saturday

	BLUE	CBS	KNX	NBC
8am	Pietro Yon, organ (7:45pm)	Cheer Up, Gang	Records (7:00am)	The Morning Parade (7:15am)
8:15				
8:30		The Glee Club		
8:45				
9am		Music	Organ Recital	
9:15				
9:30	Physical Education	Abram Chasins Orchestra		The National Farm and Home Hour
9:45		Enoch Light Orchestra		
10am		Madison Ensemble	Be Young and Happy, Eddie Albright	
10:15				
10:30		Harold Knight Orchestra		Woman's Magazine of the Air
10:45				
11am		Public Affairs	Organ Recital	
11:15				
11:30		Dancing Echoes		
11:45				
12pm		The Round Towners		
12:15	News and Views			US Agricultural Talk
12:30		Ann Leaf at the Organ		
12:45				
1pm		Jim Fettis Orchestra	Pietro Pontrelli Orchestra	Public Affairs
1:15				
1:30	The Classic Hour	Public Affairs		
1:45				

DAYTIME — SPRING, 1934

Saturday

	BLUE	CBS	KNX	NBC
2pm		Pancho Diggs Orchestra	Organ Recital	Kaltenmeryer's Kindegarten
2:15				
2:30		Maurice Sherman Orchestra		Economics in the New Deal
2:45		Music		
3pm	Wesley Tourtellotte, organ			Al Pearce and His Gang
3:15		Real Life Drama		
3:30		Organ Recital		Music
3:45				
4pm		Elder Michaux Congregation		The Three Scamps
4:15				Religion in the News
4:30		The American Mixed Quartet		News
4:45		Isham Jones Orchestra		Hotel Palace Orchestra

EVENING — SUMMER, 1934

Sunday

	BLUE	CBS	KNX	NBC
5pm	Public Affairs (2:30PM)	Sanctuary Symphony	(N/A)	The Manhattan Merry-Go-Round
5:15				
5:30		Fred Waring Orchestra		The American Album of Familiar Music
5:45	Franz Hoffman, piano			
6pm	Twilight Revelries	Lady Esther Serenade		Hind's Hall of Fame
6:15				
6:30		Americana		Music
6:45				
7pm	The Pierce Brothers Quartet	The Romance of Travel		Irene Beasley, songs
7:15				Madame Schumann-Heink, manners
7:30	Charlie Davis Orchestra	Merrymakers Orchestra		
7:45				
8pm	The Burr McIntosh Show			
8:15	Russ Columbo, songs			
8:30	Hollywood on the Air	Orville Knapp Orchestra		
8:45				
9pm	Countess De Li Guaro, songs	The Mummers		USC Symphony Orchestra
9:15				
9:30		Jan Garber Orchestra		The Reader's Guide
9:45				
10pm		The Ten o'Clock Wire		
10:15		Music		Bridge to Dreamland
10:30				
10:45				

EVENING — SUMMER, 1934

Monday

BLUE	CBS	KNX	NBC	
Studio Chatter	Evan Evans, songs	(N/A)	Music (4:45 PM)	*5pm*
	Roy Helton, songs			*5:15*
	Dance Orchestra		The Colgate House Party	*5:30*
				5:45
Public Affairs	Lady Esther Serenade		The Carnation Contented Hour	*6pm*
News				*6:15*
Music	All for You		The MJB Demi-Tasse Revue	*6:30*
	Military Band			*6:45*
	Public Affairs		Bring 'Em Back Alive	*7pm*
	Glen Gray Orchestra		Gene and Glenn	*7:15*
Albert Bergman, legal talk			Tne Voice of Firestone	*7:30*
	Music			*7:45*
	The Blue Monday Jamboree		The Shell Show	*8pm*
The Stove Poker Philosopher				*8:15*
SERA Orchestra				*8:30*
				8:45
	Dance Orchestra		The Parade of Champions	*9pm*
Fishing and Hunting Talk				*9:15*
Songs	Jan Garber Orchestra		Waltz Time	*9:30*
				9:45
	The Ten o'Clock Wire			*10pm*
Music	Russ Carlson Orchestra			*10:15*
	Music			*10:30*
				10:45

EVENING — SUMMER, 1934

Tuesday

	BLUE	CBS	KNX	NBC
5pm	The Golden Sword	The George Givot Show	(N/A)	Edwin Franko Goldman Band (4:30 PM)
5:15	Duluth Symphony Orchestra			
5:30		The Little Theater of the Air		
5:45	Alexander W. Dodge, talk			
6pm		Fray and Braggiotti, piano		The Palmolive Beauty Box Theater
6:15	News	Songs		
6:30	Twilight Reveries	Melodic Strings		
6:45				
7pm	Paul Roberts, songs	Richard Himber Orchestra		Bring 'Em Back Alive
7:15	Romance at Fifty			Gene and Glenn
7:30		Music		Johnny Presents
7:45		Joe Reichman Orchestra		
8pm	Vivian Johnson Orchestra	The Inglewood Park Concert		Music
8:15	Charles Bowes, songs			Public Affairs
8:30	Dr. Liebling, health	Rube Wolf Orchestra		Death Valley Days
8:45				
9pm	Music	The Hodge Podge Lodge		Music
9:15				
9:30	Tom Coakley Orchestra	Jan Garber Orchestra		
9:45				Tom Coakley Orchestra
10pm		The Ten o'Clock Wire		
10:15	Mark Hopkins Orchestra	Russ Carlson Orchestra		
10:30		Music		
10:45				

LISTINGS FOR 1934

EVENING — SUMMER, 1934

Wednesday

BLUE	CBS	KNX	NBC	
Edwin Franko Goldman Band	Detroit Symphony Orchestra	(N/A)	Sports Talk	*5pm*
				5:15
Records			Edwin Franko Goldman Band	*5:30*
				5:45
	The Adventures of Admiral Byrd			*6pm*
News			Eddy Duchin Orchestra	*6:15*
Twilight Reveries	California Melodies			*6:30*
				6:45
Opera Records	Calling All Cars		Bring 'Em Back Alive	*7pm*
			Gene and Glenn	*7:15*
	Half Forgotten Americans		Memory Lane	*7:30*
	Frank Dailey Orchestra			*7:45*
	Treasures of Time		The Hour of Smiles, Fred Allen	*8pm*
				8:15
	Rube Wolf Orchestra			*8:30*
Popular Science				*8:45*
Hotel Bismarck	Everett Hoagland		Music	*9pm*
				9:15
	Jan Garber Orchestra		Tom Coakley Orchestra	*9:30*
				9:45
	The Ten o'Clock Wire			*10pm*
Mark Hopkins Orchestra	Russ Carlson Orchestra			*10:15*
	Joe Sullivan Orchestra			*10:30*
	Music			*10:45*

EVENING — SUMMER, 1934

Thursday

	BLUE	CBS	KNX	NBC
5pm	The Golden Sword	Freddie Hinkel Orchestra	(N/A)	The Maxwell House Showboat
5:15				
5:30		Melody Masterpieces		
5:45	Dr. Ernest Caldecott, talk	The Fats Waller Rhythm Club		
6pm		The Romance of Travel		The Kraft Music Hall
6:15	News			
6:30	Organ Recital	Public Affairs		
6:45		Full Speed Ahead		
7pm	Records	Vera Van, songs		Bring 'Em Back Alive
7:15		The Pacific Geographic Society		Gene and Glenn
7:30		Carey's Copers		Winning of the West
7:45		Henry Busse Orchestra		
8pm		Joe Reichman Orchestra		The Standard Symphony Hour
8:15				
8:30	Nick Harris	Rube Wolf Orchestra		
8:45				
9pm	Clyde Lucas Orchestra	Jimmy Davis Orchestra		Music
9:15				
9:30		Jan Garber Orchestra		French Casino Orchestra
9:45				
10pm		The Ten o'Clock Wire		
10:15	Mark Hopkins Orchestra	Russ Carlson Orchestra		
10:30		Everett Hoagland Orchestra		
10:45				

EVENING — SUMMER, 1934

Friday

BLUE	CBS	KNX	NBC	
News and Views	Everett Hoagland Orchestra	(N/A)	Let's Listen to Harris	5pm
	The Los Angeles Fire Department			5:15
	Johnny Green Orchestra		The Armour Star Jester, Phil Baker	5:30
				5:45
	Music		The First Nighter Program	6pm
News	Songs			6:15
Twilight Reveries	Music		The General Tire Show, Jack Benny	6:30
	Military Band			6:45
Music	Edith Murray, songs		Bring 'Em Back Alive	7pm
	Women's Slant on the News		Gene and Glenn	7:15
The Burr McIntosh Show	The Court of Human Relations			7:30
			The Philistines	7:45
			The Caswell Concert	8pm
Music	Harry Sosnik Orchestra		One Man's Family	8:15
	Rube Wolf Orchestra			8:30
			Public Affairs	8:45
Melody Masquerade	Orville Knapp Orchestra			9pm
				9:15
Tom Coakley Orchestra	Jan Garber Orchestra			9:30
				9:45
	The Ten o'Clock Wire			10pm
Mark Hopkins Orchestra	From Me To You, Julie Cruze			10:15
	Everett Hoagland Orchestra		Jimmy Grier Orchestra	10:30
				10:45

EVENING — SUMMER, 1934

Saturday

	BLUE	CBS	KNX	NBC
5pm	Mickey Gillette Orchestra	The Philadelphia Summer Concert (4:30PM)	(N/A)	Hands Across the Border (4:30PM)
5:15				
5:30	Temple Baptist Church			Edwin Franko Goldman Band
5:45				
6pm	Songs			The Cuckoo Hour, Ray Knight
6:15	News			Guy Lombardo Orchestra
6:30	The Lyric Trio	Elder Michaux Congregation		The National Barn Dance
6:45				
7pm	Poet of the Air	Sylvia Froos, songs		
7:15		Glen Gray Orchestra		
7:30				
7:45		Ferde Grofe' Orchestra		
8pm	Recreation	Orville Knapp Orchestra		Hotel Biltmore Orchestra
8:15				Carefree Carnival
8:30		Jan Garber Orchestra		
8:45				
9pm	Mark Hopkins Orchestra	Everett Hoagland Orchestra		
9:15				William Walsh Orchestra
9:30		Jackie Sounder Orchestra		Tom Coakley Orchestra
9:45		The Old Music Master		
10pm		The Ten o'Clock Wire		Blue Moonlight
10:15		Russ Carlson Orchestra		
10:30	Hal Grayson Orchestra	Rube Wolf Orchestra		
10:45				

DAYTIME — SUMMER, 1934

Sunday

	BLUE	CBS	KNX	NBC
8am	Major Bowes' Capitol Family	The Times Comics Pages	(N/A)	(Off the Air)
8:15				
8:30	The Radio City Music Hall	The Romany Trio		
8:45				
9am		Ann Leaf at the Organ		
9:15				
9:30		The Compinsky Trio		The Sunday Forum
9:45	The Hollywood Conservatory of Music			
10am	Music	The Randall String Trio		
10:15		Abram Chasin's Power Pointers		
10:30		The Windy City Revue		Concert Artists
10:45	Temple Baptist Church	Music		
11am		Detroit Symphony Orchestra		Music
11:15				
11:30				Chatauqua Symphony Orchestra
11:45				
12pm		The Buffalo Variety Workshop		
12:15				
12:30		Oregon on Parade		
12:45				
1pm		The Playboys		Natonal Vespers
1:15		Poet's Gold		
1:30	Dr. Bernard, health	Organ Recital		Walter Preston, songs
1:45		Professor Lindsay, readings		Boyer Rendezvous

DAYTIME — SUMMER, 1934

Monday-Friday

BLUE	CBS	KNX	NBC	
Music (7:45AM)	Music	(N/A)	(Off the Air)	8am
Fields and Hall, songs				8:15
Vic and Sade	Al Kavelin Orchestra			8:30
Words and Music				8:45
	Velazco Orchestra			9am
Charlie Wellman and Company				9:15
	Music / Betty Crocker, cooking		Talk and Music	9:30
Music	Music			9:45
	Music / Ann Leaf at the Organ			10am
				10:15
	Music		Woman's Magazine of the Air	10:30
				10:45
Music / Language Lesson				11am
				11:15
Music	Music / Dancing by the Sea			11:30
				11:45
	Music		Betty and Bob	12pm
News			The National Farm and Home Hour	12:15
Music				12:30
				12:45
			Music	1pm
	Music / Between the Bookends			1:15
	Music		Ma Perkins	1:30
			Music / Dreams Come True	1:45

DAYTIME — SUMMER, 1934

Sunday

	BLUE	CBS	KNX	NBC
2pm	The Catholic Hour	Music		
2:15				
2:30	Public Affairs			Music
2:45		Carlisle and London, piano		
3pm		Peter the Great		The Silken Strings
3:15				
3:30		Music		Music
3:45		Newspaper Adventures		
4pm		The Columbia Variety Hour		The Chase and Sanborn Hour, Jimmy Durante
4:15				
4:30				
4:45				

DAYTIME — SUMMER, 1934

Monday-Friday

BLUE	CBS	KNX	NBC	
	The Happy Go Lucky Hour		Al Pearce and His Gang	*2pm*
				2:15
				2:30
				2:45
Music / The Italian Language	Feminine Fancies		Music	*3pm*
				3:15
	Stimulating Soothers			*3:30*
USC Symphony Orchestra	The Texas Rangers			*3:45*
	Music / Kate Smith and Her Swanee Music		Music / The Jack Pearl Show / The Fleischmann Yeast Hour, Rudy Vallee / The Cities Service Concerts	*4pm*
				4:15
Talk and Music	Music / The Dramatic Guild			*4:30*
				4:45

DAYTIME — SUMMER, 1934

Saturday

	BLUE	CBS	KNX	NBC
8am	Down Lovers Lane (7:45PM)	Connie Gates, songs	(N/A)	Down Lovers Lane (7:30AM)
8:15		Emery Deutsch Orchestra		Fields and Hall, songs
8:30	Vic and Sade	Al Kavelin Orchestra		Music
8:45	Words and Music			
9am		Emil Velasco Orchestra		
9:15	Public Affairs			
9:30		Organ Recital		The National Farm and Home Hour
9:45				
10am		Jack Russell Orchestra		
10:15		The Austria Music Festival		
10:30		The Round Towners		Woman's Magazine of the Air
10:45				
11am		Columbia Salon Orchestra		
11:15				
11:30	The Weekend Revue	Dancing by the Sea		
11:45				
12pm		Ann Leaf at the Organ		Cliff Navarro, songs
12:15	News and Views			US Agricultural Talk
12:30		Russ Carlson Orchestra		
12:45		Scott Fisher Orchestra		
1pm	Public Affairs	Little Jack Little Orchestra		
1:15				
1:30		Wurtzebach's Music		Ross Fenton Orchestra
1:45		Mischa Raginsky Orchestra		

DAYTIME — SUMMER, 1934

Saturday

	BLUE	CBS	KNX	NBC
2pm		Music		Al Pearce and His Gang
2:15				
2:30		The Wanderers Quartet		Tom Coakley Orchestra
2:45		Gene Kardos Orchestra		
3pm	Wesley Tourtellotte, organ	Mary Eastman, songs		The Three X Sisters
3:15		Isham Jones Orchestra		Al Williams, songs
3:30				
3:45		The Fats Waller Rhythm Club		
4pm	The Golden Sword			Hotel Plaza Orchestra
4:15				
4:30	Records	The Philadelphia Summer Concert		Hands Across the Border
4:45				

EVENING — FALL, 1934

Sunday

	BLUE	CBS	KNX	NBC
5pm	Records	The Ford Sunday Evening Hour	(N/A)	The Chase and Sanborn Hour, Eddie Cantor
5:15				
5:30				
5:45				
6pm	Twilight Revelries	The Town Crier		The Manhattan Merry-Go-Round
6:15		Music		
6:30		The United for California League		The American Album of Familiar Music
6:45		Songs		
7pm	The Pierce Brothers Quartet	Lady Esther Serenade		Hind's Hall of Fame
7:15				
7:30	The Classic Hour	Merrymakers Orchestra		The Pontiac Show, Jane Froman
7:45				
8pm	Music			Wendell Hall, songs
8:15				Songs
8:30		Ben Pollack Orchestra		The Jello Program, Jack Benny
8:45		Voices of the Evening		
9pm	Countess De Li Guaro, piano	Johnny Murray's Hi-Jinks		The Silken Strings
9:15	Music			
9:30				The Philistines
9:45				Big Ben Dream Dramas
10pm	Records	The Ten o'Clock Wire		The Richfield Reporter
10:15		Joe Sullivan Orchestra		Fiesta
10:30		Vincent Lopez Orchestra		
10:45				Claudia Dell and Reginald Denny, songs

EVENING — FALL, 1934

Monday

BLUE	CBS	KNX	NBC	
How Songs Grew	Bar X Days	(N/A)	Jan Garber Orchestra	5pm
Hermes, the Story Teller	Wheatenaville Sketches			5:15
Songs	The Radio Hour		The Stamp Club	5:30
The Catholic Mission Hour			Little Orphan Annie	5:45
Public Affairs	Rosa Ponselle, songs		The Sinclair Wiener Minstrels	6pm
News	Public Affairs			6:15
Organ Recital			The Colgate House Party	6:30
	Raymond Knight Orchestra			6:45
	Lady Esther Serenade		The Carnation Contented Hour	7pm
				7:15
Music	Public Health		Music	7:30
Albert Bergman, legal talk	Unsolved Mysteries			7:45
Paul Roberts, songs	The Story of Myrt and Marge		Amos 'n' Andy	8pm
The Stove Poker Philosopher	Edwin C. Hill, news		Gene and Glenn	8:15
SERA Orchestra	The Blue Monday Jamboree		The Voice of Firestone	8:30
				8:45
			The Shell Show	9pm
Fishing and Hunting Talk				9:15
Songs	The Witch's Tale			9:30
				9:45
Records	The Ten o'Clock Wire		The Richfield Reporter	10pm
	Ben Pollack Orchestra		Red Davis	10:15
Marshall's Mavericks			Jimmy Grier Orchestra	10:30
				10:45

EVENING — FALL, 1934

Tuesday

	BLUE	CBS	KNX	NBC
5pm	Music	Carlos Molina Orchestra	(N/A)	The Nomads
5:15	The Nomads	Wheatenaville Sketches		Songs
5:30	The Word Detective	Dance Orchestra		Pal Jimmy
5:45	Music	The Adventures of Robin Hood		Little Orphan Annie
6pm	Children of All Lands	Bing Crosby Entertains		The Four Blackbirds
6:15	News			Charles Hamp, songs
6:30	Twilight Reveries	Isham Jones Orchestra		The Texaco Star Theater, Ed Wynn
6:45				
7pm	Claudia Dell, songs	The Camel Caravan		The Palmolive Beauty Box Theater
7:15	Records			
7:30	The Borowsky Concert Quartet	Bolero's		
7:45		Unsolved Mysteries		
8pm		The Story of Myrt and Marge		Amos 'n' Andy
8:15		Parko Pals		Gene and Glenn
8:30	Dr. Liebling, health	Calling All Cars		Johnny Presents
8:45				
9pm	Music	Music		Ben Bernie, the Old Maestro
9:15		Spotlight		
9:30		Raymond Knight Orchestra		Death Valley Days
9:45				
10pm		The Ten o'Clock Wire		The Richfield Reporter
10:15		Claudia Dell, songs		Drama
10:30	Tom Coakley Orchestra	Vincent Lopez Orchestra		Jimmy Grier Orchestra
10:45				

EVENING — FALL, 1934

Wednesday

BLUE	CBS	KNX	NBC	
Records	Al Roth Orchestra	(N/A)	Mary Pickford Dramas	5pm
	Wheatenaville Sketches			5:15
Cliff Nazarro, songs	Broadway Varieties		The Stamp Club	5:30
Harriet Andrews Bremner, songs			Little Orphan Annie	5:45
Edward W. Houck, talk	The Chesterfield Show		Twenty Thousand Years in Sing Sing	6pm
News				6:15
Twilight Reveries	The Adventures of Gracie, Burns and Allen		Our Home on the Range, John C. Thomas	6:30
				6:45
Ladies Laugh Last	The Adventures of Admiral Byrd		Dennis King, songs	7pm
			Madame Sylvia, gossip	7:15
Records	King's Serenade		Memory Lane	7:30
	Unsolved Mysteries			7:45
	The Story of Myrt and Marge		Amos 'n' Andy	8pm
	Edwin C. Hill, news		Gene and Glenn	8:15
	The Voice of Experience		The Log Cabin Jamboree, Lanny Ross	8:30
	Treasures of Time			8:45
Musicale			The Hour of Smiles, Fred Allen	9pm
	Tapestries of Life			9:15
				9:30
Records	Hal Grayson Orchestra			9:45
	The Ten o'Clock Wire		The Richfield Reporter	10pm
	Drama		Red Davis	10:15
Tom Coakley Orchestra	Vincent Lopez Orchestra		Jimmy Grier Orchestra	10:30
				10:45

EVENING — FALL, 1934

Thursday

	BLUE	CBS	KNX	NBC
5pm	Records	The PTA Program	(N/A)	The Fleischmann Yeast Hour, Rudy Vallee
5:15		Wheatenaville Sketches		
5:30		Dance Orchestra		
5:45		Sports		
6pm	Drama	The Romance of Travel		The Maxwell House Showboat
6:15				
6:30	Organ Recital	Fred Waring Orchestra		
6:45				
7pm	Records	Barnyard Serenade		The Kraft Music Hall
7:15				
7:30		The Inglewood Park Concert		
7:45				
8pm		The Story of Myrt and Marge		Amos 'n' Andy
8:15		Music		The Standard Symphony Hour
8:30	Nick Harris	The Camel Caravan		
8:45				
9pm	Hermes, the Story Teller	Music		
9:15	Records			Winning the West
9:30				
9:45				Music
10pm		The Ten o'Clock Wire		The Richfield Reporter
10:15	The Big Ten	The Melody Man		The Four Blackbirds
10:30		Vincent Lopez Orchestra		Jimmy Grier Orchestra
10:45	Tom Coakley Orchestra			

EVENING — FALL, 1934

Friday

BLUE	CBS	KNX	NBC	
Flirtation	Al Hoth Orchestra	(N/A)	Rev. Fuller, religion	5pm
	Wheatenaville Sketches			5:15
Ricardo and His Violin	The Adventures of Robin Hood		The Stamp Club	5:30
James Samuel Lacy, talk	Sports		Little Orphan Annie	5:45
The Board of Education	The March of Time		Let's Listen to Harris	6pm
News				6:15
Twilight Reveries	Hollywood Hotel		The Armour Star Jester, Phil Baker	6:30
				6:45
Scotland in Song and Story			The First Nighter Program	7pm
Records				7:15
Mickey Gillette Orchestra	Friday Frolics		Enos Crime Clues	7:30
				7:45
Records	The Story of Myrt and Marge		Amos 'n' Andy	8pm
	Edwin C. Hill, news		Gene and Glenn	8:15
	The Court of Human Relations		One Man's Family	8:30
				8:45
	The Los Angeles Police Band		The Caswell Concert	9pm
Hotel Congress Orchestra	Dance Orchestra		Charles Hamp, songs	9:15
Ted Fiorito Orchestra	United for California League		Richelieu	9:30
	Ben Pollack Orchestra			9:45
Records	The Ten o'Clock Wire		The Richfield Reporter	10pm
	Drama		Red Davis	10:15
Tom Coakley Orchestra	Vincent Lopez Orchestra		Jimmy Grier Orchestra	10:30
				10:45

EVENING — FALL, 1934

Saturday

	BLUE	CBS	KNX	NBC
5pm	Music	The Roxy Revue	(N/A)	The Swift Hour
5:15				
5:30	Temple Baptist Church			
5:45		Sports		
6pm		The Chesterfield Show		The Radio City Party
6:15	News			
6:30	Music	All for You		The Gibson Family
6:45		The Canadian Grenadiers		
7pm		Music		
7:15				
7:30		Mona Lowe, songs		Enos Crime Clues
7:45		Music		
8pm	Recreation	Richard Himber Orchestra		The National Barn Dance
8:15				
8:30		The Hodge Podge Lodge		
8:45				
9pm	Music	Music		Floyd Gibbons, news
9:15	Carefree Carnival	Dance Orchestra		Music
9:30				
9:45		Ben Pollack Orchestra		
10pm		The Ten o'Clock Wire		Blue Moonlight
10:15		The Melody Man		
10:30	Tom Coakley Orchestra	Vincent Lopez Orchestra		Jimmy Grier Orchestra
10:45				

DAYTIME — FALL, 1934

Sunday

	BLUE	CBS	KNX	NBC
8am	(Off the Air)	The Times Comics Pages	(N/A)	The Church Quarter-Hour
8:15				Morning Musicale
8:30	The Classic Hour	The Salt Lake Tabernacle Choir		Major Bowes' Capitol Family
8:45				
9am	Records			The Sunday Morning Special
9:15				
9:30		Melodies Organistique		The Radio City Music Hall
9:45		A Visitor Looks at America		
10am	Maurice Zam, piano	The CBS Church of the Air		
10:15				
10:30	Highlights of the Bible	Colonial Minuets		Charles Hamp, songs
10:45		Pat Kennedy, songs		Dr. Casselbury, health
11am	Records	Lazy Dan, the Minstrel Man		Treasure Chest
11:15				
11:30		The Imperial Hawaiian Band		Public Affairs
11:45				
12pm		New York Philharmonic Orchestra		
12:15				
12:30	USC College of Music			Musical Romance
12:45				
1pm				Kansas City Symphony Orchestra
1:15				

DAYTIME — FALL, 1934

Monday-Friday

BLUE	CBS	KNX	NBC	
Music / Johnny O'Brien, songs	Stock Reports	(N/A)	The Church Quarter-Hour	*8am*
Music	Connie Gates, songs		Music / Your Child / Tony Wons' Scrapbook	*8:15*
	The Country Church of Hollywood		Music / Helen Guest, songs	*8:30*
			Music / The All-Americans	*8:45*
Records	The Voice of Experience		Music / Fields and Hall, songs	*9am*
	Talk and Music		Talk and Music / Josephine Gibson, food	*9:15*
Talk and Music	Music / Betty Crocker, cooking		Music	*9:30*
	Talk and Music		News	*9:45*
Records	Just Plain Bill		Talk and Music	*10am*
	Talk / George Hall Orchestra			*10:15*
	Music		Woman's Magazine of the Air	*10:30*
				10:45
Music / Language Lesson	Marie, the Little French Princess		Music / The Standard School Broadcast	*11am*
	The Romance of Helen Trent			*11:15*
Talk and Music	The American School of the Air		Music / Smackout	*11:30*
			Talk / Fashion Tour	*11:45*
	Music / The Kate Smith Matinee Hour		Stock Market Reports	*12pm*
News			The National Farm and HomeHour	*12:15*
Records				*12:30*
				12:45
	Visiting America's Little House		Betty and Bob	*1pm*
The Borowsky Concert Quartet	Talk and Music		Songs / Charlie Wellman and Company	*1:15*

DAYTIME — FALL, 1934

Sunday

	BLUE	CBS	KNX	NBC
1:30	Dr. Bernard, health	Chicago Symphony Orchestra		The House By the Side of the Road
1:45	The Hollywood Conservatory of Music			
2pm	The Classic Hour	Vick's Open House		The Hoover Sentinels
2:15				
2:30		Music		The Radio Explorer's Club
2:45		Rabbi Magnin, religion		A. P. Terhune's Dog Dramas
3pm	The Catholic Hour	Music By Gershwin		The Makers of History
3:15				
3:30	Records	Smilin' Ed McConnell, songs		Grand Hotel
3:45		Newspaper Adventures		
4pm	Music	California Melodies		Organ Recital
4:15				
4:30		Edgewater Beach Orchestra		The Baker's Broadcast, Joe Penner
4:45				

DAYTIME — FALL, 1934

Monday-Friday

BLUE	CBS	KNX	NBC	
			Ma Perkins	1:30
			Betty Harlow, songs / Dreams Come True	1:45
The Classic Hour	The Happy Go Lucky Hour		Al Pearce and His Gang	2pm
				2:15
				2:30
				2:45
Music / The Italian Language	Feminine Fancies		Pictorial	3pm
			Music / John and Ned, songs	3:15
Music	Talk and Music		Ann Warner Chats	3:30
Music / The Singing Strings				3:45
Music / The Cuckoo Hour, Ray Perkins			Music / Nick Harris / Irvin S. Cobb, stories	4pm
	University of the Air		Music	4:15
Talk and Music	Talk and Music			4:30
Music / Coquettes	Between the Bookends			4:45

DAYTIME — FALL, 1934

Saturday

	BLUE	CBS	KNX	NBC
8am	Johnny O'Brien, songs	George Johnson, songs	(N/A)	The Church Quarter-Hour
8:15	Records			Music
8:30		The Country Church of Hollywood		
8:45				
9am	The Armchair Quartet	Songs		County Medical Association Talks
9:15	Genia Fonariova, songs	Russian Music		News
9:30		News		The National Farm and Home Hour
9:45		Abraham Chasin's Piano Pointers		
10am		George Hall Orchestra		
10:15				
10:30	The Classic Hour	Esther Velas Ensemble		Claudia Dell and Reginald Denny, songs
10:45				Woman's Magazine of the Air
11am		Sports		
11:15				Sports
11:30				
11:45				
12pm				
12:15	News			
12:30	Records			
12:45				
1pm				
1:15				
1:30	Biltmore Concert Orchestra			
1:45				

DAYTIME — FALL, 1934

Saturday

	BLUE	CBS	KNX	NBC
2pm	The Classic Hour			
2:15				
2:30	Our American Schools			
2:45				
3pm	Music			
3:15				
3:30				
3:45				
4pm	Religion in the News			
4:15	Jamboree			
4:30				
4:45	The Pickens Sisters, songs			

LISTINGS FOR 1935

EVENING — WINTER, 1935

Sunday

	BLUE	CBS	MBS	NBC
5pm	Belmar Edmonson, news	Club Romance	(N/A)	The Opera Guild
5:15	Records			
5:30		California Melodies		
5:45				
6pm	Burt Shepard, violin	The Ford Sunday Evening Hour		The Manhattan Merry-Go-Round
6:15				
6:30				The American Album of Familiar Music
6:45				
7pm	The Pierce Brothers Quartet	Lady Esther Serenade		The Pontiac Show, Jane Froman
7:15				
7:30	Nick Harris	Raymond Paige Presents		K-7, Secret Service Spy Stories
7:45	Records			
8pm		Dance Orchestra		Wendell Hall, songs
8:15				Walter Winchell's Jergens Journal
8:30	Bartlett-Frankel String Quartet	Salon Moderne		The Jello Program, Jack Benny
8:45				
9pm	Countess De Li Guaro, piano	Johnny Murray's Hi-Jinks		The Silken Strings
9:15	Records			
9:30	The Reader's Guide			The Four Blackbirds
9:45				Big Ben Dream Dramas
10pm	Musical Celebrities	The Ten o'Clock Wire		The Richfield Reporter
10:15		Joe Sullivan Orchestra		Bridge to Dreamland
10:30		Orville Knapp Orchestra		
10:45				

EVENING — WINTER, 1935

Monday

BLUE	CBS	MBS	NBC	
How Songs Grew	Diane and Her Life Saver	(N/A)	Jan Garber Orchestra	5pm
Hermes, the Story Teller	Wheatenaville Sketches			5:15
Records	Songs		Carefree Carnival	5:30
The KECA Flying Club	Clinic of the Air			5:45
The Board of Education	The Chesterfield Show		Flirtations	6pm
News				6:15
Liberal Arts Series	Leonardo Da Vinci		The Colgate House Party	6:30
Music				6:45
Organ Recital	Lady Esther Serenade		The Carnation Contented Hour	7pm
Records				7:15
	Public Health		The Princess Pat Players	7:30
Albert Bergman, legal talk	Unsolved Mysteiries			7:45
Paul Roberts, songs	The Story of Myrt and Marge		Amos 'n' Andy	8pm
The Stove Poker Philosopher	Edwin C. Hill, news		Red Davis	8:15
Songs	Kate Smith's New-Star Revue		The Voice of Firestone	8:30
				8:45
News	The Blue Monday Jamboree		The Shell Show	9pm
Music				9:15
				9:30
				9:45
Records	The Ten o'Clock Wire		The Richfield Reporter	10pm
Blue Moonlight	Moonlight Melodies		Walkalkians	10:15
	Lionel Hamptoni Orchestra		Jimmy Grier Orchestra	10:30
Music				10:45

EVENING — WINTER, 1935

Tuesday

	BLUE	CBS	MBS	NBC
5pm	The Five Cards	The Adventures of Robin Hood	(N/A)	The Latvian Singers
5:15		Wheatenaville Sketches		The Stamp Club
5:30	The Word Detective	What Would You Do		The Packard Show, Lawrence Tibbett
5:45	The KECA Flying Club	The DSS Club Mystery		
6pm	Children of All Lands	Bing Crosby Entertains		Vick's Open House
6:15	News			
6:30	Liberal Arts Series	Isham Jones Orchestra		The Texaco Star Theater, Ed Wynn
6:45	Organ Recital			
7pm	Records	The Camel Caravan		The Palmolive Beauty Box Theater
7:15				
7:30	The Borowsky Concert Quartet	Bolero's		
7:45		Voice of the Crusaders		
8pm	Records	The Story of Myrt and Marge		Amos 'n' Andy
8:15		Music		The Night Editor
8:30	Music	Calling All Cars		Johnny Presents
8:45				
9pm	News	Voices of the Evening		Ben Bernie, the Old Maestro
9:15	Fishing and Hunting Talk	Oliver Knapp Orchestra		
9:30	Records	The University Expllorer		Death Valley Days
9:45				
10pm		The Ten o'Clock Wire		The Richfield Reporter
10:15	Tom Coakley Orchestra	Fred Skinner, songs		The Four Blackbirds
10:30		Orville Knapp Orchestra		Jimmy Grier Orchestra
10:45				

EVENING — WINTER, 1935

Wednesday

BLUE	CBS	MBS	NBC	
Songs	Diane and Her Life Saver	(N/A)	Mary Pickford Dramas	5pm
Song Recital	Wheatenaville Sketches			5:15
Just Around the Corner	Broadway Varieties		The Stamp Club	5:30
The KECA Flying Club			Just Around the Corner	5:45
The Board of Education	The Chesterfield Show		Twenty Thousand Years in Sing Sing	6pm
News				6:15
Liberal Arts Series	The Adventures of Gracie, Burns and Allen		Our Home on the Range, John C. Thomas	6:30
Organ Recital				6:45
Records	The Adventures of Admiral Byrd		Jimmy Fidler, gossip	7pm
			Madame Sylvia, gossip	7:15
	Barnyard Serenade		One Man's Family	7:30
				7:45
	The Story of Myrt and Marge		Amos 'n' Andy	8pm
	Edwin C. Hill, news		Red Davis	8:15
	The Voice of Experience		The Log Cabin Jamboree, Lanny Ross	8:30
	Treasures of Time			8:45
News			The Hour of Smiles, Fred Allen	9pm
The Junior Colllege Program	Tapestries of Life			9:15
				9:30
	Lionel Hampton Orchestra			9:45
Records	The Ten o'Clock Wire		The Richfield Reporter	10pm
Tom Coakley Orchestra	Joe Sullivan Orchestra		Public Affairs	10:15
	Orville Knapp Orchestra		Jimmy Grier Orchestra	10:30
				10:45

EVENING — WINTER, 1935

Thursday

	BLUE	CBS	MBS	NBC
5pm	Records	The Hour of Charm	(N/A)	The Fleischmann Yeast Hour, Rudy Vallee
5:15				
5:30	Tuning in With Our Children	Wheatenaville Sketches		
5:45	The KECA Flying Club	The DSS Mystery Club		
6pm	Children of All Lands	Let's Go to Europe		The Maxwel House Showboat
6:15	News	Piano Fantasies		
6:30	Liberal Arts Series	Fred Waring Orchestra		
6:45	Burt Shepard, violin			
7pm	Records			The Kraft Music Hall
7:15	Paul Roberts, songs			
7:30	Walkalkians	The Inglewood Park Concert		
7:45				
8pm	Property Studies	The Story of Myrt and Marge		Amos 'n' Andy
8:15	Records	Little Jack Little Orchestra		The Standard Symphony Hour
8:30		The Camel Caravan		
8:45	The Nation's Songs			
9pm	News	Dramatic Sketch		
9:15	Hermes, the Story Teller	George Hamilton Orchestra		Winning of the West
9:30	Records			
9:45		Bill Fleck Orchestra		Dancing in Twin Cities
10pm		The Ten o'Clock Wire		The Richfield Reporter
10:15	Tom Coakley Orchestra	Fred Skinner, songs		Manchester Boddy, news
10:30		Orville Knapp Orchestra		Jimmy Grier Orchestra
10:45				

EVENING — WINTER, 1935

Friday

BLUE	CBS	MBS	NBC	
Care of the Eyes	The Adventures of Robin Hood	(N/A)	The Beaux Arts Trio	5pm
Records	Wheatenaville Sketches			5:15
Music	What Would You Do		The Stamp Club	5:30
	The Master Music Room		Young People's Concert	5:45
The Board of Education	The March of Time		The Beatrice Lillie Show	6pm
News				6:15
Liberal Arts Series	Hollywood Hotel		The Armour Star Jester, Phil Baker	6:30
Organ Recital				6:45
			The First Nighter Program	7pm
Leo McDonald, sports				7:15
Scotland in Song and Story	The Cleveland Entertainers		The Pause That Refreshes	7:30
	The Wilshire Presbyterian Choir			7:45
The Classic Hour	The Story of Myrt and Marge		Amos 'n' Andy	8pm
	Edwin C. Hill, news		Red Davis	8:15
	The Court of Human Relations		The Intimate Revue	8:30
				8:45
News	The Witch's Tale		The Caswell Concert	9pm
Victor Allen, piano			Richard Himber Orchestra	9:15
Records	George Hamilton Orchestra			9:30
			The Philistines	9:45
	The Ten o'Clock Wire		The Richfield Reporter	10pm
Tom Coakley Orchestra	Joe Sullivan Orchestra		The Four Blackbirds	10:15
	Orville Knapp Orchestra		Jimmy Grier Orchestra	10:30
				10:45

EVENING — WINTER, 1935

Saturday

	BLUE	CBS	MBS	NBC
5pm	Records	The Roxy Revue	(N/A)	The Swift Hour
5:15				
5:30				
5:45		Luden's Musical Revue		
6pm		The Chesterfield Show		The Radio City Party
6:15	News			
6:30	Organ Recital	The Country Church of Hollywood		The Gibson Family
6:45				
7pm	Raine Bennett, rhymes	Wannamaker Mile, sports		
7:15		The Saturday Revue		
7:30	Records			Ladies Laugh Last
7:45		Public Affairs		
8pm	Recreation	Richard Himber Orchestra		The National Barn Dance
8:15	Opera			
8:30		Johnny Green Orchestra		
8:45				
9pm		Del White Orchestra		Walkalkians
9:15		Gordon Henderson Orchestra		Studio Program
9:30		George Hamilton Orchestra		Let's Dance
9:45				
10pm		The Ten o'Clock Wire		
10:15		Bill Fleck Orchestra		
10:30		Orville Knapp Orchestra		
10:45				

DAYTIME — WINTER, 1935

Sunday

	BLUE	CBS	MBS	NBC
8am	(Off the Air)	The Times Comics Pages	(N/A)	The Church Quarter-Hour
8:15				Roger Whitman, songs
8:30	The Classic Hour	The Salt Lake Tabernacle Choir		Major Bowes' Capitol Family
8:45				
9am				
9:15				What Home Means for Me
9:30		The Sunday Breakfast Club		The Radio City Music Hall
9:45				
10am	Maurice Zam, piano			
10:15				
10:30	Young People's Conference	Harold Rhodes, piano		Walkalkians
10:45		Pat Kennedy, songs		Dr. Casselbury, health talk
11am	First Unitarian Church of Hollywood	Lazy Dan, the Minstrel Man		Immortal Dramas
11:15				
11:30		The Hammerstein Music Hall		The Lux Radio Theater
11:45				
12pm	Records	New York Philharmonic Orchestra		
12:15				
12:30				Penthouse Serenade
12:45				
1pm				Kansas City Symphony Orchestra
1:15				
1:30	Vocational Adjustment			The Sunday Special
1:45	The Hollywood Conservatory of Music			

DAYTIME — WINTER, 1935

Monday-Friday

BLUE	CBS	MBS	NBC	
Music / Johnny O'Brien, songs	Rise and Shine (7:00AM)	(N/A)	The Church Quarter-Hour	8am
Records			Talk / Your Child / Tony Wons' Scrapbook	8:15
	The Country Church of Hollywood		Music / Helen Guest, songs	8:30
	Lil' Joe Warner's Jolly Journal		Hints to Housewives	8:45
	The Voice of Experience		The Story of Mary Marlin	9am
	The Gumps		Talk and Music	9:15
Talk and Music	Music / Betty Crocker, cooking			9:30
	Talk and Music		News	9:45
Music / Johnny O'Brien, songs			Talk and Music	10am
Music	Wife Begins at 10:15			10:15
	Talk and Music		Woman's Magazine of the Air	10:30
	Music / Pat Kennedy, songs			10:45
Music / Language Lesson	Marie, the Little French Princess		Music / The Standard School Broadcast	11am
	The Romance of Helen Trent			11:15
Music	The American School of the Air		Charlie Wellman and Company	11:30
			Fashion Tour	11:45
Music / Edna Fisher, songs	Music / The Kate Smith Matinee Hour		Stock Market Reports	12pm
News			The National Farm and HomeHour	12:15
Records				12:30
	Easy Aces			12:45
	Visiting America's Little House		Betty and Bob	1pm
	Talk and Music		Vic and Sade	1:15
The Borowsky Concert Quartet			Ma Perkins	1:30
			Betty Harlow, songs / Dreams Come True	1:45

DAYTIME — WINTER, 1935

Sunday

	BLUE	CBS	MBS	NBC
2pm	The Classic Hour	Vick's Open House		The Hoover Sentinels
2:15				
2:30		Rose Hills Ensemble		The House By the Side of the Road
2:45				
3pm	The Catholic Hour	National Amateur Night		Burt Shepherd, violin
3:15				
3:30	The DAR Program	Smilin' Ed MdConnell, songs		Grand Hotel
3:45	Spirituals	Newspaper Adventures		
4pm	Martha Mears, songs	The Town Crier		Judge Yankwich, legal talk
4:15	Records			A. P. Terhune's Dog Dramas
4:30	USC College of Music	The Magic Music Box		The Baker's Broadcast, Joe Penner
4:45		Rabbi Magnin, religion		

DAYTIME — WINTER, 1935

Monday-Friday

BLUE	CBS	MBS	NBC	
The Classic Hour	The Happy Go Lucky Hour		Al Pearce and His Gang	*2pm*
				2:15
				2:30
	Between the Bookends			*2:45*
Music / The Italian Language	Feminine Fancies		Pictorial	*3pm*
Mickey Gillette Orchestra			Music	*3:15*
	Talk and Music		Ann Warner Chats	*3:30*
				3:45
Talk and Music	Music / Louis Panico Orchestra		Liberal Arts Series	*4pm*
			Talk and Music	*4:15*
	Music / Buck Rogers of the 25th Century			*4:30*
	University of the Air		Just Plain Bill	*4:45*

DAYTIME — WINTER, 1935

Saturday

	BLUE	CBS	MBS	NBC
8am	Johnny O'Brien, songs	Cincinatti Conservatory Symphony	(N/A)	The Church Quarter-Hour
8:15	Records			The Vass Family, songs
8:30	Down Lovers Lane			Charles Wellman and Company
8:45	Records			Down Lovers Lane
9am	The Minute Men Quartet	Al Kavelin Orchestra		County Medical Association Talks
9:15	Genia Fonariova, songs			News
9:30	Public Schools	News		The National Farm and Home Hour
9:45		Abrham Chasin's Piano Pointers		
10am		Frederick William Wile, news		
10:15		George Hall Orchestra		
10:30	Young People's Philharmonic Orchestra	Esther Velas Ensemble		Words and Music
10:45				The Metropolitan Opera
11am	Records	Music / Public Affairs		
11:15				
11:30		Poetic Strings		
11:45		Beauty Talk		
12pm		The Modern Minstrels		
12:15	News			
12:30	Records			
12:45				
1pm		Are Women to Blame		
1:15		The Pro Arts String Quartet		
1:30	The Borowsky Concert Quartet			
1:45				

DAYTIME — WINTER, 1935

Saturday

	BLUE	CBS	MBS	NBC
2pm	The Classic Hour	Little Jack Little Orchestra		
2:15				Eddy Duchin Orchestra
2:30		Rabbi Wise, religion		Our American Schools
2:45		Between the Bookends		
3pm	Records	Lilac Time with the Night Singer		Kaltenmeyer's Kindegarten
3:15				
3:30		Bob Allen, piano		The Ranch Boys
3:45		Organ Interlude		
4pm		Dance Orchestra		Religion in the News
4:15				Music
4:30		Louis Panico Orchestra		
4:45				

EVENING — SPRING, 1935

Sunday

	BLUE	CBS	MBS	NBC
5pm	Records	The Eddie Cantor Show	(N/A)	Major Bowes' Original Amateur Hour
5:15				
5:30	The Voice of Healiing	Beyond the Blue Horizon		
5:45	News			
6pm	Burt Shepard, violin	The Ford Sunday Evening Hour		The Manhattan Merry-Go-Round
6:15				
6:30				The American Album of Familiar Music
6:45				
7pm	The Pierce Brothers Quartet	Lady Esther Serenade		The Gibson Family
7:15				
7:30	Nick Harris	Raymond Paige Presents		
7:45		Strange As It Seems		
8pm	Irish Folk Songs	Music		Wendell Hall, songs
8:15	Mexican Music			Walter Winchell's Jergens Journal
8:30	The Compinsky Trio			The Jello Program, Jack Benny
8:45				
9pm	News	Orville Knapp Orchestra		The Silken Strings
9:15	Piano Recital			
9:30	Records	Salon Moderne		One Man's Family
9:45				
10pm	Musical Celebrities	The Ten o'Clock Wire		The Richfield Reporter
10:15	Bridge to Dreamland	Dance Orchestra		The Three Musketeers
10:30		Orville Knapp Orchestra		Wesley Tortellotte, organ
10:45				

EVENING — SPRING, 1935

Monday

BLUE	CBS	MBS	NBC	
How Songs Grew	Fray and Braggiotti, piano	(N/A)	Music	5pm
Hermes, the Story Teller	Songs of Old			5:15
Records	Charles Long, songs		Carefree Carnival	5:30
The KECA Flying Club	Melodies Organistique			5:45
The Board of Education	Howard Barlow Orchestra		Pan Americana	6pm
News			Charles Hamp, songs	6:15
Liberal Arts Series	The Inglewood Park Concert		Music at the Hadyns	6:30
Eleanor Rennie, songs				6:45
Wesley Tourtellotte, organ	Lady Esther Serenade		The Carnation Contented Hour	7pm
				7:15
	Lilac Time with the Night Singer		The Music Masters	7:30
Albert Bergman, legal talk			The Caswell Concert	7:45
Opera	The Story of Myrt and Marge		Amos 'n' Andy	8pm
	Edwin C. Hill, news		Red Davis	8:15
	Kate Smith's New-Star Revue		The Voice of Firestone	8:30
				8:45
News	The Blue Monday Jamboree		The Shell Show	9pm
County Relief Association Talks				9:15
				9:30
				9:45
Fishing and Hunting Talk	The Ten o'Clock Wire		The Richfield Reporter	10pm
Musical Celebrities	Ray Herbeck Orchestra		Ben Alexander, stories	10:15
	Dick Jurgen Orchestra		Jimmy Grier Orchestra	10:30
				10:45

EVENING — SPRING, 1935

Tuesday

	BLUE	CBS	MBS	NBC
5pm	Records	The Adventures of Robin Hood	(N/A)	Walkalkians
5:15		Keith Beecher Orchestra		The Stamp Club
5:30	The Word Detective	What Would You Do		Tunes of the Times
5:45	The KECA Flying Club	The DSS Club Mystery		
6pm	Children of All Lands	Bing Crosby Entertains		Red Trails
6:15	News			
6:30	Liberal Arts Series	The Hour of Charm		The Texaco Star Theater, Ed Wynn
6:45	Twilight Reveries			
7pm	Wesley Tourtellotte, organ	The Camel Caravan		The Palmolive Beauty Box Theater
7:15	The Blind Singers			
7:30	The Borowsky Concert Quartet	Captain Dobbsie's Ship of Joy		
7:45		Voice of the Crusaders		
8pm	Music	The Story of Myrt and Marge		Amos 'n' Andy
8:15		Music		The Night Editor
8:30	Walkalkians	Calling All Cars		Johnny Presents
8:45				
9pm	News	Voices of the Evening		Ben Bernie, the Old Maestro
9:15	Music	True Confessions		
9:30	Records	The University Expllorer		Death Valley Days
9:45				
10pm	Musical Celebrities	The Ten o'Clock Wire		The Richfield Reporter
10:15		Anson Weeks Orchestra		Music
10:30		Orville Knapp Orchestra		Jimmy Grier Orchestra
10:45				

EVENING — SPRING, 1935

Wednesday

BLUE	CBS	MBS	NBC	
Songs	St. Louis Blues	(N/A)	One Man's Family	5pm
	D'Arteagua Orchestra			5:15
Records	Broadway Varieties		The Stamp Club	5:30
The KECA Flying Club			Music	5:45
Our National Parks	Leith Stevens Harmonies		Twenty Thousand Years in Sing Sing	6pm
News				6:15
Liberal Arts Series	The Adventures of Gracie, Burns and Allen		Our Home on the Range, John C. Thomas	6:30
Twilight Reveries				6:45
The Opera Hour	Peter Pfeiffer		Jimmy Fidler, gossip	7pm
			Charles Hamp, songs	7:15
	Raymond Paige Presents		Pleasure Island	7:30
	Strange As It Seems			7:45
	The Story of Myrt and Marge		Amos 'n' Andy	8pm
	Edwin C. Hill, news		Red Davis	8:15
	The Voice of Experience		Rainbow Gardens Orchestra	8:30
	Treasures of Time			8:45
News			The Hour of Smiles, Fred Allen	9pm
The Junior Colllege Program	Tapestries of Life			9:15
				9:30
Records	Ray Herbleck Orchestra			9:45
Musical Celebrities	The Ten o'Clock Wire		The Richfield Reporter	10pm
	Anson Weeks Orchestra		Dance Orchestra	10:15
	Orville Knapp Orchestra		Jimmy Grier Orchestra	10:30
				10:45

EVENING — SPRING, 1935

Thursday

	BLUE	CBS	MBS	NBC
5pm	Records	Romance	(N/A)	The Fleischman Yeast Hour, Rudy Vallee
5:15				
5:30	Tuning in With Our Children	Dance Orchestra		
5:45	The KECA Flying Club	The DSS Mystery Club		
6pm	Records	Let's Go to Europe		The Maxwell House Showboat
6:15	News	Movie Column of the Air		
6:30	Liberal Arts Series	Fred Waring Orchestra		
6:45	Wesley Tourtellotte, organ			
7pm				The Kraft Music Hall
7:15	The Compinsky Trio			
7:30		Captain Dobbsie's Ship of Joy		
7:45	Paul Roberts, songs	Voice of the Crusaders		
8pm	Property Studies	The Story of Myrt and Marge		Amos 'n' Andy
8:15	Good Old Songs	Music		The Standard Symphony Hour
8:30	Records	The Camel Caravan		
8:45				
9pm	News	Mobil Magazine		
9:15	Public Affairs			Winning of the West
9:30	Records	Ray Herbleck Orchestra		
9:45				Dancing in Twin Cities
10pm	Musical Celebrities	The Ten o'Clock Wire		The Richfield Reporter
10:15		Anson Weeks Orchestra		The Four Blackbirds
10:30		Orville Knapp Orchestra		Jimmy Grier Orchestra
10:45				

EVENING — SPRING, 1935

Friday

BLUE	CBS	MBS	NBC	
Records	It's a Woman's World	(N/A)	The Beaux Arts Trio	5pm
Care of the Eyes	The Phantom Emperor			5:15
Songs	What Would You Do		The Stamp Club	5:30
	Music		Music	5:45
Records	The March of Time		The Beatrice Lillie Show	6pm
News				6:15
Liberal Arts Series	Hollywood Hotel		The Armour Star Jester, Phil Baker	6:30
Wesley Tourtellotte, organ				6:45
			The First Nighter Program	7pm
Leo McDonald, sports				7:15
Music	Milion Dollar Smiles		The Pause That Refreshes	7:30
	Strange As It Seems			7:45
Famous Songs	The Story of Myrt and Marge		Amos 'n' Andy	8pm
	Edwin C. Hill, news		Red Davis	8:15
Records	Bolero's		Circus Night in Silvertown, Joe Cook	8:30
	Pasadena Orchestra			8:45
News	The Witch's Tale			9pm
Records			Enrico Madriguera Orchestra	9:15
	Bob Kinney Orchestra		Oriental Garden Orchestra	9:30
			The Philistines	9:45
Musical Celebrities	The Ten o'Clock Wire		The Richfield Reporter	10pm
	Anson Weeks Orchestra		Tom Coakley Orchestra	10:15
	Orville Knapp Orchestra		Jimmy Grier Orchestra	10:30
				10:45

EVENING — SPRING, 1935

Saturday

	BLUE	CBS	MBS	NBC
5pm	Records	The Roxy Revue	(N/A)	Your Hit Parade
5:15				
5:30				
5:45		St. Louis Blues		
6pm		Melody Masterpieces, Mary Eastman		The Radio City Party
6:15				
6:30	Twilight Reveries	The Country Church of Hollywood		Joe Hornick Orchestra
6:45				
7pm	Raine Bennett, rhymes	Song Time in Tennessee		Organ Recital
7:15				
7:30	Neil Russell and Margaret Duncan, piano	California Melodies		Blythe Taylor Burns, songs
7:45	Records			
8pm	Playground Department Music	Richard Himber Orchestra		The National Barn Dance
8:15				
8:30	Records	Hotel Del Monte Orchestra		
8:45	Wild Flowers			
9pm	Waltz Time	Orville Knapp Orchestra		Charles Hamp, songs
9:15				The Four Blackbirds
9:30	Records	Ray Herbleck Orchestra		Let's Dance
9:45				
10pm	Musical Celebrities	The Ten o'Clock Wire		
10:15		Dance Orchestra		
10:30		Dick Jurgens Orchestra		
10:45				

DAYTIME — SPRING, 1935

Sunday

	BLUE	CBS	MBS	NBC
8am	(Off the Air)	The Times Comics Pages	(N/A)	The Church Quarter-Hour
8:15				Walberg Brown String Quartet
8:30	The Classic Hour	The Salt Lake Tabernacle Choir		Major Bowes' Capitol Family
8:45				
9am				
9:15		The Garden Guide		What Home Means for Me
9:30		Romany Trail		The Radio City Music Hall
9:45	Roaming in the South Seas	Poetic Strings		
10am	Maurice Zam, piano	The Sunday Breakfast Club		
10:15				
10:30	Young People's Conference			Stanley L. McMichael, real estate
10:45				Dr. Casselbury, health
11am	Records	Lazy Dan, the Minstrel Man		Immortal Moments
11:15				
11:30		Harold Rhodes' Music School		The Lux Radio Theater
11:45		Organ and Vibroharp		
12pm		New York Philharmonic Orchestra		
12:15				
12:30				Penthouse Serenade
12:45				
1pm				Kansas City Symphony Orchestra
1:15				
1:30	Vocational Adjustment			The Sunday Special
1:45	The Hollywood Conservatory of Music			

DAYTIME — SPRING, 1935

Monday-Friday

BLUE	CBS	MBS	NBC	
Music / Johnny O'Brien, songs	Rise and Shine (7:00AM)	(N/A)	The Church Quarter-Hour	8am
Records	The Country Church of Hollywood		Talk and Music / Your Child / Tony Wons' Scrapbook	8:15
			Music	8:30
	The Story of Mary Marlin		Hints to Housewives	8:45
Talk and Music	The Voice of Experience		Music / Fields and Hall, songs	9am
Records	The Gumps		Music	9:15
	Five-Star Jones			9:30
	Talk and Music		News	9:45
			Talk and Music	10am
	Wife Begins at 10:15			10:15
	Talk and Music			10:30
			.	10:45
	Marie, the Little French Princess		Music / The Standard School Broadcast	11am
	The Romance of Helen Trent			11:15
	Talk and Music		Charlie Wellman and Company	11:30
			Music	11:45
	Music / The Kate Smith Matinee Hour		Stock Market Reports	12pm
News			The National Farm and Home Hour	12:15
Records				12:30
				12:45
	Visiting America's Little House		Betty and Bob	1pm
	Talk and Music		Vic and Sade	1:15
The Borowsky Concert Quartet			Ma Perkins	1:30
			Music / Dreams Come True / The Girl Next Door	1:45

DAYTIME — SPRING, 1935

Sunday

	BLUE	CBS	MBS	NBC
2pm	The Classic Hour	The Country Church of Hollywood		The Hoover Sentinels
2:15				
2:30		Rose Hills Ensemble		The House By the Side of the Road
2:45				
3pm	The Catholic Hour	National Amateur Night		The Makers of History
3:15				
3:30	The DAR Program	Smilin' Ed MdConnell, songs		Grand Hotel
3:45	Spirituals	Newspaper Adventures		
4pm	K-7, Secret Service Spy Story	Roadways of Romance		The Friendly Counselor
4:15				Judge Yankwich, legal talk
4:30	USC College of Music	Rabbi Magnin, religion		The Baker's Broadcast, Joe Penner
4:45		Cameos of Melody		

DAYTIME — SPRING, 1935

Monday-Friday

BLUE	CBS	MBS	NBC	
The Classic Hour	The Happy Go Lucky Hour		Woman's Magazine of the Air	*2pm*
				2:15
				2:30
	Between the Bookends			*2:45*
Talk / The Italian Language	Feminine Fancies		Pictorial	*3pm*
Music			Music / Easy Aces	*3:15*
	Music		Ann Warner Chats	*3:30*
				3:45
	Music / Louis Panico Orchestra		Liberal Arts Series	*4pm*
			Liberal Arts Series / Stories of the Black Chamber	*4:15*
	Music / Buck Rogers of the 25th Century		Wesley Tourtellotte, organ	*4:30*
	University of the Air		Just Plain Bill	*4:45*

DAYTIME — SPRING, 1935

Saturday

	BLUE	CBS	MBS	NBC
8am	Johnny O'Brien, songs	Cincinatti Conservatory Symphony	(N/A)	The Church Quarter-Hour
8:15	Records			Music
8:30				
8:45	Music			Charles Wellman and Company
9am		Music		County Medical Association Talks
9:15	Genia Fonariova, songs			News
9:30	Public Schools	News		The National Farm and Home Hour
9:45		Saturday Syncopators		
10am	Records	Poetic Strings		
10:15				
10:30	The Classic Hour	The People's Lobby		Music
10:45				
11am		Louis Panico Orchestra		
11:15				
11:30		Mickey of the Circus		The Weekend Revue
11:45				
12pm	Records	Emery Deutch's Dance Rhythms		Stock Market Reports
12:15	News			US Agricultural Talks
12:30	Records	Buffalo Presents		
12:45				
1pm		Music		Couquettes
1:15				Our National Parks
1:30	The Borowsky Concert Quartet			
1:45				Music

DAYTIME — SPRING, 1935

Saturday

	BLUE	CBS	MBS	NBC
2pm	The Classic Hour			Kearney Walton Orchestra
2:15				
2:30		Romany Trails		Our American Schools
2:45		Between the Bookends		
3pm	Records	Frederick William Wile, news		Music
3:15		Freddie Berrin Orchestra		
3:30				Songs
3:45		Milton Charles, songs		The Master Builder
4pm		Leonardo Da Vinci		Religion in the News
4:15				American Prosperity
4:30		Charles Lung, songs		
4:45		Tea Dasant		Ricardo and His Violin

EVENING — SUMMER, 1935

Sunday

	BLUE	CBS	KNX	NBC
5pm	Records	America's Hour	(N/A)	The Manhattan Merry-Go-Round
5:15				
5:30				The American Album of Familiar Music
5:45	The Lutheran Bureau of Southern California			
6pm	News	Lady Esther Serenade		Uncle Charlie's Tent Show
6:15	Burt Shepard, violin			
6:30		Benay Venuta's Variety Show		
6:45		Congressional Opinion		
7pm	Sacred Concert	Musical Mirrors		Sunset Dreams, The Morin Sisters
7:15				Cornelius Otis Skinner, talk
7:30	Nick Harris	Minute Melodies		Lanny Ross and His State Fair
7:45	Light Opera	Johnny Hamp Orchestra		
8pm	Records	Old Hymnal		Dance Orchestra
8:15		Dance Orchestra		
8:30		Salon Moderne		One Man's Family
8:45				
9pm	News and Views	Thomas Lee Presents		Dance Orchestra
9:15				
9:30	The Reader's Guide	Jan Garber Orchestra		The Three Musketeers
9:45		Musical Moments		
10pm	Musical Celebrities	The Ten o'Clock Wire		The Richfield Reporter
10:15		Les Hite Orchestra		The Backyard Astronomer
10:30		Orville Knapp Orchestra		Bridge to Dreamland
10:45				

EVENING — SUMMER, 1935

Monday

BLUE	CBS	KNX	NBC	
How Songs Grew	Six-Gun Justice	(N/A)	The Radio Pen Friend Club	5pm
The Beaux Arts Trio			Robert Hurd, songs	5:15
	St. Louis Orchestra		Meredith Willson Orchestra	5:30
Once Upon a Time				5:45
	Lady Esther Serenade		The Carnation Contented Hour	6pm
News				6:15
A Dog's Eye View	Lilac Time with the Night Singer		Lucky Smith	6:30
Blythe Taylor Burns, songs	Music			6:45
	Abe Lyman Orchestra		Amos 'n' Andy	7pm
			Tony and Gus	7:15
	Pick and Pat		The Voice of Firestone	7:30
Albert Bergman, legal talk				7:45
	Delmar Edmundsen, news		Ted Fiorito Orchestra	8pm
	Music		Captain Wilkie's Crime Lab	8:15
	Road to Fame		Musical Revue	8:30
Culbertson Club Bridge Talk			Dance Orchestra	8:45
News	Comedy Stars of Hollywood		Heartbreaks of the City	9pm
County Relief Association Orchestra	Bill Fleck Orchestra			9:15
	Jan Garber Orchestra		Albert Bergman, legal talk	9:30
			Marshall's Mavericks	9:45
Fishing and Hunting Talk	The Ten o'Clock Wire		The Richfield Reporter	10pm
Musical Celebrities	Jimmy Davis Orchestra		Ben Alexander, stories	10:15
	Merle Carlson Orchestra		Culbertson Club Bridge Talk	10:30
			Jimmy Grier Orchestra	10:45

EVENING — SUMMER, 1935

Tuesday

	BLUE	CBS	KNX	NBC
5pm	Music (4:30PM)	Lud Gluskin Presents on the Air	(N/A)	NTG and His Girls
5:15				
5:30		Fred Waring Orchestra		Eddy Duchin Orchestra
5:45				
6pm	Children of All Lands			The Palmolive Beauty Box Theater
6:15	News			
6:30	Organ Recital	The Jerry Cooper Show		
6:45	Twilight Revelries	Fiddler's Three		
7pm		Fred Stark Orchestra		Amos 'n' Andy
7:15				Tony and Gus
7:30	The Borowsky Concert Quartet	Calliing All Cars		Johnny Presents
7:45				
8pm	Composers Series	Music		Dance Orchestra
8:15				
8:30	Music	Jan Garber Orchestra		Death Valley Days
8:45				
9pm	News	Jay Erlick Orchestra		Fan Fare
9:15	Records			
9:30		The University Expllorer		Dance Orchestra
9:45		Bill Fleck Orchestra		
10pm	Musical Celebrities	The Ten o'Clock Wire		The Richfield Reporter
10:15		Jimmy Davis Orchestra		Dance Orchestra
10:30		Orville Knapp Orchestra		
10:45				Jimmy Grier Orchestra

EVENING — SUMMER, 1935

Wednesday

BLUE	CBS	KNX	NBC	
Time Clock of Ideas	Music	(N/A)	Our Home on the Range, John C. Thomas	5pm
				5:15
	Mark Warnow Orchestra			5:30
Once Upon a Time	Life Stories		Education in the News	5:45
Children of All Lands	The Adventures of Gracie, Burns and Allen		The Hits and Bits Revue	6pm
News				6:15
Public Affairs	He, She and They, Mary Eastman		Pleasure Island	6:30
Twilight Reveries				6:45
	Claude Honkin Orchestra		Amos 'n' Andy	7pm
The Opera Hour			Tony and Gus	7:15
	Ted Fiorito Orchestra		The House of Glass	7:30
	Strange As It Seems			7:45
	Raymond Paige Presents		Victor Young Orchestra	8pm
	Music		Dance Orchestra	8:15
	Jan Garber Orchestra		Lights Out	8:30
Culbertson Club Bridge Talk				8:45
News	Comedy Stars of Hollywood		Songs	9pm
Records	Bill Fleck Orchestra			9:15
	Sterling Young Orchestra		The Wandering Minstrels	9:30
				9:45
Musical Celebrities	The Ten o'Clock Wire		The Richfield Reporter	10pm
	Jay Erlick Orchestra		Al Gayle, songs	10:15
			Culbertson Club Bridge Talk	10:30
	Dance Orchestra		Jimmy Grier Orchestra	10:45

EVENING — SUMMER, 1935

Thursday

	BLUE	CBS	KNX	NBC
5pm	Hermes, the Story Teller (4:00 PM)	Music	(N/A)	The Maxwell House Showboat
5:15		Charles H. Towne, talk		
5:30		Marty May Time		
5:45				
6pm		Horace Heidt Orchestra		The Kraft Music Hall
6:15	News			
6:30	A Dog's Eye View	Dance Orchestra		
6:45	Wesley Tourtellotte, organ			
7pm				Amos 'n' Andy
7:15	Light Opera	Midge Williams, songs		Tony and Gus
7:30		Music		Winning of the West
7:45				
8pm	Records	Music		Blythe Taylor Burns, songs
8:15				The Standard Symphony Hour
8:30		Tapestries of Life		
8:45				
9pm	News	Mobil Magazine		
9:15	Good Old Songs			John Pennington, violin
9:30		Musical Moments		
9:45		Jan Garber Orchestra		Wesley Tourtellotte, organ
10pm	Musical Celebrities	The Ten o'Clock Wire		The Richfield Reporter
10:15		Lynn Daniels Orchestra		Bill Roberts, songs
10:30		Orville Knapp Orchestra		Paul Pendarvis Orchestra
10:45				Jimmy Grier Orchestra

EVENING — SUMMER, 1935

Friday

BLUE	CBS	KNX	NBC	
Music (4:15 PM)	Hollywood Hotel	(N/A)	Music	5pm
Care of the Eyes				5:15
			The Armour Star Jester, Phil Baker	5:30
Once Upon a Time				5:45
Los Angeles Traffic Association Talks	Among My Souvenirs		The First Nighter Program	6pm
News	The Canadian Grenadiers			6:15
Liberal Arts Series	Leith Stevens Harmonies		Circus Night in Silvertown, Joe Cook	6:30
Wesley Tourtellotte, organ				6:45
Leo MacDonald, sports	Carl Hoff Orchestra		Amos 'n' Andy	7pm
Waltz			Tony and Gus	7:15
	Music		Helene Hill piano	7:30
The Classic Hour	Strange As It Seems		Heart Beats of the City	7:45
	Bolero's			8pm
	Bill Fleck Orchestra		The Caswell Concert	8:15
	Richard Himber Orchestra		Victor Young Orchestra	8:30
Culbertson Club Bridge Talk			Leonard Keller Orchestra	8:45
News	The Witch's Tale		Reflections	9pm
Records				9:15
	Jan Garber Orchestra		Roy Maxon Orchestra	9:30
			Ben Pollack Orchestra	9:45
Musical Celebrities	The Ten o'Clock Wire		The Richfield Reporter	10pm
	Sterling Young Orchestra		Music	10:15
	Orville Knapp Orchestra		Culbertson Club Bridge Talk	10:30
			Walkalkians	10:45

EVENING — SUMMER, 1935

Saturday

	BLUE	CBS	KNX	NBC
5pm	Records (4:00PM)	The Columbia Concert Hall	(N/A)	G-Men
5:15				
5:30		California Melodies		Shell Chateau, Al Jolson
5:45				
6pm		Fiesta		
6:15				
6:30	Twilight Reveries	Jan Garber Orchestra		Carefree Carnival
6:45				
7pm	Raine Bennett, rhymes	Spanish Serenade		The National Barn Dance
7:15				
7:30	Neil Russell and Margaret Duncan, piano	Claude Hopkins Orchestra		
7:45				
8pm	Playground Department Music	Ray Kinney Orchestra		Dance Orchestra
8:15				
8:30		Orville Knapp Orchestra		Jimmy Grier Orchestra
8:45				
9pm	Records	Hollywood Comedy Stars		Waltz Time
9:15		Dance Orchestra		
9:30		Musical Moments		Jose Ramirez Orchestra
9:45		Jay Castle Orchestra		
10pm	Musical Celebrities	The Ten o'Clock Wire		Frank Andrews, news
10:15		Dance Orchestra		Henry King Orchestra
10:30				
10:45				

DAYTIME — SUMMER, 1935

Sunday

	BLUE	CBS	KNX	NBC
8am	(Off the Air)	The Times Comics Pages	(N/A)	The Church Quarter-Hour
8:15				Major Bowes' Capitol Family
8:30	Records	Romany Trails		The Radio City Music Hall
8:45				
9am		The Compinsky Trio		
9:15				
9:30	The Sunday Forum	Eddie Dundstedter, organ		Stanley L. McMichael, real estate
9:45		The Californians		Dr. Casselbury, health
10am	Maurice Zam, piano	Johnny Augustine's Music		Bible Dramas
10:15				
10:30	Records	Between the Bookends		The NBC Light Opera Guild
10:45		Music		
11am		New York Philharmonic Orchestra		
11:15				
11:30				National Vespers
11:45				
12pm				Willard Robinson Orchestra
12:15				
12:30				The Sunday Special
12:45				
1pm		Jackie and Earl Hatch, songs		Kansas City Symphony Orchestra
1:15		The Islanders		
1:30	Vocational Adjustment	Eunice Steel, songs		Music
1:45	The Hollywood Conservatory of Music	Helene Hughes, songs		Ray Heatherton and Lucille Manners, songs

DAYTIME — SUMMER, 1935

Monday-Friday

BLUE	CBS	KNX	NBC	
(Off the Air)	Music / Fred Friebel, organ	(N/A)	The Church Quarter-Hour	*8am*
Music	Music / The Gumps		Talk and Music	*8:15*
	The Story of Mary Marlin			*8:30*
	Five-Star Jones			*8:45*
Music / Language Lesson	Talk and Music		Music / Fields and Hall, songs	*9am*
	Music / Looking Forward		Music	*9:15*
Talk and Music	Talk and Music		Music / Helen Guest, songs	*9:30*
	Music / Betty Crocker, cooking		News	*9:45*
	Marie, the Little French Princess		Music / Ann Warner Chats	*10am*
	The Romance of Helen Trent			*10:15*
	Between the Bookends		Talk and Music	*10:30*
	Happy Hollow			*10:45*
	Music / The Kate Smith Matinee Hour		Talk and Music	*11am*
			Vic and Sade	*11:15*
			Ma Perkins	*11:30*
			Music / Dreams Come True	*11:45*
	Music / Visiting America's Little House		Betty and Bob	*12pm*
News	Talk and Music		The National Farm and HomeHour	*12:15*
Music / Culbertson Club Bridge Talk				*12:30*
Music				*12:45*
	Music		Stock Market Reports	*1pm*
			Al Lyon Orchestra	*1:15*
The Borowsky Concert Quartet	University of the Air		Talk and Music	*1:30*
	Talk and Music			*1:45*

DAYTIME — SUMMER, 1935

Sunday

	BLUE	CBS	KNX	NBC
2pm	The Catholic Hour	National Amateur Night		The Makers of History
2:15				
2:30	Records	The Three Browns Bears		Grand Hotel
2:45	Roaming the South Seas	The Dictators		
3pm	The Classic Hour	Vivian Della Chiesa, songs		Sarah Kriendler, violin
3:15				Paul Martin and Jean Allen, songs
3:30		Summer Serenade		The Moody Institute Singers
3:45				
4pm		Rhythm at Eight, Ethel Merman		Major Bowes' Original Amateur Hour
4:15				
4:30	USC College of Music	Rabbi Magnin, religion		
4:45		Marshall Sohl, songs		

DAYTIME — SUMMER, 1935

Monday-Friday

BLUE	CBS	KNX	NBC	
The Classic Hour	The Happy Go Lucky Hour		Woman's Magazine of the Air	2pm
				2:15
				2:30
				2:45
Talk and Music	Feminine Fancies		Pictorial	3pm
			Music	3:15
	Talk and Music		Dot and Will, songs	3:30
			Music	3:45
	Music		Fibber McGee and Molly / One Man's Family / The Fleischman Yeast Hour, Rudy Vallee / Irene Rich Dramas /	4pm
			Music /	4:15
				4:30
			Music / Easy Aces	4:45

DAYTIME — SUMMER, 1935

Saturday

	BLUE	CBS	KNX	NBC
8am	Bibie Fellowship (7:30AM)	Music	(N/A)	The Church Quarter-Hour
8:15				Genia Fonariova, songs
8:30				Words and Music
8:45				
9am		Jack Shannon, songs		County Medical Association Talks
9:15		Looking Forward		News
9:30		News		The National Farm and Home Hour
9:45		Billy Mills and Company		
10am	The Classic Hour	Madison Ensemble		
10:15				
10:30		Maurice Sherman Orchestra		The Weekend Revue
10:45				
11am		On the Village Green		
11:15				
11:30		Buffalo Presents		The NBC Music Guild
11:45				
12pm		Three Little Words		
12:15	News	Among Our Souvenirs		US Agricultural Talks
12:30	Records	Chicagoans Orchestra		
12:45				
1pm		Frank Dailey Orchestra		Stock Market Reports
1:15				Music
1:30	The Borowsky Concert Quartet	Elsie Thompson, organ		Austin Wylie Orchestra
1:45				

DAYTIME — SUMMER, 1935

Saturday

	BLUE	CBS	KNX	NBC
2pm	The Classic Hour	Frederick William Wile, news		Kearney Walton Orchestra
2:15		The Dalton Brothers, songs		
2:30		Dance Orchestra		Songs
2:45				The Master Builder
3pm		Music		The Art of Living
3:15				Jamboree
3:30				
3:45				Music
4pm	Records	The Modern Minstrels		Your Hit Parade
4:15				
4:30				
4:45		H. V. Kaltenborn, news		

EVENING — FALL, 1935

Sunday

	BLUE	CBS	KNX	NBC
5pm	Music	The Country Church of Hollywood	Ethel Huber, talk	Major Bowes' Original Amateur Hour
5:15			The Jewel Box	
5:30		The Leslie Howard Theater	Father Vaughn, religion	
5:45			John Brown Univerisity	
6pm	News	The Ford Sunday Evening Hour	The Lubovisiki Trio	The Manhattan Merry-Go-Round
6:15	Burt Shepard, violin			
6:30			Rev. Fuller, religion	The American Album of Familiar Music
6:45				
7pm	Sacred Concert	Lady Esther Serenade		The General Motors Concert
7:15				
7:30	Nick Harris	The Old Hymnal	Christian Epic	
7:45	Light Opera	The Bella Schafer Concert	Judge Rutherford, legal talk	
8pm	Records	The Eddie Cantor Show	The First Presbyterian Church of Hollywood	Sunset Dreams, The Morin Sisters
8:15				Walter Winchell's Jergens Journal
8:30		The Voice of Experience		The Jello Program, Jack Benny
8:45		The Bella Schafer Concert		
9pm		The University Explorer	News	Life is a Song
9:15			Dr. Thomas, religion	
9:30		Musical Moments	The Dude Ranch	One Man's Family
9:45		Dance Orchestra		
10pm	Musical Celebrities	The Ten o'Clock Wire		The Richfield Reporter
10:15	Bridge to Dreamland	Edwin Schallert, interview		Twenty Years After
10:30		Larry Lee Orchestra		
10:45				The Backyard Astronomer

EVENING — FALL, 1935

Monday

BLUE	CBS	KNX	NBC	
How Songs Grew	Music	Dick Tracy	Fibber McGee and Molly	5pm
		Tom Mix and His Ralston Straight Shooters		5:15
	The Harmonettes	Kearney Walton Orchestra	The Southern Harmony Four	5:30
Once Upon a Time	The Harmonica Harlequins	Little Orphan Annie	Popeye, the Sailor	5:45
	The Lux Radio Theater	Jack Armstrong, the All-American Boy	Music	6pm
News and Views		News		6:15
		The Lucea Concert	Vick's Open House	6:30
Wesley Tourtellotte, organ		The Air Adventures of Jimmy Allen		6:45
	Lady Esther Serenade	Frank Watanabe and Honorable Archie	The Carnation Contented Hour	7pm
		Lane and Woodruff, songs		7:15
	The March of Time	The In-Laws	Your Program	7:30
Albert Bergman, legal talk	Public Affairs	King's Cowboy Revue		7:45
	The Story of Myrt and Marge	The Emil Baffa Concert	Amos 'n' Andy	8pm
	Singin' Sam, the Barbasol Man	Lilac Time	Lum and Abner	8:15
Ports of Call	Pick and Pat	Songs	The Voice of Firestone	8:30
		The Townsend Plan		8:45
News and Views	Seymour Simon Orchestra	News	The New Penny	9pm
	Those O'Malleys	Musical Moments		9:15
	Laurie Higgins Orchestra	Character Analysis	Hawthorne House	9:30
		The Dude Ranch		9:45
Fishing and Hunting Talk	The Ten o'Clock Wire		The Richfield Reporter	10pm
Musical Celebrities	The National Emergency Council		Ben Alexander, stories	10:15
	Dance Orchestra		Jimmy Grier Orchestra	10:30
				10:45

EVENING — FALL, 1935

Tuesday

	BLUE	CBS	KNX	NBC
5pm	Records (3:30pm)	The Harmonettes	Dick Tracy	Music
5:15		Edith Karen, songs	Kearney Walton Orchestra	
5:30		The Packard Show, Lawrence Tibbett		Robert Hurd, songs
5:45			Little Orphan Annie	Popeye, the Sailor
6pm		Trails of Yankee Trade	Jack Armstrong, the All-American Boy	NTG and His Girls
6:15	News and Views	Music	News	
6:30		The Country Church of Hollywood	The Lucea Concert	Eddy Duchin Orchestra
6:45	Wesley Tourtellotte, organ		The Air Adventures of Jimmy Allen	
7pm		Sterling Young Orchestra	Frank Watanabe and Honorable Archie	Studio Party
7:15		Public Affairs	Drury Lane, songs	
7:30	The Borowsky Concert Quartet	The March of Time	The In-Laws	The Night Editor
7:45		Bolero's	King's Cowboy Revue	The Old Memory Box
8pm		The Story of Myrt and Marge	The Emil Baffa Concert	Amos 'n' Andy
8:15		Tapestries of Life	Lilac Time	Lum and Abner
8:30		The Camel Caravan, Walter O'Keefe	Homer Canfield, songs	Johnny Presents
8:45				
9pm	News	Fred Waring Orchestra	News	Death Valley Days
9:15	The Community Chest		Elinor Gail, songs	
9:30			P. L. Ferguson, talk	Enos Crime Clues
9:45			The Dude Ranch	
10pm	Musical Masterpieces	The Ten o'Clock Wire		The Richfield Reporter
10:15		Eddie Oliver Orchestra		Music
10:30		Larry Lee Orchestra		
10:45		Sterling Young Orchestra	Pietro Pontrelli Orchestra	Jimmy Grier Orchestra

EVENING — FALL, 1935

Wednesday

BLUE	CBS	KNX	NBC	
Time Clock of Ideas	The Cavalcade of America	Dick Tracy	One Man's Family	5pm
		Tom Mix and His Ralston Straight Shooters		5:15
	Public Affairs	Kearney Walton Orchestra	Tea Time	5:30
Once Upon a Time	Stories of Life	Little Orphan Annie	Popeye, the Sailor	5:45
	The Chesterfield Show	Jack Armstong, the All-American Boy	Our Home on the Range, John C. Thomas	6pm
News		News		6:15
The Chamber of Commerce	Six-Gun Justice	The Lucea Concert	Twenty Thousand Years in Sing Sing	6:30
Twilight Reveries		The Air Adventures of Jimmy Allen		6:45
	Calling All Cars	Frank Watanabe and Honorable Archie	The Log Cabin Revue	7pm
The Opera Hour		Syud Hosnian, talk		7:15
	The March of Time	The In-Laws	Jimmy Fidler, gossip	7:30
	Strange As It Seems	King's Cowboy Revue	The Caswell Concert	7:45
	The Story of Myrt and Marge	Music	Amos 'n' Andy	8pm
	The Male Chorus Parade	Lilac Time	Lum and Abner	8:15
	The Campbell's Tomato Juice Program, Burns and Allen	The News Parade	The House of Glass	8:30
		Rosicrucians		8:45
News	Raymond Paige Presents	News	Town Hall Tonight, Fred Allen	9pm
Maurice Zam, piano	Those O'Malleys	Musical Moments		9:15
	Sterling Young Orchestra	Music		9:30
	Anson Weeks Orchestra	The Dude Ranch		9:45
Concert Favorites	The Ten o'Clock Wire		The Richfield Reporter	10pm
	Eddie Oliver Orchestra		Rendezvous	10:15
	Larry Lee Orchestra	The Russian Eagle Quartet		10:30
	Sterling Young Orchestra	Pietro Pontrelli Orchestra	Jimmy Grier Orchestra	10:45

EVENING — FALL, 1935

Thursday

	BLUE	CBS	KNX	NBC
5pm	James Samuel Lacy, talk	The Community Chest	Dick Tracy	The Fleischmann Yeast Hour, Rudy Vallee
5:15		Music	Kearney Walton Orchestra	
5:30		Wiliam Daly Orchestra		
5:45			Little Orphan Annie	
6pm		Laurie Higgins Orchestra	Jack Armstong, the All-American Boy	The Maxwell House Showboat
6:15	News and Views	Public Affairs	News	
6:30		To Arms for Peace	The Lucea Concert	
6:45	Wesley Tourtellotte, organ		The Air Adventures of Jimmy Allen	
7pm		The Alemite Half-Hour	Frank Watanabe and Honorable Archie	The Kraft Music Hall, Bing Crosby
7:15			Drury Lane, songs	
7:30		The March of Time	The In-Laws	
7:45		Music	King's Cowboy Revue	
8pm		The Story of Myrt and Marge	Three-Quarter Time	Amos 'n' Andy
8:15		Frank Prince, songs	Lilac Time	The Standard Symphony Hour
8:30		The Camel Caravan, Walter O'Keefe	Songs	
8:45			Smilin' Ed McConnell, songs	
9pm	News and Views	Mobil Magazine	News	
9:15			The Dude Ranch	Winning of the West
9:30		Musical Moments		
9:45	John Teel, songs	Sterling Young Orchestra		Wesley Tourtellotte, organ
10pm	Musical Celebrities	The Ten o'Clock Wire		The Richfield Reporter
10:15		The Times Sports Edition	Sue Douglas, songs	Al Gayle, accordian
10:30			The Russian Eagle Quartet	Jimmy Grier Orchestra
10:45		Larry Lee Orchestra	Pietro Pontrelli Orchestra	

EVENING — FALL, 1935

Friday

BLUE	CBS	KNX	NBC	
Records (3:30PM)	Spanish Troubadours	The American Legion	Irene Rich Dramas	5pm
Care of the Eyes	World Affairs	Tom Mix and His Ralston Straght Shooters	Dr. Dougall, health	5:15
	Broadway Varieties	Kearney Walton Orchestra	College Prom, Ruth Etting	5:30
Once Upon a Time		Little Orphan Annie		5:45
	Hollywood Hotel	Jack Armstrong, the All-American Boy	Men and Empire	6pm
News and Views		News		6:15
		The Lucea Concert	The Court of Human Relations	6:30
Wesley Tourtellotte, organ		The Air Adventures of Jimmy Allen		6:45
Leo McDonald, sports	The Inglewood Park Concert	Frank Watanabe and Honorable Archie	The First Nighter Program	7pm
Jerry Joyce Orchestra		Woodruff and Lane, songs		7:15
Behind the Headlines	The March of Time	The In-Laws	The Elgin Campus Revue	7:30
Public Affairs	Strange As It Seems	King's Cowboy Revue		7:45
	The Story of Myrt and Marge	Rheba Crawford, songs	Amos 'n' Andy	8pm
	Lazy Dan, the Minstrel Man	Lilac Time	Lum and Abner	8:15
		Dramatized News	The Palmolive Beauty Box Theater	8:30
	Music	The Townsend Plan		8:45
News and Views	Richard Himber Orchestra	News		9pm
		Musical Moments		9:15
	The Witch's Tale	Character Analysis	The Galaxy of Stars	9:30
		The Hollywood Legion Fights		9:45
Musical Celebrities	The Ten o'Clock Wire		The Richfield Reporter	10pm
	Anson Weeks Orchestra		Norman Sper, sports	10:15
	Larry Lee Orchestra		Culbertson Club Bridge Talk	10:30
	Sterling+G1381 Young Orchestra		Jimmy Grier Orchestra	10:45

EVENING — FALL, 1935

Saturday

	BLUE	CBS	KNX	NBC
5pm	The Classic Hour (2:00PM)	Public Affairs	Kearney Walton Orchestra	Your Hit Parade
5:15				
5:30		California Melodies	The Sunday School Class	
5:45				
6pm		The Chesterfield Show	Musical Auction	The Chevrolet Show
6:15			News	
6:30		Marty May Time	The Emil Baffa Concert	Shell Chateau, Wallace Beery
6:45			The Lubovisiki Trio	
7pm	Raine Bennett, rhymes	Music		
7:15			Ethel Huber, talk	
7:30			Music	Carefree Carnival
7:45				
8pm		Eddie Oliver Orchestra	The Hollywood Barn Dance	The National Barn Dance
8:15		Tapestries of Life		
8:30				
8:45		Larry Lee Orchestra		
9pm	News	Merle Carlson Orchestra	News	Strange Cases
9:15	Records	Those O'Malleys	The Hollywood Barn Dance	
9:30		Musical Moments		Al Lyon Orchestra
9:45		Sterliing Young Orchestra		
10pm	Musical Celebrities	The Ten o'Clock Wire	Pasadena Dance Orchestra	Waltz Time
10:15		Bert Woodward Orchestra		
10:30			The Russian Eagle Quartet	Frank Andrews, news
10:45		Dance Orchestra	Pietro Pontrelli Orchestra	Jimmy Grier Orchestra

DAYTIME — FALL, 1935

Sunday

	BLUE	CBS	KNX	NBC
8am	(Off the Air)	The Times Comics Pages	The Solemn Pontifical Mass	The Church Quarter-Hour
8:15				Neighbor Nell
8:30	Records	Toni D'Orazi, cartoons		Major Bowes' Capitol Family
8:45		The Salt Lake Tabernacle Choir		
9am			Lal Chand Mehra, india talk	
9:15		Songs Across the Border		
9:30			Rabbi Winkler, religion	The Radio City Music Hall
9:45		International Broadcast		
10am	Maurice Zam, piano	The CBS Church of the Air	Dr. King, religion	
10:15				
10:30	Highlights of the Bible	Eddie Dunstedter, organ		Victor Allen, piano
10:45		Sisters of the Skillet	Temple Baptist Church	Dr. Casselbury, health
11am	Records	The Canadian Grenadiers		The Magic Key of RCA
11:15				
11:30		Between the Bookends		
11:45		Blue Flames		
12pm		New York Philharmonic Orchestra		Words to the Wise
12:15			The Emil Baffa Concert	Music
12:30				The Widow's Sons
12:45				
1pm	Old Age Pension Talk			The Sunday Special
1:15				

DAYTIME — FALL, 1935

Monday-Friday

BLUE	CBS	KNX	NBC	
Bible Fellowship (7:30AM)	Talk / Hymns of All Churches	Music / Sharpsville (7:45AM)	The Church Quarter-Hour	*8am*
	Music		Music / Happy Ktichen	*8:15*
	Music / Mary Mantell, songs		Music / Your Child	*8:30*
	Just Plain Bill		Talk and Music	*8:45*
Talk and Music	The Voice of Experience	Dr. Thomas, religion		*9am*
	The Gumps / Betty Crocker, cooking			*9:15*
	The Story of Mary Marlin			*9:30*
	Five-Star Jones	News	News	*9:45*
	Music / Hostess Counsel	The Ten O' Clock Family	Talk and Music	*10am*
	Music		Music / The Community Chest	*10:15*
	Talk and Music / How to Be Charming	Talk and Music	Music	*10:30*
	The Newlyweds		Music / Ann Warner Chats	*10:45*
Talk	Between the Bookends	Fletcher Wiley, talk	Talk and Music / The Standard School Broadcast	*11am*
	Happy Hollow			*11:15*
	The American School f the Air	Music	The National Farm and HomeHour	*11:30*
				11:45
	News	News		*12pm*
News	Talk and Music	Music	Ma Perkins	*12:15*
Talk and Music	Talk and Music / Whoa, Oincus		Vic and Sade	*12:30*
			The O'Neills	*12:45*
	Talk and Music	Pietro Pontrelli Orchestra	Betty and Bob	*1pm*
			Music / Charlie Wellman and Company	*1:15*

DAYTIME — FALL, 1935

Sunday

	BLUE	CBS	KNX	NBC
1:30	Vocational Adjustment		Carefree Capers	Design for Living
1:45	The Hollywood Conservatory of Music			
2pm	The Classic Hour	Maric Golden, piano	The Exposition Park Concert	Penthouse Serenade
2:15		Music		
2:30		Eunice Steele, songs		What's New
2:45		Music		
3pm	The Catholic Hour	National Amateur Night		Transcription
3:15				Walkikians
3:30	Records	Smilin' Ed MdConnell, songs		Grand Hotel
3:45		Rabbi Magnin, religion		
4pm		The Town Crier	Charles Lindsley, literary talk	Music
4:15				A. P. Terhune's Dog Dramas
4:30		The Mummers	Dr. Thomas, religion	Believe It or Not
4:45				

DAYTIME — FALL, 1935

Monday-Friday

BLUE	CBS	KNX	NBC	
The Radio Guild / The Borowsky Concert Quartet	University of the Air		Music	*1:30*
	Music			*1:45*
The Classic Hour	The Happy Go Lucky Hour	The Bookworm	Music / Al Pearce and His Gang	*2pm*
				2:15
		Music	Music	*2:30*
			Clara, Lu and Em	*2:45*
Talk / The Italian Language	Feminine Fancies	Talk and Music	Women's Magazine of the Air	*3pm*
				3:15
Records	Music	Fletcher Wiley, talk		*3:30*
				3:45
		Hometown Sketches	Sports / Easy Aces	*4pm*
		Music	Talk and Music	*4:15*
				4:30
		Music / Dr. McCoy, health	Pictorial	*4:45*

DAYTIME — FALL, 1935

Saturday

	BLUE	CBS	KNX	NBC
8am	Bible Fellowship (7:30AM)	Hymns of All Churches	The Sharples Gang (7:45AM)	The Church Quarter-Hour
8:15		Cincinatti Conservatory Symphony		Happy Kitchen
8:30				Mexican Marimba Typica Band
8:45		John T. Whitaker, songs		
9am		The Salvation Army	Dr. Thomas, religion	County Medical Association Talks
9:15				News
9:30	Public Schools	Allen Roth's Syncopators	Jose Manzanares Orchestra	The National Farm and Home Hour
9:45			News	
10am		Jack Shannon, songs	The Ten O'Clock Family	
10:15		Poetic Strings		
10:30		Football Souvenir	Sue Douglas, songs	Lick Fidler Orchestra
10:45		Sports		Sports
11am			Frances Patton, piano	
11:15				
11:30				
11:45				
12pm			News	
12:15	News		Pauline Holden, songs	
12:30	Records		Marshall Grant, organ	
12:45				
1pm			Pietro Pontrelli Orchestra	
1:15				
1:30	The Borowsky Concert Quartet	Frank Dailey Orchestra		Fascinating Rhythm
1:45				The Vagabonds Quartet

DAYTIME — FALL, 1935

Saturday

	BLUE	CBS	KNX	NBC
2pm	The Classic Hour	Buffalo Presents		
2:15		Sports	Sports	Sports
2:30				
2:45				
3pm				
3:15				
3:30				
3:45				
4pm				
4:15				
4:30				
4:45		Sunset Serenade		

LISTINGS FOR 1936

EVENING — WINTER, 1936

Sunday

	BLUE	CBS	KNX	NBC
5pm	Records (4:00PM)	The Sunday Free-for-All	Ethel Huber, talk	Major Bowes' Original Amateur Hour
5:15			Rev. Schuler, religion	
5:30			Father Vaughn, religion	
5:45			The Lamplighter	
6pm	News	The Ford Sunday Evening Hour	The Lubovisiki Trio	The Manhattan Merry-Go-Round
6:15	Burt Shepard, violin			
6:30			Rev. Fuller, religion	The American Album of Familiar Music
6:45				
7pm	The Reader's Guide	Lady Esther Serenade		The General Motors Concert
7:15				
7:30	Sunday Evening at Seth Parker's	The Bella Schafer Concert	New Tunes	
7:45		The Old Hymnal	Judge Rutherford, legal talk	
8pm		The Eddie Cantor Show	The First Presbyterian Church of Hollywood	Sunset Dreams, The Morin Sisters
8:15	Walter Winchell's Jergens Journal			Walkikians
8:30	Paul Whiteman's Musical Varieties	The Voice of Experience		The Jello Program, Jack Benny
8:45		The Bella Schafer Concert		
9pm		The Leslie Howard Theater	News	Life is a Song
9:15	Records		Music	
9:30		The University Explorer	The Crockett Family	One Man's Family
9:45				
10pm		The Ten o'Clock Wire		The Richfield Reporter
10:15	Musical Celebrities	Edwin Schallert, interview		Twenty Years After
10:30		Larry Lee Orchestra		
10:45				Bridge to Dreamland

EVENING — WINTER, 1936

Monday

BLUE	CBS	KNX	NBC	
Hermes, the Story Teller	Trails of Yankee Trade	Dick Tracy	Fibber McGee and Molly	5pm
How Songs Grew	Los Angeles Fire Department Orchestra	Tom Mix and His Ralston Straight Shooters		5:15
	Sports	Congo Bartlett	An Evening in Paris	5:30
Chansonette	Johnny Burkhart Orchestra	Little Orphan Annie		5:45
News and Views	The Lux Radio Theater	Jack Armstrong, the All-American Boy	Dinner Concert	6pm
		News	Musical Moments	6:15
Wesley Tourtellotte, organ		Songs	Vick's Open House	6:30
		The Air Adventures of Jimmy Allen		6:45
	Lady Esther Serenade	Elmer Goes Hollywood	The Carnation Contented Hour	7pm
		The Laff Parade		7:15
	The March of Time	The In-Laws	Your Program	7:30
Albert Bergman, legal talk	The Modern Treasure Hunters	King's Cowboy Revue		7:45
	The Story of Myrt and Marge	Music	Amos 'n' Andy	8pm
	Singin' Sam, the Barbasol Man	Famous Jury Trials	Lum and Abner	8:15
Ports of Call	Pick and Pat		The Voice of Firestone	8:30
		The Townsend Plan		8:45
News and Views	The California Sunshine Hour	News	The New Penny	9pm
		Musical Moments		9:15
Records	Those O'Malleys		Hawthorne House	9:30
	Jimmy Bittick Orchestra	The Crockett Family		9:45
Fishing and Hunting Talk	The Ten o'Clock Wire		The Richfield Reporter	10pm
Musical Celebrities	Ted Dawson Ordhestra		Ben Alexander, stories	10:15
	Dance Orchestra		Dance Orchestra	10:30
			Mark Hopkins Orchestra	10:45

EVENING — WINTER, 1936

Tuesday

	BLUE	CBS	KNX	NBC
5pm	Hermes, the Story Teller	The National Emergency Council	Dick Tracy	The Beaux Arts Trio
5:15	Once Upon a Time	Sports	Kearney Walton Orchestra	
5:30		The Packard Show, Lawrence Tibbett		Robert Hurd, songs
5:45			Little Orphan Annie	Popeye, the Sailor
6pm	News and Views	Trails of Yankee Trade	Jack Armstong, the All-American Boy	NTG and His Girls
6:15		Garlord Carter, organ	News	
6:30	Twilight Revelries	The Country Church of Hollywood	Music	The Jumbo Fire Chief Show, Jimmy Durante
6:45			The Air Adventures of Jimmy Allen	
7pm		Drums	Elmer Goes Hollywood	Studio Party
7:15	Records		Drury Lane, songs	
7:30		The March of Time	The In-Laws	Jimmy Fidler, gossip
7:45		Tapestries of Life	King's Cowboy Revue	Salon Moderne
8pm		The Story of Myrt and Marge	Music	Amos 'n' Andy
8:15		Frank Prince, songs		Lum and Abner
8:30	Theater Echoes	The Camel Caravan, Walter O'Keefe		Johnny Presents
8:45				
9pm	News and Views	Fred Waring Orchestra	News	Death Valley Days
9:15			Music	
9:30	Tone Poems	Will Osborn Orchestra		Enos Crime Clues
9:45		Musical Moments	The Crockett Family	
10pm	Command Performance	The Ten o'Clock Wire		The Richfield Reporter
10:15		Dance Orchestra		Ben Bernie, the Old Maestro
10:30		Larry Lee Orchestra	Reflections of Romance	
10:45		Sterling Young Orchestra	Pietro Pontrelli Orchestra	Jimmy Grier Orchestra

EVENING — WINTER, 1936

Wednesday

BLUE	CBS	KNX	NBC	
Hermes, the Story Teller	The Cavalcade of America	Dick Tracy	One Man's Family	5pm
Time Clock of Ideas		Tom Mix and His Ralston Straight Shooters		5:15
	Sports	Congo Bartlett	Tea Dance	5:30
	Stories of Life	Little Orphan Annie	Popeye, the Sailor	5:45
The Versailies Peace Conference Program	The Chesterfield Show	Jack Armstong, the All-American Boy	Music	6pm
		News		6:15
	Refreshment Time	Music	Twenty Thousand Years in Sing Sing	6:30
		The Air Adventures of Jimmy Allen		6:45
Music	Gangbusters	Elmer Goes Hollywood	Our Home on the Range, John C. Thomas	7pm
		The Laff Parade		7:15
	The March of Time	The In-Laws	Musical Moments	7:30
	Strange As It Seems	King's Cowboy Revue	The Caswell Concert	7:45
The Opera Hour	The Story of Myrt and Marge	Music	Amos 'n' Andy	8pm
	The Male Chorus Parade		Lum and Abner	8:15
	The Campbell's Tomato Juice Program, Burns and Allen	The News Parade	Rendezous	8:30
		Tunes		8:45
News and Views	Music	News	Town Hall Tonight, Fred Allen	9pm
		Music		9:15
Maurice Zam, piano	Those O'Malleys	The Crockett Family		9:30
	Sterling Young Orchestra			9:45
Concert Favorites	The Ten o'Clock Wire		The Richfield Reporter	10pm
	Ted Dawson Orchestra		Tom Coakley Orchestra	10:15
	Larry Lee Orchestra	The Haven of Rest	Eddie Fitzpatrick Orchestra	10:30
	Sterling Young Orchestra			10:45

EVENING — WINTER, 1936

Thursday

	BLUE	CBS	KNX	NBC
5pm	Hermes, the Story Teller	Sports	Dick Tracy	The Fleischmann Yeast Hour, Rudy Vallee
5:15	NBC String Symphony	Music	Kearney Walton Orchestra	
5:30		Phil Cook, Just Another Amateur		
5:45	James Samuel Lacy, talk		Little Orphan Annie	
6pm	News and Views	Public Affairs	Jack Armstrong, the All-American Boy	The Maxwell House Showboat
6:15			News	
6:30	Wesley Tourtellotte, organ		Music	
6:45			The Air Adventures of Jimmy Allen	
7pm		The Alemite Half-Hour	Elmer Goes Hollywood	The Kraft Music Hall Bing Crosby
7:15	Tone Poems		Music	
7:30		The March of Time	The In-Laws	
7:45	Public Affairs	Bolero's	King's Cowboy Revue	
8pm	Concert Favorites	The Story of Myrt and Marge	Music	Amos 'n' Andy
8:15		The Other Woman's Diary		The Standard Symphony Hour
8:30		The Camel Caravan, Walter O'Keefe		
8:45				
9pm	News and Views	Mobil Magazine	News	
9:15			Music	Winning of the West
9:30		Musical Moments	The Crockett Family	
9:45		Sterling Young Orchestra		Blythe Taylor Burns, songs
10pm	Musical Celebrities	The Ten o'Clock Wire		The Richfield Reporter
10:15		The Times Sports Edition		Music
10:30		Larry Lee Orchestra	The Red Dagger Cafe'	Jimmy Grier Orchestra
10:45				

EVENING — WINTER, 1936

Friday

BLUE	CBS	KNX	NBC	
Hermes, the Story Teller	Paul Keast, songs	The Lamplighter	Irene Rich Dramas	5pm
Once Upon a Time	World Affairs	Tom Mix and His Ralston Straight Shooters	Music	5:15
	Broadway Varieties	Congo Bartlett		5:30
Romance		Little Orphan Annie		5:45
News and Views	Hollywood Hotel	Jack Armstong, the All-American Boy	Al Pearce and His Gang	6pm
		News		6:15
Wesley Tourtellotte, organ		Music	Concert Hall	6:30
		The Air Adventures of Jimmy Allen	The California Safety Council	6:45
	Calling All Cars	Elmer Goes Hollywood	The First Nighter Program	7pm
The College Music Series		Yesteryear Songs		7:15
	The March of Time	The In-Laws	Musical Moments	7:30
	Strange As It Seems	King's Cowboy Revue	Helene Hill, piano	7:45
Masters Immortal	The Story of Myrt and Marge	Rheba Crawford, songs	Amos 'n' Andy	8pm
	Lazy Dan, the Minstrel Man	Music	Lum and Abner	8:15
			The Court of Human Relations	8:30
	Sterling Young Orchestra	The Townsend Plan		8:45
News and Views	Richard Himber Orchestra	News	Fred Waring Orchestra	9pm
		Musical Moments		9:15
Music	The Witch's Tale	Stage and Screen Echoes	The Galaxy of Stars	9:30
		The Hollywood Legion Fights		9:45
Command Performance	The Ten o'Clock Wire		The Richfield Reporter	10pm
	Jimmy Bittick Orchestra		Music	10:15
	Larry Lee Orchestra		Eddie Fitzpatrick Orchestra	10:30
	Sterlnig Young Orchestra			10:45

EVENING — WINTER, 1936

Saturday

	BLUE	CBS	KNX	NBC
5pm	Tea Time (4:30PM)	Sports	Kearney Walton Orchestra	Your Hit Parade
5:15	Boston Symphony Orchestra	Tom Coakley Orchestra		
5:30		Salon Moderne	The Lamplighter	
5:45			The Monitor Children's Program	
6pm		The Chesterfield Show	Musical Auction	The Chevrolet Show
6:15	News		News	
6:30	Wesley Tourtellotte, organ	The Pacific School of Music	Music	Shell Chateau, Al Jolson
6:45		Tapestries of Life	The Lubovisiki Trio	
7pm	Raine Bennett, rhymes	Public Affairs		
7:15			The World Revue	
7:30				The Corn Cob Pipe Club
7:45			Let's Go Places	
8pm	The Music Hall	The Palmolive Beauty Box Theater	The Hollywood Barn Dance	The National Barn Dance
8:15				
8:30				
8:45				
9pm	News and Views	Musical Moments	News	The Packard Fiesta
9:15		Larry Lee Orchestra	The Hollywood Barn Dance	
9:30	Music	Those O'Malleys		Frank Andrews, news
9:45		Jimmy Bittick Orchestra		Hotel Fifth Avenue Orchestra
10pm	Musical Celebrities	The Ten o'Clock Wire	Pasadena Dance Orchestra	Waltz Time
10:15		Sterling Young Orchestra		
10:30		Jimmy Bain Orchestra		Tom Coakley Orchestra
10:45		Gigi Royee Orchestra	Pietro Pontrelli Orchestra	

DAYTIME — WINTER, 1936

Sunday

	BLUE	CBS	KNX	NBC
8am	Sacred Concert	The Times Comics Pages	Dr. Phillips and the Forty Voice Choir	The Church Quarter-Hour
8:15				The Peerless Trio
8:30	The Classic Hour	Tony D'Orazi, cartoons	The Jewel Box	Major Bowes' Capitol Family
8:45		The Salt Lake Tabernacle Choir	Rev. Shuler, religion	
9am			Lal Chand Mehra, india talk	
9:15				
9:30		Romany Trail	Rabbi Winkler, religion	The Radio City Music Hall
9:45		International Broadcast		
10am	Maurice Zam, piano	The CBS Church of the Air	Dr. King, religion	
10:15			Music	
10:30	Young People's Conference	Musical Footnotes		Heartbeats of the City
10:45		Between the Bookends	Temple Baptist Church	Dr. Casselbury, health
11am	The First Unitarian Church of Hollywood	Murray and Harris, songs		The Magic Key of RCA
11:15		Helene Hughes, songs		
11:30		Walks of Life		
11:45		Bob Allen, piano		
12pm		New York Philharmonic Orchestra	Music	Your English
12:15				Nick Harris
12:30				The Metropolitan Opera Auditions
12:45				
1pm	National Vespers		Father Charles Couglin, religion	The Sunday Special

DAYTIME — WINTER, 1936

Monday-Friday

BLUE	CBS	KNX	NBC	
Music	Talk / Hymns of All Churches	Music / Family Altar	The Church Quarter-Hour	*8am*
	The Romance of Helen Trent	Polly Patterson's Pantry	Music / Happy Ktichen	*8:15*
	Just Plain Bill	Music	Music / Your Child	*8:30*
	The Ozark Mountaineers		Music / Hints to Housewives	*8:45*
Talk and Music	The Voice of Experience	Dr. Thomas, religion	Music / Helen Guest, songs	*9am*
	Music / Betty Crocker, cooking		Honeyboy and Sassafras	*9:15*
	The Story of Mary Marlin	Talk and Music	Talk and Music	*9:30*
	Five-Star Jones	News	News	*9:45*
	Music / Hostess Counsel	The Ten o'Clock Family	Talk and Music	*10am*
	Music			*10:15*
	Music / How to Be Charming	Mary Holmes, songs	Music	*10:30*
	The Fred Wild String Trio	Topic Tunes	Music / Ann Warner Chats	*10:45*
	Between the Bookends	Fletcher Wiley, talk	Talk and Music / The Standard School Broadcast	*11am*
	Happy Hollow			*11:15*
	The American School of the Air	Music	The National Farm and HomeHour	*11:30*
				11:45
News	News	News	Forever Young	*12pm*
Talk and Music	Talk and Music	Lataner's Facts	Ma Perkins	*12:15*
		Music	Vic and Sade	*12:30*
			The O'Neills	*12:45*
Talk and Music / The Woman's Radio Revue		Pietro Pontrelli Orchestra	Betty and Bob	*1pm*

DAYTIME — WINTER, 1936

Sunday

	BLUE	CBS	KNX	NBC
1:15				
1:30	Vocational Adjustment			Music
1:45	The Hollywood Conservatory of Music		Music	
2pm	The Classic Hour	Public Affairs	The Exposition Park Concert	Penthouse Serenade
2:15		The Harmonettes		
2:30		Jose Manzaneras Orchestra		Tea-Cup Tunes
2:45				
3pm	The Catholic Hour	National Amateur Night		Music
3:15				
3:30	Fifeld's Friendly Forum	Smilin' Ed MdConnell, songs		Grand Hotel
3:45		Rabbi Magnin, religion		
4pm	Records	Gaylord Carter, organ	Charles Lindsley, literary talk	Popeye, the Sailor
4:15				A. P. Terhune's Dog Dramas
4:30		The Country Church of Hollywood	Dr. Thomas, religion	Believe It or Not
4:45				

DAYTIME — WINTER, 1936

Monday-Friday

BLUE	CBS	KNX	NBC	
			Music / Charlie Wellman and Company	1:15
Talk and Music / The Radio Guild	University of the Air		Talk and Music	1:30
	Music			1:45
The Classic Hour	Music	The Bookworm	Music / Al Pearce and His Gang	2pm
				2:15
	Nothing But the Truth	Music / Francis Patton, piano	Music	2:30
	The Goldbergs			2:45
Talk and Music / The Italian Language	Feminine Fancies	Talk and Music	Women's Magazine of the Air	3pm
				3:15
Talk and Music	Music	Fletcher Wiley, talk		3:30
	Music / H. V. Kaltenborn, news			3:45
	Talk and Music / Buck Rogers of the 25th Century	Hometown Sketches	Talk and Music / Easy Aces	4pm
	Music	Music	Music / Wesley Tortellotte, organ	4:15
Talk / Tea Time	News	Music / Haven of Rest	Charlie Wellman and Company	4:30
	Talk		Pictorial	4:45

DAYTIME — WINTER, 1936

Saturday

	BLUE	CBS	KNX	NBC
8am	Bible Fellowship (7:30AM)	Hymns of All Churches	Melody Palette	Our American Schools
8:15		Cincinatti Conservatory Symphony	Polly Patterson's Pantry	Happy Kitchen
8:30			Music	Mexican Marimba Typica Band
8:45				
9am		St. Andrews Glee Club	Dr. Thomas, religion	County Medical Association Talks
9:15		Musical Reveries		News
9:30	Public Schools	George Hall Orchestra	Jose Manzanares Orchestra	The National Farm and Home Hour
9:45			News	
10am		Jack Shannon, songs	The Ten O'Clock Family	Vladimir Brenner, piano
10:15		Jack and Jill, songs		
10:30		Buffalo Presents	The Song Market	
10:45			Tunes	
11am	The Metropolitan Opera	The Townsend Plan	Frances Patton, piano	The Metropolitan Opera
11:15				
11:30		Tito Guizar, guitar	Carefree Capers	
11:45		St. Dunstan Singers		
12pm		Down by Hermans	News	
12:15			Lataner's Facts	
12:30		Isle of Dreams		
12:45			Russian Ensemble	
1pm		Motor City Melodies	Pietro Pontrelli Orchestra	
1:15				
1:30		Frank E. Hering, talk		
1:45		Music		

DAYTIME — WINTER, 1936

Saturday

	BLUE	CBS	KNX	NBC
2pm	The Classic Hour	Jimmy Bittick Orchestra	Music	Blue Room Echoes
2:15				Clark Dennis, songs
2:30		Vincent Lopez Orchestra		US Agricultural Talks
2:45				
3pm	The Hawaiian Coast Guard Band	Frederick William Wile, news	New Tunes	
3:15		Men of Note	Memory Paths	Otto Thurn Orchestra
3:30	Records	Allen Roth Orchestra	The KNX Show Window	Musical Moments
3:45		Gogo de Lys, songs		Religion in the News
4pm		Nayar Kurkdjie Ensemble	Metropolitan Moods	The New Yorkers
4:15				The Master Builder
4:30	Tea Time	Sunset Serenade	The Haven of Rest	Edwin C. Hill, news
4:45				The Hampton Institute Singers

EVENING — SPRING, 1936

Sunday

	BLUE	CBS	KNX	NBC
5pm	Records	World Dances	Ethel Huber, talk	Major Bowes' Original Amateur Hour
5:15			Rev. Schuler, religion	
5:30	Organ Recital	Public Affairs	Father Vaughn, religion	
5:45			Judge Rutherford, legal talk	
6pm	News and Views	The Ford Sunday Evening Hour	Music	The Manhattan Merry-Go-Round
6:15				
6:30	Walter Winchell's Jergens Journal		Rev. Fuller, religion	The American Album of Familiar Music
6:45	Paul Whiteman's Musical Varieties			
7pm		Musical Tapestries	The Lubovisiki Trio	The General Motors Concert
7:15		Bolero's		
7:30	Dreams of Long Ago	Drums		
7:45				
8pm	Moment Musicale	The Eddie Cantor Show	The First Presbyterian Church of Hollywood	Sunset Dreams, The Morin Sisters
8:15	The Music Master			Music
8:30		The Voice of Experience		The Jello Program, Jack Benny
8:45		The Bela Schaefer Concert		
9pm	The Reader's Guide	The California Sunshine Hour	News	Jack Hylton Orchestra
9:15			Larry Lee Orchestra	
9:30	Operatic Gems	The University Explorer	The Crockett Family	One Man's Family
9:45				
10pm		The Ten o'Clock Wire		The Richfield Reporter
10:15	Musical Celebrities	Edwin Schallert, interview		The Great Gunns
10:30		Nocturnal Serenade	Larry Lee Orchestra	
10:45				Bridge to Dreamland

EVENING — SPRING, 1936

Monday

BLUE	CBS	KNX	NBC	
Ann Arthur's Story Hour	Trails of Yankee Trade	Dick Tracy	Fibber McGee and Molly	5pm
How Songs Grew		Kearney Walton Orchestra		5:15
Music of All Countries	Tony D'Orazi, cartoons	Congo Bartlett	An Evening in Paris	5:30
	Musical Magic	Little Orphan Annie		5:45
News	The Lux Radio Theater	Jack Armstong, the All-American Boy	Dinner Concert	6pm
The Board of Education		News		6:15
Wesley Tourtellotte, organ		Pinto Pete	Studio Party	6:30
		The Air Adventures of Jimmy Allen		6:45
Public Affairs	Lady Esther Serenade	Elmer Goes Hollywood	The Carnation Contented Hour	7pm
		The House in the Sun		7:15
The National Radio Forum	The March of Time	The Newlyweds	Your Program	7:30
	The Goose Creek Parson	King's Cowboy Revue		7:45
Albert Bergman, legal talk	Jack Denny Orchestra	Famous Jury Trials	Amos 'n' Andy	8pm
Frank Watanabe and Honorable Archie	Singin' Sam, the Barbasol Man		Lum and Abner	8:15
	Pick and Pat		The Voice of Firestone	8:30
		The Townsend Plan		8:45
News	The California Sunshine Hour	News	Hawthorne House	9pm
Moment Musicale		Musical Moments		9:15
Scenes de Ballet		The Crockett Family	Public Affairs	9:30
			Dan Emmett, interview	9:45
John P. Cassidy, news	The Ten o'Clock Wire		The Richfield Reporter	10pm
Musical Celebrities	Dick Jurgens Ordhestra		Ben Alexander, stories	10:15
	Merle Carlson Orchestra	Marshall Grant, organ	Jimmy Grier Orchestra	10:30
				10:45

EVENING — SPRING, 1936

Tuesday

	BLUE	CBS	KNX	NBC
5pm	Ann Arthur's Story Hour	The National Emergency Council	Dick Tracy	Music
5:15	Folk Music	Eddie Dudstedter, organ	Kearney Walton Orchestra	The Beaux Arts Trio
5:30	Ebony and Ivory	Laugh with Ken		Robert Hurd, songs
5:45	Creative Education		Little Orphan Annie	Popeye, the Sailor
6pm	News	Musical Moments	Jack Armstrong, the All-American Boy	Ben Bernie, the Old Maestro
6:15	California Safety Talk	Mel Buick, songs	News	
6:30	Organ Recital	Frederick Stark Orchestra	Let's Go Places	The Jumbo Fire Chief Show, Jimmy Durante
6:45			The Air Adventures of Jimmy Allen	
7pm	Silhouette	Parties at Pickfair	Elmer Goes Hollywood	The Eddie Dowling Revue
7:15			Frank Luther, songs	
7:30	Los Angeles Music Appreciation	The March of Time	The Newlyweds	Jimmy Fidler, gossip
7:45	The Pasadena Civic Chorus	Harry Balkin, talk	King's Cowboy Revue	The All-Star Revue
8pm		Music	Famous Jury Trials	Amos 'n' Andy
8:15	Frank Watanabe and Honorable Archie	The Male Chorus Parade		Lum and Abner
8:30	Records	The Camel Caravan, Walter O'Keefe	The Watch Dogs	Johnny Presents
8:45			Pinto Pete	
9pm	News	Fred Waring Orchestra	News	Death Valley Days
9:15	Opera Night		Musical Moments	
9:30		Music	The Crockett Family	Enos Crime Clues
9:45		Musical Moments		
10pm		The Ten o'Clock Wire		The Richfield Reporter
10:15		Dance Orchestra		Dance Orchestra
10:30		Sterling Young Orchestra	Pietro Pontrelli Orchestra	Jimmy Grier Orchestra
10:45				

EVENING — SPRING, 1936

Wednesday

BLUE	CBS	KNX	NBC	
Ann Arthur's Story Hour	The Cavalcade of America	Dick Tracy	One Man's Family	*5pm*
Time Clock of Ideas		Kearney Walton Orchestra		*5:15*
	Music	Congo Bartlett	Tea Dance	*5:30*
	Moving Stories of Life	Little Orphan Annie	Popeye, the Saiilor	*5:45*
News	The Chesterfield Show	Jack Armstong, the All-American Boy	The Corn Cob Pipe Club	*6pm*
The Chamber of Commerce		News		*6:15*
Twilight Reveries	Refreshment Time	Drury Lane, songs	The Blue Prelude	*6:30*
		The Air Adventures of Jimmy Allen		*6:45*
Your Hit Parade	Gangbusters	Elmer Goes Hollywood	Our Home on the Range, John C. Thomas	*7pm*
		The House in the Sun		*7:15*
	The March of Time	The Newlyweds	Winning of the West	*7:30*
	Strange As It Seems	King's Cowboy Revue		*7:45*
Music	Music		Amos 'n' Andy	*8pm*
Fra nk Watanabe and Honorable Archie		Tudor Williams Orchestra	Lum and Abner	*8:15*
Music	The Campbell's Tomato Juice Program, Burns and Allen	Larry Lee Orchestra	Death Rides the Highway	*8:30*
		Harry Balkin, talk		*8:45*
News	Ports of Call	News	Town Hall Tonight, Fred Allen	*9pm*
Records		Musical Moments		*9:15*
Maurice Zam, piano	Sterling Young Orchestra	The Crockett Family		*9:30*
				9:45
Command Performance	The Ten o'Clock Wire		The Richfield Reporter	*10pm*
	Dance Orchestra		The Olympic Games Preview	*10:15*
	Eddie Oliver Orchestra	The Haven of Rest	Dance Orchestra	*10:30*
				10:45

EVENING — SPRING, 1936

Thursday

	BLUE	CBS	KNX	NBC
5pm	Ann Arthur's Story Hour	The Air Show	Dick Tracy	The Fleischmann Yeast Hour, Rudy Vallee
5:15			Kearney Walton Orchestra	
5:30		Fray and Baum, piano		
5:45		Rev. Maverick, religion	Little Orphan Annie	
6pm	News and Views	At Sundown	Jack Armstong, the All-American Boy	The Maxwell House Showboat
6:15		Tapestries of Life	News	
6:30	America's Town Meeting of the Air	Gulliver, Ed Wynn	Let's Go Places	
6:45			The Air Adventures of Jimmy Allen	
7pm		The Alemite Half-Hour	Elmer Goes Hollywood	The Kraft Music Hall, Bing Crosby
7:15			Music	
7:30	Rochester Philharmonic Orchestra	The March of Time	The Newlyweds	
7:45		The Goose Creek Parson	King's Cowboy Revue	
8pm	The First Congregational Church Choir	Music	Calling All Cars	Amos 'n' Andy
8:15	Records			The Standard Symphony Hour
8:30		The Camel Caravan, Walter O'Keefe	The Tree of Knowledge	
8:45			Pinto Pete	
9pm	News	Mobil Magazine	News	
9:15	Records		Drury Lane, songs	The Hollywood Talent Parade
9:30		Musical Moments	The Crockett Family	
9:45		Music		Blythe Taylor Burns, songs
10pm	Musical Celebrities	The Ten o'Clock Wire		The Richfield Reporter
10:15		The Times Sports Edition		The Motion Picture Revue
10:30			Officer of the Day	Jimmy Grier Orchestra
10:45		Sterling Young Orchestra		

EVENING — SPRING, 1936

Friday

BLUE	CBS	KNX	NBC	
Ann Arthur's Story Hour	Elbert Lachelle, songs	Kearney Walton Orchestra	Irene Rich Dramas	5pm
Music	Public Affairs		Harry Stanton, talk	5:15
	Broadway Varieties	Congo Bartlett	Music	5:30
		Little Orphan Annie		5:45
News	Hollywood Hotel	Jack Armstong, the All-American Boy		6pm
Music		News		6:15
Wesley Tourtellotte, organ		Music	The Opportunity Parade	6:30
		The Air Adventures of Jimmy Allen		6:45
Music	Calling All Cars	Elmer Goes Hollywood	The First Nighter Program	7pm
		The House in the Sun		7:15
	The March of Time	The Newlyweds	Ry-Krisp Presents Marion Talley	7:30
	Strange As It Seems	King's Cowboy Revue	Music	7:45
	Music	Rheba Crawford, songs	Amos 'n' Andy	8pm
Music			Lum and Abner	8:15
	Paris Night Life	Pinto Pete	The Court of Human Relations	8:30
	The Success Doctor	The Townsend Plan		8:45
News	Richard Himber Orchestra	News	Fred Waring Orchestra	9pm
Records		Musical Moments		9:15
	Guy Lombardo Orchestra	Stage and Screen Echoes	Slices of Life	9:30
		The Hollywood Legion Fights		9:45
Musical Celebrities	The Ten o'Clock Wire		The Richfield Reporter	10pm
	Dance Orchestra		Musical Moments	10:15
	Sterling Young Orchestra		Jimmy Grier Orchestra	10:30
				10:45

EVENING — SPRING, 1936

Saturday

	BLUE	CBS	KNX	NBC
5pm	Jesse Crawford, organ (3:00PM)	Two Piano Concert	Kearney Walton Orchestra	Your Hit Parade
5:15	Boston Symphony Orchestra	Music		
5:30			Fireside Fantasies	
5:45			The Monitor Children's Program	
6pm		The Chesterfield Show	Musical Auction	The Frank Fay Show
6:15	News		News	
6:30	Wesley Tourtellotte, organ	The Pacific School of Music	Music	Shell Chateau, Smith Ballew
6:45			The Lubovisiki Trio	
7pm	Raine Bennett, rhymes	Salon Moderne		
7:15			Public Affairs	
7:30		Gateway to Hollywood	Stage and Screen Echoes	Celebrity Night
7:45			Music	
8pm	Tone Poems		The Hollywood Barn Dance	The National Barn Dance
8:15				
8:30		Musical Moments		
8:45				
9pm	News and Views	The Ziegfeld Follies of the Air	News	Fiesta
9:15			The Hollywood Barn Dance	
9:30	Records			The Galaxy of Stars
9:45				
10pm	Command Performance	The Ten o'Clock Wire	Pasadena Dance Orchestra	Frank Andrews, news
10:15		Cole McElroy Orchestra		Waltz Time
10:30		Bart Woodward Orchestra	Pietro Pontrelli Orchestra	Dance Orchestra
10:45				

DAYTIME — SPRING, 1936

Sunday

	BLUE	CBS	KNX	NBC
8am	Records	The Times Comics Pages	Music	The Church Quarter-Hour
8:15			Lal Chand Mehra, india talk	The Peerless Trio
8:30	The Classic Hour	The Salt Lake Tabernacle Choir		Major Bowes' Capitol Family
8:45			Rev. Shuler, religion	
9am			Dr. Gardener, religion	
9:15				
9:30	The Radio City Music Hall	Garden Chat	Rabbi Winkler, religion	The University of Chicago Round Table
9:45		International Broadcast		
10am		The CBS Church of the Air	Memory Paths	Road to Romany
10:15			Judge Rutherford, legal talk	
10:30	Young People's Conference	Your Little Girls	Dr. King, religion	Music
10:45		Music	Temple Baptist Church	Dr. Casselbury, health
11am	The Magic Key of RCA	Music		Say It With a Song
11:15				
11:30				Peter Absolute
11:45				
12pm	Records	New York Philharmonic Orchestra		Your English
12:15			Metropolitan Moods	Nick Harris
12:30				Ed Younger's Mountaineers
12:45	Henri Deering, piano			
1pm	National Vespers		Father Charles Couglin, religion	The Sunday Special

DAYTIME — SPRING, 1936

Monday-Friday

BLUE	CBS	KNX	NBC	
Music	Music / Hymns of All Churches	Talk and Music / Family Altar	The Church Quarter-Hour	*8am*
	The Romance of Helen Trent	Polly Patterson's Pantry	Music	*8:15*
	Just Plain Bill	Music	Music / Your Child	*8:30*
	Rich Man's Darling		Music	*8:45*
Talk and Music	The Voice of Experience	Dr. Thomas, religion	Music / Gene Arnold and the Ranch Boys	*9am*
	Talk and Music / Betty Crocker, cooking	Music	Talk and Music / Helen Guest, songs	*9:15*
	The Story of Mary Marlin		Music	*9:30*
	Five-Star Jones	News	News	*9:45*
	News	The Ten O'Clock Family	Talk and Music	*10am*
	Talk and Music			*10:15*
		Mary Holmes, songs	Music	*10:30*
		Topic Tunes	Music / Ann Warner Chats	*10:45*
	Between the Bookends	Fletcher Wiley, talk	Talk and Music / The Standard School Broadcast	*11am*
	Happy Hollow			*11:15*
Talk and Music / The Radio Guild	The American School of the Air	Talk and Music		*11:30*
			Mrs. Wiggs of the Cabbage Patch	*11:45*
The National Farm and Home Hour	News	News	Forever Young	*12pm*
	Talk and Music	Music	Ma Perkins	*12:15*
			Vic and Sade	*12:30*
			The O'Neills	*12:45*
Talk / The Woman's Radio Revue		Pietro Pontrelli Orchestra	Betty and Bob	*1pm*

DAYTIME — SPRING, 1936

Sunday

	BLUE	CBS	KNX	NBC
1:15				
1:30	Vocational Adjustment			The Noble Cain A Cappella Choir
1:45			Music	
2pm	The Classic Hour	Public Affairs	The Exposition Park Concert	Music
2:15		The Harmonettes		
2:30		Jose Manzaneras Orchestra		
2:45				
3pm	The Catholic Hour	The Hour of Charm		
3:15				
3:30	Music	Smilin' Ed MdConnell, songs		
3:45		Organ Recital		
4pm	Records	Music	Charles Lindsley, literary talk	Popeye, the Sailor
4:15		The Townsend Place		Walkikians
4:30		Maurice Zam, piano	Dr. Thomas, religion	Believe It or Not
4:45				

DAYTIME — SPRING, 1936

Monday-Friday

BLUE	CBS	KNX	NBC	
			Music / Charlie Wellman and Company	1:15
Talk / The Radio Guild / How to Be Charming	University of the Air		Talk and Music	1:30
	Music			1:45
The Classic Hour	Music	The Bookworm	Music	2pm
				2:15
		Music / Frances Patton, piano		2:30
	The Goldbergs		Happy Kitchen	2:45
Talk and Music / The Italian Language	Feminine Fancies	Talk and Music	Women's Magazine of the Air	3pm
				3:15
Talk and Music	Music	Fletcher Wiley, talk		3:30
				3:45
	New Models and Talent	Hometown Sketches	Talk and Music / Easy Aces	4pm
		Music / The Haven of Rest	Talk and Music / Wesley Tourtellotte, organ	4:15
Tea Time	News			4:30
	Renfrew of the Mounted	Talk and Music	Pictorial	4:45

DAYTIME — SPRING, 1936

Saturday

	BLUE	CBS	KNX	NBC
8am	Concert Favorites	Hymns of All Churches	Melody Palette	Our American Schools
8:15		Cincinatti Conservatory Symphony	Polly Patterson's Pantry	The Norsemen Quartet
8:30	The Junior Radio Journal		Music	Anthony Antobal Orchestra
8:45				Helen Guest, songs
9am		The St. Andrews Glee Club	Dr. Thomas, religion	County Medical Association Talks
9:15		Stewart Churchill, news		News
9:30	Public Schools	George Hall Orchestra	The Song Market	The National Farm and Home Hour
9:45			News	
10am		Jack Shannon, songs	The Ten O'Clock Family	
10:15		Buffalo Presents		
10:30			Metropolitan Moods	Ernie Gill Orchestra
10:45	News	Horse Racing		
11am	Public Affairs	The Notre Dame Glee Club	France s Patton, piano	Horse Racing
11:15				
11:30		The Three Stars	Carefree Capers	Carnegie Tech Symphony
11:45		Concert Miniature		
12pm		Down by Herman's	News	The Merry Madcaps
12:15	Horse Racing		Music	US Agricultural Talk
12:30		Horse Racing	Sports	
12:45				
1pm				The Southern Harmony Four
1:15				The Weekend Revue
1:30			Pietro Pontrelli Orchestra	Rainbow Grill Orchestra
1:45				

DAYTIME — SPRING, 1936

Saturday

	BLUE	CBS	KNX	NBC
2pm	The Classic Hour	The Hartford College Glee Club	Organ Recital	Blue Room Echoes
2:15		Sea Stories		
2:30		Joe Haymes Orchestra	Music	Ted White, songs
2:45		Horse Racing		A Pair of Pianos
3pm	Jesse Crawford, organ	Frederick William Wile, news		Otto Thurn Orchestra
3:15		Gertrude Ross, talk		
3:30		New Models and Talent	The KNX Show Window	Alma Kitchell, talk
3:45				Religion in the News
4pm		Annals of the Ages	Musical Scrapbook	Music
4:15				Tea Dasante
4:30		Music		The Hampton Institute Singers
4:45			Heartbeats of the City	

EVENING — SUMMER, 1936

Sunday

	BLUE	CBS	KNX	NBC
5pm	Cornelia Otis Skinner, talk	The Robin Hood Dell Concerts (4:30PM)	Reunion of the Stars	The Manhattan Merry-Go-Round
5:15	Paul Whiteman's Musical Varieties			
5:30				The American Album of Familiar Music
5:45				
6pm	The Colonial Quartet		The Jones Boys, songs	The National Music Camp
6:15	News		Ethel Huber, talk	
6:30	Dreams of Long Ago	The Gillette Community Sing	Rev. Fuller, religion	
6:45				
7pm	Wesley Tourtellotte, organ	Cocktails of Melody		Sunset Dreams, The Morin Sisters
7:15		Vincent Lopez Orchestra		Comedy Capers
7:30	Records	Bob Crosby Orchestra	The Townsend Plan	The Jello Summer Show, Tim and Irene
7:45			Music	
8pm	The Music Masters	The American Campaign	The First Presbyterian Church of Hollywood	Dance Orchestra
8:15		Johnny Johnson Orchestra		
8:30	Music of All Countries	The Bela Schaefer Concert		One Man's Family
8:45				
9pm	Viennese Interlude	Music	News	The Passing Parade
9:15	Moving Stories		Larry Lee Orchestra	Stringtime
9:30	The Reader's Guide	The University Explorer	The Crockett Family	The Barnstormers
9:45		Franklin McCormick, news		
10pm	Musical Celebrities	The Ten o'Clock Wire		The Richfield Reporter
10:15		Edwin Schallert, interview	Hal Grayson Orchestra	Bridge to Dreamland
10:30		Jan Garber Orchestra	Larry Lee Orchestra	
10:45				

EVENING — SUMMER, 1936

Monday

BLUE	CBS	KNX	NBC	
Ann Arthur's Story Hour	The Lux Radio Theater	Dick Tracy	Captain Dobbs	*5pm*
How Songs Grew		Maurlee Orchestra		*5:15*
Edwin Franko Goldman Band		Music	The Blue Prelude	*5:30*
				5:45
Carefree Carnival	Lady Esther Serenade	Music	The Carnation Contented Hour	*6pm*
		News		*6:15*
	The March of Time	Music	Great Lakes Symphony Orchestra	*6:30*
	Best Bets in Music	Vagabonds Orchestra		*6:45*
News	Clyde Lucas Orchestra	Elmer Goes Hollywood	Amos 'n' Andy	*7pm*
The Stanford Program	Renfrew of the Mounted	Drury Lane, songs	Lum and Abner	*7:15*
Music	Pick and Pat	The Newlyweds	The Voice of Firestone	*7:30*
Albert Bergman, legal talk		King's Cowboy Revue		*7:45*
Henry Busse Orchestra	Public Affairs	Officer of the Day	Fibber McGee and Molly	*8pm*
Frank Watanabe and Honorable Archie	Vincent Lopez Orchestra	Music		*8:15*
	Hawaii Calls		The Champions	*8:30*
News	Donald Novis, songs	The Townsend Plan		*8:45*
Music	The California Sunshine Hour	News	Hawthorne House	*9pm*
		Musical Moments		*9:15*
		The Crockett Family	Keith Beener Orchestra	*9:30*
				9:45
Fishing and Hunting Talk	The Ten o'Clock Wire		The Richfield Reporter	*10pm*
Musical Celebrities	Gaylord Carter, organ	Hal Grayson Orchestra	Marshall's Mavericks	*10:15*
	Jan Garber Orchestra	Marshall Grant, organ	Jimmy Grier Orchestra	*10:30*
				10:45

EVENING — SUMMER, 1936

Tuesday

	BLUE	CBS	KNX	NBC
5pm	Ann Arthur's Story Hour	The Interpreter	Dick Tracy	Ben Bernie, the Old Maestro
5:15	Folk Music	Sonny and Buddy, songs	Maurice Winnick Orchestra	
5:30	Edwin Franko Goldman Band	Benny Goodman's Swiing School	Buddy and Ginger, songs	Ed Wynn and His Grab Bag
5:45	News		Music	
6pm	String Symphony			Nickelodean
6:15			News	
6:30		The March of Time	Peter Kent and Betty Borden, songs	Public Affairs
6:45		The Corner Store Philosopher	Music	
7pm	California Safety Talk	Williard Robison Orchestra	Elmer Goes Hollywood	Amos 'n' Andy
7:15	Twilight Revelries	Renfrew of the Mounted	D. A. Fitts, talk	Lum and Abner
7:30		Laugh with Ken	The Newlyweds	Johnny Presents
7:45			King's Cowboy Revue	
8pm	Andy Sanella Orchestra	Fred Waring Orchestra	Music	Death Valley Days
8:15	Frank Watanabe and Honorable Archie			
8:30		Music		Ben Pollack Orchestra
8:45	News			
9pm	Records	Old Age Revolving Pension	News	The Bank Program
9:15		Rubinoff and His Violin	Jay Whidden Orchestra	
9:30	Opera Night	Rhythm on the Range	The Crockett Family	Music
9:45		Jan Garber Orchestra		
10pm		The Ten o'Clock Wire		The Richfield Reporter
10:15		Ellis Kimball Orchestra	Hal Grayson Orchestra	Ran Wilde Orchestra
10:30		Harry Lewis Orchestra	Pietro Pontrelli Orchestra	Jimmy Grier Orchestra
10:45				

EVENING — SUMMER, 1936

Wednesday

BLUE	CBS	KNX	NBC	
The Concert Hour	The Chesterfield Show	Dick Tracy	US Army Band	5pm
		Maurice Winnick Orchestra		5:15
	Come On, Let's Sing		Marshall's Mavericks	5:30
		Music		5:45
Your Hit Parade	Gangbusters		Your Hit Parade	6pm
		News		6:15
	The March of Time	Music		6:30
	Strange As It Seems			6:45
Pop Concert	Best Bets in Music	Elmer Goes Hollywood	Amos 'n' Andy	7pm
	Renfrew of the Mounted	Drury Lane, songs	Lum and Abner	7:15
	Dance Orchestra	The Newlyweds	Winning of the West	7:30
	Music	King's Cowboy Revue		7:45
Million Dollar Pier Orchestra	Jan Garber Orchestra	Officer of the Day	Stoopnagle and Budd	8pm
Fra nk Watanabe and Honorable Archie	D. A. Fitts, talk	Tudor Williams Orchestra		8:15
	Burns and Allen	Music		8:30
News				8:45
Josef Hornik, songs	Ports of Call	News	Al Pearce and His Gang	9pm
Back Stage with Pritchard		The Hollywood Parade		9:15
Maurice Zam, piano	Harry Lewis Orchestra	The Crockett Family	Sterling Young Orchestra	9:30
				9:45
Command Performance	The Ten o'Clock Wire	Hall Grayson Orchestra	The Richfield Reporter	10pm
	Ellis Kimball Orchestra	Jay Whidden Orchestra	World Affairs	10:15
	Jan Garber Orchestra	The Haven of Rest	Jimmy Grier Orchestra	10:30
				10:45

EVENING — SUMMER, 1936

Thursday

	BLUE	CBS	KNX	NBC
5pm	Ann Arthur's Story Hour	Trail of Yankee Trade	Dick Tracy	Beverly King, songs
5:15	The California Zoological Society	Sonny and Buddy, songs	Maurice Winnick Orchestra	Robert Hurd, songs
5:30	The Great Lakes Concert	The Armand Hand Band	Buddy and Ginger, songs	Stringtime
5:45		Moving Stories of Life	Music	
6pm			World Dances	The Kraft Music Hall, Bing Crosby
6:15	The Better Business Bureau	The Grant Park Concert	News	
6:30	Twilight Revelries	The March of Time	Song Souvenirs	
6:45		The Anti Monopoly League	Music	
7pm	Evening Edition	Mary Martin, songs	Elmer Goes Hollywood	Amos 'n' Andy
7:15		Renfrew of the Mounted	The Hollywood Parade	The Maxwell House Showboat
7:30	Rochester Philharmonic Orchestra	Vincent Lopez Orchestra	The Newlyweds	
7:45			King's Cowboy Revue	
8pm	Larchmont Casino Orchestra	The Concerteers	Calling All Cars	
8:15	Frank Watanabe and Honorable Archie			The Standard Symphony Hour
8:30		The Passing Parade	Music	
8:45	News	Music	The Jones Boys, songs	
9pm	Harbor Lights	Mobil Magazine	News	
9:15			Jay Whidden Orchestra	The Talent Parade
9:30	Waltz Time	Jan Garber Orchestra	The Crockett Family	
9:45		The Olympic Reporter		Mark Fisher Orchestra
10pm	Musical Celebrities	The Ten o'Clock Wire		The Richfield Reporter
10:15		Gaylord Carter, organ	Hal Grayson Orchestra	Carl Ravazza Orchestra
10:30		Harry Lewis Orchestra	Marshall Grant, organ	Jimmy Grier Orchestra
10:45				

EVENING — SUMMER, 1936

Friday

BLUE	CBS	KNX	NBC	
Ann Arthur's Story Hour	Hollywood Hotel	Maurice Winnick Orchestra	Wesley Tourtellotte, organ	5pm
Sharps and Fints, songs				5:15
Clara, Lu and Em		Behind the Mike	Clara, Lu and Em	5:30
		Music		5:45
The Grant Park Concert	The Chesterfield Show		Ry-Krisp Presents Marion Talley	6pm
		News	Ella Schallert, movies	6:15
Twilight Revelries	The March of Time	Song Souvenirs	The Great Lakes Concert	6:30
	Strange As It Seems	Music		6:45
Records	Best Bets in Music	Elmer Goes Hollywood	Amos 'n' Andy	7pm
	Renfrew of the Mounted	Music	Lum and Abner	7:15
	The Juvenile Revue	The Newlyweds	D.A. Fitts, talk	7:30
		King's Cowboy Revue	Secret Service Secrets	7:45
Andy Sanella Orchestra	Calling All Cars	Public Affairs	Fred Waring Orchestra	8pm
Frank Watanabe and Honorable Archie				8:15
	The Country Fair	Hal Grayson Orchestra	The Court of Human Relations	8:30
News		The Townsend Plan		8:45
The Drama Hour	Music	News	Fletcher Henderson Orchestra	9pm
		Rubinoff and His Violin	Carl Omeron, songs	9:15
Ricardo and His Caballeros	Jan Garber Orchestra	Jay Whidden Orchestra	Jimmy Grier Orchestra	9:30
		The Hollywood Legion Fights		9:45
Musical Celebrities	The Ten o'Clock Wire		The Richfield Reporter	10pm
	Ellis Kimball Orchestra		Carl Ravazza Orchestra	10:15
Charles Runyan, songs	Harry Lewis Orchestra		Henry King Orchestra	10:30
		The Ringside Club		10:45

EVENING — SUMMER, 1936

Saturday

	BLUE	CBS	KNX	NBC
5pm	Edwin Franko Goldman Band (4:30PM)	Bruno Castagna, songs	Maurice Winnick Orchestra	Jamboree
5:15		Sonny and Buddy, songs		
5:30	Misha Elman, songs	Salon Moderne	Buddy and Ginger, songs	Shell Chateau, Al Jolson
5:45			The Monitor Children's Program	
6pm	Twilight Revelries	Your Hit Parade		
6:15			News	
6:30			Song Souvenirs	The Galaxy of Stars
6:45			The Lubovisiki Trio	
7pm	News and Views	Gateway to Hollywood		The National Barn Dance
7:15			Peter Kent and Betty Borden, songs	
7:30	The Poet's Corner	Hal Kemp Orchestra	The Hollywood Parade	
7:45			Phantasies	
8pm	Records	Jan Garber Orchestra	The Hollywood Barn Dance	Eddy Duchin Orchestra
8:15				
8:30		Benny Goodman Orchestra		Charles Stenross Orchestra
8:45	News and Views			
9pm		Harry Lewis Orchestra	News	Fletcher Henderson Orchestra
9:15		Rubinoff and His Violin	The Hollywood Barn Dance	
9:30	Records	Jan Garber Orchestra		Keith Beecher Orchestra
9:45				
10pm	Command Performance	The Ten o'Clock Wire	Pasadena Dance Orchestra	Frank Andrews, news
10:15		Eddie Fitzpatrick Orchestra		Carl Ravazza Orchestra
10:30		Cole McElroy Orchestra	Jay Whidden Orchestra	Tom Brown Orchestra
10:45				

DAYTIME — SUMMER, 1936

Sunday

	BLUE	CBS	KNX	NBC
8am	Sacred Concert	The Salt Lake Tabernacle Choir	Music	The Church Quarter-Hour
8:15			Lal Chand Mehra, india talk	Major Bowes' Capitol Family
8:30	The Radio City Music Hall	The Times Comics Pages		The University of Chicago Round Table
8:45			Rev. Shuler, religion	
9am		The CBS Church of the Air	Dr. Gardener, religion	Harold Nagel Orchestra
9:15				
9:30	The Sunday Forum	Music	Rabbi Winkler, religion	Joan and the Escorts
9:45		Eddie Dunstedter, organ		Physical Well-Being
10am	The Magic Key of RCA	The Kreiner String Quartet		Music
10:15			Judge Rutherford, legal talk	
10:30		St. Louis Orchestra	Dr. King, religion	Peter Absolute
10:45		Donald Novis, songs	Temple Baptist Church	
11am	Records	Everybody's Music		Chatauqua Symphony Orchestra
11:15				
11:30				
11:45			Donald Novis, songs	
12pm	National Vespers	Sunday Serenade		Dr. Casselbury, health
12:15			Music	Nick Harris
12:30	Vocational Adjustment	Songs of Russia		Words and Music
12:45			Song Souvenirs	
1pm	The Classic Hour	Ann Leaf at the Organ	Charles Lindsley, literary talk	The Sunday Special
1:15				
1:30		Johnson and Sheasgroen, songs	Behind the Mike	The Noble Cain A Cappella Choir
1:45			Judge Rutherford, legal talk	

DAYTIME — SUMMER, 1936

Monday-Friday

BLUE	CBS	KNX	NBC	
Financial Service	Music	Talk and Music	Music	*8am*
Talk and Music			The Merry Madcaps	*8:15*
		Ben Sweetland, comment	The Church Quarter-Hour	*8:30*
		Music	Music	*8:45*
	Betty and Bob	Dr. Thomas, religion		*9am*
	Modern Cinderella	Talk and Music		*9:15*
	Talk / The Times Radio Reporter			*9:30*
	Betty Crocker, cooking / Hymns of All Churches	News	News	*9:45*
	Between the Bookends	The Ten O'Clock Family	Talk and Music	*10am*
	Talk / Happy Hollow			*10:15*
	Easy Home Decorations	Mary Holmes, songs		*10:30*
	Music	Marshall Grant, organ	Music / Ann Warner Chats	*10:45*
News	Talk and Music	Fletcher Wiley, talk	Pepper Young's Family	*11am*
Music			Ma Perkins	*11:15*
The National Farm and Home Hour		Talk and Music	Vic and Sade	*11:30*
			The O'Neills	*11:45*
	News	News	The Woman's Radio Revue	*12pm*
	Talk and Music	Music		*12:15*
Music		Sports	Talk and Music	*12:30*
				12:45
Talk and Music	Stock Market Reports			*1pm*
	Talk and Music			*1:15*
		Pietro Pontrelli Orchestra		*1:30*
	Wilderness Road			*1:45*

DAYTIME — SUMMER, 1936

Sunday

	BLUE	CBS	KNX	NBC
2pm	The Catholic Hour	Ma and Pa	The Exposition Park Concert	Wesley Tourtellotte, organ
2:15				
2:30	Book Review	Chicagoans Orchestra		Orchestra Pit Echoes
2:45	Alistair Cooke, talk	Between the Bookends		Donald Novis, songs
3pm	The Symphony Hour	Clyde Lucas Orchestra		K-7, Secret Service Spy Story
3:15				
3:30		Annals of the Ages		Jose Ramirez Orchestra
3:45				
4pm	Records	America Dances	News	Major Bowes' Original Amateur Hour
4:15			Music	
4:30	Edwin Franko Goldman Band	The Robin Hood Dell Concerts	Dr. Thomas, religion	
4:45				

DAYTIME — SUMMER, 1936

Monday-Friday

BLUE	CBS	KNX	NBC	
The Classic Hour	Music	The Bookworm	Women's Magazine of the Air	2pm
	University of the Air			2:15
	Talk and Music	Music / Frances Patton, piano		2:30
				2:45
Talk and Music / The Italian Language	Feminine Fancies	Talk and Music	Talk / Easy Aces	3pm
			Talk / The Lamplighter	3:15
Talk and Music	Music	Fletcher Wiley, talk	Talk / Happy Kitchen	3:30
	News		Pictorial	3:45
	Music / The Alemite Half-Hour	Hometown Sketches	Music / One Man's Family / The Royal Gelatin Hour, Rudy Vallee / Irene Rich Dramas /	4pm
		Music / The Haven of Rest	Music /	4:15
	Music		Music / The Frank Fay Show	4:30
		Talk and Music		4:45

DAYTIME — SUMMER, 1936

Saturday

	BLUE	CBS	KNX	NBC
8am	Financial Service	Larry Vincent, songs	Music	Concert Miniature
8:15	Genia Fonariova, songs	Poetic Strings	Almanac	
8:30	Words and Music	George Hall Orchestra	Bill Sweetland Orchestra	The Church Quarter-Hour
8:45			Your Home	The Merry Madcaps
9am		Jack Shannon, songs	Dr. Thomas, religion	County Medical Association Talks
9:15		Jack and Jill, songs	Music	Rex Battle Orchestra
9:30	The National Farm and Home Hour	Buffalo Presents		Peggy Cochrane, songs
9:45			News	News
10am		Allen Roth Orchestra	The Ten O'Clock Family	The Southern Tavern
10:15				
10:30	Whitney Ensemble	Easy Home Decorations	Americana Musical	Sammy Watkins Orchestra
10:45		Clyde Barrie, songs		
11am	News and Views	Down by Herman's		Brad and Al, songs
11:15				Don Jose, songs
11:30	Pop Concert	Tours in Tone	Donald Novis, songs	The Weekend Revue
11:45			What's New	
12pm		The Olympic Games	News	
12:15			Behind the Mike	US Agricultural Talk
12:30	Opera Comique	Isle of Dreams	Sports	
12:45				
1pm	Sports	Angelo Vitale Orchestra		Blue Room Echoes
1:15				
1:30	Ken Shannon Orchestra	Looks at Books	Pietro Pontrelli Orchestra	The Blue Prelude
1:45		Great Lakes Spelling Bee		

DAYTIME — SUMMER, 1936

Saturday

	BLUE	CBS	KNX	NBC
2pm	Sports	H. V. Kaltenborn, news	The World Revue	Otto Thurn Orchestra
2:15		Hal Munro Orchestra		
2:30		Allen Roth Orchestra	Light Opera	Sonia Esson, songs
2:45				The Art of Living
3pm		Patti Chapin, songs	Organ Recital	Saturdays at Connie's
3:15		The Song Stylists		The Canadian Grenadiers
3:30	Records	The Victor Bay Concert	The Acceptance Desk	
3:45				Thornton Fisher, sports
4pm	El Chico	The Saturday Swing Session	Warren Gale, guitar	Carl Ravazza Orchestra
4:15			The Haven of Rest	
4:30	Edwin Franko Goldman Band	The Columbia Workshop		Meredith Wilson Orchestra
4:45			Heartbeats of the City	

EVENING — FALL, 1936

Sunday

	BLUE	CBS	MBS	NBC
5pm	Symphonique Moderne	Vick's Open House	News	The Goodwill Court
5:15			Dr. Thomas, religion	
5:30	The Royal Hawaiians	Dick Tracy		
5:45		Looks at Books	Dance Orchestra	
6pm	Walter Winchell's Jergens Journal	The Ford Sunday Evening Hour	Ethel Hubler, talk	The Manhattan Merry-Go-Round
6:15	Paul Whiteman's Musical Varieties		Music	
6:30			Rev. Fuller, religion	The American Album of Familiar Music
6:45				
7pm	Edwin C. Hill, news	The Gillette Community Sing		The General Motors Concert
7:15	Public Affairs			
7:30			D, A. Fitts, talk	
7:45		History's Split Second	Public Affairs	
8pm	News	Texaco Town, Eddie Cantor	The First Presbyterian Church of Hollywood	Sunset Dreams, The Morin Sisters
8:15	Public Affairs			Larry Burke, songs
8:30	The Reader's Guide	California Chain Stores		The Jello Program, Jack Benny
8:45		Southern California Business Men		
9pm	Public Affairs	Public Affairs	News	The Passing Parade
9:15			Music	The Night Editor
9:30	Moving Stories of Life		The Crockett Family	One Man's Family
9:45		The Anti Monopoly League		
10pm	Musical Celebrities	The Ten o'Clock Wire		The Richfield Reporter
10:15		The Crusaders		Bridge to Dreamland
10:30		Dance Orchestra	Dance Orchestra	
10:45				

EVENING — FALL, 1936

Monday

BLUE	CBS	MBS	NBC	
Dance Orchestra	The Interscholastic Reporter	Junior Broadcasters	Sunset Serenade	5pm
	Invisible Trails	The Junior Nurse Corps		5:15
Armand Giraud, songs	Dick Tracy	Jack Armstong, the All-American Boy	Cross Cuts of the Day	5:30
Violin Recital	Moonglow Melodies	Little Orphan Annie		5:45
News	The Lux Radio Theater	The Catalina Quartet	Twenty Thousand Years in Sing Sing	6pm
Public Affairs		News		6:15
Carefree Carnival		Mary Martin, songs	The Old Observer	6:30
		Officer of the Day	Public Affairs	6:45
Ten Years in Retrospect	Lady Esther Serenade	Elmer Goes Hollywood	The Carnation Contented Hour	7pm
		Popeye, the Sailor		7:15
Choral Voices	Public Affairs	The Newlyweds	Hawthorne House	7:30
	The Goose Creek Parson	King's Cowboy Revue		7:45
Albert Bergman, legal talk	William Hard's Hour	Music / Public Affairs	Amos 'n' Andy	8pm
Public Affairs	Renfrew of the Mounted		Lum and Abner	8:15
News	Pick and Pat		The Voice of Firestone	8:30
Uncle Ezra's Radio Station		The Townsend Plan		8:45
Public Affairs	The Alemite Half-Hour	News	Fibber McGee and Molly	9pm
The Colonial Quartet		Rubinoff and His Violin		9:15
Helen Hayes in Bambi	The Southern California Hour	The Crockett Family	The Champions	9:30
				9:45
Fishing and Hunting Talk		Legion Wrestling	The Richfield Reporter	10pm
Musical Celebrities			The Music Parade	10:15
	The Ten o'Clock Wire		Jimmy Grier Orchestra	10:30
	Dance Ordhestra	Bob Miller Orchestra		10:45

EVENING — FALL, 1936

Tuesday

	BLUE	CBS	MBS	NBC
5pm	Paul Martin Orchestra	The Hammerstien Music Hall	Maurice Winnick Orchestra	Along About Sundown
5:15			Buddy and Ginger, songs	
5:30	The Beaux Arts Trio	Music	Jack Armstong, the All-American Boy	Cross Cuts of the Day
5:45		George Fischer, gossip	Little Orphan Annie	
6pm	News	Music	Travel Aid Drama	Ben Bernie, the Old Maestro
6:15	Music		News	
6:30	Husbands and Wives	Benny Goodman's Swing School	Dances	The Packard Hour, Fred Astaire
6:45			Gene and Charlie, songs	
7pm	Hildegarde, songs		Elmer Goes Hollywood	
7:15			Music	
7:30	Portraits in Harmony	Strange As It Seems	The Newlyweds	The California Recreation Council
7:45		The Male Chorus Parade	King's Cowboy Revue	Roy Campbell Royalists
8pm	Music	Willam Hard's Hour	Dance Orchestra	Amos 'n' Andy
8:15	News	Renfrew of the Mounted		Lum and Abner
8:30	The Log Cabin Dude Ranch	Laugh with Ken		Johnny Presents
8:45			The Rosecrucians	
9pm	Public Affairs	Fred Waring Orchestra	News	Death Valley Days
9:15	News		Bob Miller Orchestra	
9:30	Music	Music		Good Morning Tonight
9:45			The Crockett Family	
10pm	Musical Celebrities	The Ten o'Clock Wire		The Richfield Reporter
10:15		Dance Orchestra		The Music Parade
10:30		Phil Harris Orchestra	The Voice of Hollywood	Jimmy Grier Orchestra
10:45			Hits and Bits	

EVENING — FALL, 1936

Wednesday

BLUE	CBS	MBS	NBC	
The Better Business Bureau	The Hawaiian Serenade	Junior Broadcasters	One Man's Family	5pm
Hands Across the Table		The Junior Nurse Corps		5:15
Hits and Misses	Dick Tracy	Jack Armstong, the All-American Boy	The Musical Parade	5:30
News	Music	Little Orphan Annie	Cross Cuts of the Day	5:45
News	Chesterfield Presents	Lazar Samollioff Presents	The Beaux Arts Trio	6pm
Paul Carson, organ		News	The California Chain Stores	6:15
The Bishop and the Gargoyle	Come On, Let's Sing	Mary Martin, songs	Public Affairs	6:30
		The Singing Waiters		6:45
El Chico	Gangbusters	Elmer Goes Hollywood	Your Hit Parade	7pm
		Popeye, the Sailor		7:15
Judge Avery, legal talk	The Passing Parade	The Newlyweds		7:30
Public Affairs	The Goose Creek Parson	King's Cowboy Revue		7:45
	William Hard's Hour	Public Affairs	Amos 'n' Andy	8pm
	Renfrew of the Mounted		Lum and Abner	8:15
News	Burns and Allen	Larry Lee Orchestra	Winning of the West	8:30
Uncle Ezra's Radio Station		Dr. Thomas, religion		8:45
Dance Orchestra	Calling All Cars	News	Town Hall Tonight, Fred Allen	9pm
		Bob Miller Orchestra		9:15
Waltz Time	The California Service Association			9:30
	The California Chain Stores	The Crockett Family		9:45
Musical Celebrities	The Ten o'Clock Wire		The Richfield Reporter	10pm
	The Horse Sense Philosopher		World Affairs	10:15
	Phil Harris Orchestra	The Haven of Rest	Jimmy Grier Orchestra	10:30
				10:45

EVENING — FALL, 1936

Thursday

	BLUE	CBS	MBS	NBC
5pm	James Samuel Lacy, talk	Public Affairs	Maurice Winnick Orchestra	The Royal Gelatin Hour, Rudy Vallee
5:15		Invisible Trails	Buddy and Ginger, songs	
5:30	Music	Lyrics of Loneliness	Jack Armstong, the All-American Boy	
5:45		Stories of Life	Little Orphan Annie	
6pm	News	Major Bowes' Original Amateur Hour	Music	The Music Parade
6:15	The House of Peter McGregor		News	Music
6:30	America's Town Meeting of the Air		James Townsend, songs	Public Affairs
6:45			Officer of the Day	
7pm		Then and Now	Elmer Goes Hollywood	The Kraft Music Hall, Bing Crosby
7:15			The Hollywood Parade	
7:30	Public Affairs	The March of Time	The Newlyweds	
7:45			King's Cowboy Revue	
8pm		Public Affairs	Calling All Cars	Amos 'n' Andy
8:15		Renfrew of the Mounted		The Standard Symphony Hour
8:30		The Cavalcade of America	Public Affairs	
8:45	News			
9pm	The Maxwell House Showboat	Mobil Magazine	News	
9:15			Dance Orchestra	Dance Orchestra
9:30		The California Chain Stores		
9:45		Musical Moments	The Crockett Family	
10pm	Musical Celebrities	The Ten o'Clock Wire		The Richfield Reporter
10:15		Music		The Music Parade
10:30		Phil Harris Orchestra	The Voice of Hollywood	Jimmy Grier Orchestra
10:45			Music	

EVENING — FALL, 1936

Friday

BLUE	CBS	MBS	NBC	
The Beaux Arts Trio	Broadway Varieties	Junior Broadcasters	Irene Rich Dramas	5pm
		The Junior Nurse Corps	Ralina Zarova, songs	5:15
The Sazotunes	Dick Tracy	Jack Armstong, the All-American Boy	Cross Cuts of the Day	5:30
	Harold Peterson, songs	Little Orphan Annie		5:45
News	Hollywood Hotel	Lazar Samollloff Presents	Music	6pm
Musical Echoes		News		6:15
Twin Stars, Brancato and Clair		Music		6:30
			The Old Observer	6:45
Music	Calling All Cars	Elmer Goes Hollywood	The First Nighter Program	7pm
Harold Thompson, songs		Popeye, the Sailor		7:15
The California Recreation Council	Public Affairs	The Newlyweds	Public Affairs	7:30
Public Affairs	The Goose Creek Parson	King's Cowboy Revue		7:45
	Wiilam Hard's Hour	Rheba Crawford, songs	Amos 'n' Andy	8pm
The Digest Poll	Renfrew of the Mounted	The California Chain Stores	Lum and Abner	8:15
Singin' Sam, the Barbosol Man	Chesterfield Presents	Bob Miller Orchestra	The Court of Human Relations	8:30
Uncle Ezra's Radio Station		The Townsend Plan		8:45
Dance Orchestra	Lucky Stars	News	Fred Waring Orchestra	9pm
		Rubinoff and His Violin		9:15
Harbor Lights	Strange As It Seems	Hits and Bits	The House of Melody	9:30
	Sports	The Hollywood Legion Fights		9:45
Musical Celebrities	The Ten o'Clock Wire		The Richfield Reporter	10pm
	Dance Orchestra		The Music Parade	10:15
	Phil Harris Orchestra		Jimmy Grier Orchestra	10:30
		The Ringside Club		10:45

EVENING — FALL, 1936

Saturday

	BLUE	CBS	MBS	NBC
5pm	Music	Larry Kent Orchestra	Sports (2:15pm)	Music
5:15				
5:30	Meredith Willson Orchestra	The Elgin Football Revue	Music	The Blue Parade
5:45				
6pm	News	Public Affairs	The Catalina Quartet	Public Affairs
6:15	Music		News	
6:30	The Drama Hour	Saturday Night Serenade	Music	Shell Chateau, Smith Ballew
6:45			The Lubovisiki Trio	
7pm	Nickelodean	Your Hit Parade		
7:15			The Hollywood Parade	
7:30	Raine Bennett's Island Cruises		Father Charles Couglin, religion	Paducah Plantation, Irwin S. Cobb
7:45				
8pm	The National Barn Dance	Drums	The Hollywood Barn Dance	The National Barn Dance
8:15				
8:30		The Juvenile Revue		
8:45				
9pm	Dance Orchestra	Dance Orchestra	News	Public Affairs
9:15			The Hollywood Barn Dance	
9:30				
9:45				
10pm	Command Performance	The Ten o'Clock Wire	Dance Orchestra	Frank Andrews, news
10:15		Dance Orchestra		Eddie Fizpatrick Orchestra
10:30		Phil Harris Orchestra	Pasadena Dance Orchestra	Jimmy Grier Orchestra
10:45				

DAYTIME — FALL, 1936

Sunday

	BLUE	CBS	MBS	NBC
8am	Records	The Times Comics Pages	Tunes	Words and Music
8:15			Lal Chand Mehra, india talk	The Church Quarter-Hour
8:30	The World is Yours	Major Bowes' Capitol Family		Songs You Left Behind
8:45			Day Dreams	The Peerless Trio
9am	The First Unitarian Church of Hollywood		Dr. Gardener, religion	Salute to NBC
9:15	The Hihatters			
9:30	The Radio City Music Hall	The Salt Lake Tabernable Choir	Rabbi Winkler, religion	The University of Chicago Round Table
9:45				
10am		The CBS Church of the Air	Music	Lucille Manners, songs
10:15				
10:30	Highlights of the Bible	Layman's Views	Tunes	Physical Well-Being
10:45		Eddie Dunstedter, organ	Temple Baptist Church	Samovar Serenade
11am	The Magic Key of RCA	Music		Dr. Casselbury, health
11:15		Moment Musicale		Nick Harris
11:30		Public Affairs		Paul Carson, organ
11:45				The Southern Harmony Four
12pm	Better Speech	Everybody's Music		The Metropolitan Opera Auditions
12:15	Vocational Adjustment		Music	
12:30	Our Neighbors			Grand Hotel
12:45			Songs	
1pm	National Vespers	Ma and Pa	Charles Lindsley, literary talk	The Sunday Special

DAYTIME — FALL, 1936

Monday-Friday

BLUE	CBS	MBS	NBC	
Music / Neighbor Nell	Music	Keeping Fit in Hollywood	Financial Service	8am
Vagabonds Orchestra			Howdy Folks	8:15
The Honeymooners	Music / Gaylord Carter, organ	Almanac		8:30
The Gospel Singer	Music / Dr. Allen Dafoe, health		Music / The Voice of Experience	8:45
Music / Honeyboy and Sassafras	The Gumps	Dr. Thomas, religion	News	9am
Music / Jack and Loretta Clemens, songs	Between the Bookends	Music	The Story of Mary Marlin	9:15
Talk and Music	The Romance of Helen Trent		Talk and Music / How to Be Charming	9:30
	Rich Man's Darling	News	Talk and Music / The Mystery Chef	9:45
	Betty and Bob	The Ten O'Clock Family	Talk and Music	10am
	Modern Cinderella		Mrs. Wiggs of the Cabbage Patch	10:15
	John K. Watkins, news	Mary Holmes, songs	John's Other Wife	10:30
Music / Dot and Will	Hymns of All Churches / Betty Crocker, cooking	Music	Just Plain Bill	10:45
Music / Words and Music	Big Sister	Fletcher Wiley, talk	Ann Warner Chats / The Standard School Broadcast	11am
Music / Language Lesson	The American School of the Air			11:15
The National Farm and Home Hour		Talk and Music	Stock Market Report	11:30
	Music / Happy Hollow		Music / The Calendar of Memories	11:45
	Talk and Music / Magazine of the Air	News	Pepper Young's Family	12pm
		Lataner's Facts	Ma Perkins	12:15
Talk and Music	Music / The Monticello Party Line	Pietro Pontrelli Orchestra	Vic and Sade	12:30
	Ben Sweetland, comment		The O'Neills	12:45
	Music	Maurice Winnick Orchestra	Music / The Weekday Special	1pm

DAYTIME — FALL, 1936

Sunday

	BLUE	CBS	MBS	NBC
1:15				
1:30	Senator Fishface and Professor Figgsbottle	Sunday Seranade	Music	The Noble Cain A Cappella Choir
1:45			Dr. King, religion	
2pm	We, the People	Wings of Song	The Exposition Park Concert	Ry-Krisp Presents Marion Talley
2:15				
2:30	Stoopnagle and Budd	Rabbi Magnin, religion		Home Harmonies
2:45		Margaret Hegedus, organ		
3pm	The Catholic Hour	The Park Avenue Penners		Barnstormers Drama
3:15				
3:30	Alistaire Cooke, talk	Rubinoff and His Violin		The Sunday Concert
3:45	Music			
4pm	Pittsburgh Symphony Orchestra	Television Broadcast	Reunion of the Stars	Mickey Gillette Orchestra
4:15		The Townsend Plan		
4:30	Reflections	Previews and Encores		Believe It or Not
4:45				

DAYTIME — FALL, 1936

Monday-Friday

BLUE	CBS	MBS	NBC	
	Dale Armstrong, news			1:15
News	Music	The Bookworm	Music / The Landon Radio Club	1:30
Music / Young Hickory			Talk and Music / Grandpa Burton	1:45
The Classic Hour	Music	The Cliff Dwellers	Music	2pm
	University of the Air		Country Cousins	2:15
	News Through a Woman's Eyes	Music	Music	2:30
	Talk and Music			2:45
Talk and Music	Feminine Fancies	Talk and Music	Women's Magazine of the Air	3pm
		Music / Day Dreams		3:15
Happy Kitchen	Talk and Music	Fletcher Wiley, talk		3:30
Flying Time	Dale Armstrong, news			3:45
Talk and Music	Talk / Sunset Serenade	Hometown Sketches	Talk and Music / Easy Aces	4pm
	Talk and Music	Music / The Haven of Rest	The Voice of Experience / Back Seat Driver	4:15
			Music	4:30
		Music	Pictorial	4:45

DAYTIME — FALL, 1936

Saturday

	BLUE	CBS	MBS	NBC
8am	Julia Hoyt, songs	Cincinatti Conservatory Symphony	Music	Our American Schools
8:15	Bill Krentz Orchestra			Financial Service
8:30	The Magic of Speech		Almanac	Bromley House, songs
8:45				The Home Town
9am		Captivators Orchestra	Dr. Thomas, religion	News
9:15	Genia Fonarovia, songs	Orientale	Range Rhythms	County Medical Association Talks
9:30	The National Farm and Home Hour	George Hall Orchestra		Concert Miniatures
9:45			News	
10am		Music	The Ten O'Clock Family	Rex Battle Orchestra
10:15				
10:30	News	Buffalo Presents	Americana Music	Campus Capers
10:45	Old Skipper's Gang			
11am	Music	Football Souvenir	Musicomedy	Music
11:15		Sports		
11:30	Sports		The Monitor Children's Program	Sports
11:45			Music	
12pm			News	
12:15			Lataner's Facts	
12:30			Music	
12:45				
1pm				
1:15				
1:30			The Cliff Dwellers	
1:45				

DAYTIME — FALL, 1936

Saturday

	BLUE	CBS	MBS	NBC
2pm		Al Roth Orchestra	Blue Ballads	
2:15		Sports	Sports	
2:30				Music
2:45				
3pm				Otto Thurn Orchestra
3:15				
3:30				Sonia Esson, songs
3:45				The Art of Living
4pm				Ricardo and His Violin
4:15				The Hampton Institute Singers
4:30				
4:45				Sports

LISTINGS FOR 1937

EVENING — WINTER, 1937

Sunday

	BLUE	CBS	MBS	NBC
5pm	The Hour of Charm	Vick's Open House	Music	Do You Want to Be an Actor
5:15				
5:30	News	Popeye, the Sailor		
5:45	Al Gayle Orchestra	News	The Townsend Plan	
6pm	Walter Winchell's Jergens Journal	The Ford Sunday Evening Hour	Rabbi Magnin, religion	The Manhattan Merry-Go-Round
6:15	The Rippling Rhythm Revue		Piano Team	
6:30			Dance Orchestra	The American Album of Familiar Music
6:45	Edwin C. Hill, news			
7pm	Music	The Gillette Community Sing	Rev. Fuller, religion	The General Motors Concert
7:15	The Southern California Hour			
7:30				
7:45		Music		
8pm		Texaco Town, Eddie Cantor	Dance Orchestra	Sunset Dreams, The Morin Sisters
8:15	News			French Casino Orchestra
8:30	The Reader's Guide	Larry Lee Orchestra	The Inglewood Park Concert	The Jello Program, Jack Benny
8:45		News		
9pm	The Chamber Music Ensemble	Moments You Never Forget	News	The Passing Parade
9:15			Dance Orchestra	The Night Editor
9:30	Music	The Morgan Family		One Man's Family
9:45				
10pm	Musical Celebrities			The Richfield Reporter
10:15			House Undivided	Bridge to Dreamland
10:30		Tommy Tucker Orchestra	Dance Orchestra	
10:45		The Three Knights		

EVENING — WINTER, 1937

Monday

BLUE	CBS	MBS	NBC	
Sunset Melodies	Popeye, the Sailor	Dance Orchestra	Music	5pm
	The Junior Nurse Corps	Invisible Trails		5:15
Music	Jack Armstrong, the All-American Boy	Tony D'Orazi, cartoons	The Packard Parade	5:30
Sports	Little Orphan Annie	Piano Duo	Famous Songs	5:45
The Bishop and the Gargoyle	The Lux Radio Theater	Tom Sawyer, comment	Twenty Thousand Years in Sing Sing	6pm
		The Story Teller		6:15
The Raleigh-Kool Program, Jack Pearl		Rendezvous	Music	6:30
		Drums	The Old Observer	6:45
Good Time Society	Lady Esther Serenade	George Fisher, gossip	The Carnation Contented Hour	7pm
Music is My Hobby		Buried Treasure		7:15
King's Cowboy Revue	Captains of Industry		Hawthorne House	7:30
Albert Bergman, legal talk	News	Music		7:45
News	Poetic Melodies	French Casino Orchestra	Amos 'n' Andy	8pm
Lum and Abner	Renfrew of the Mounted		Uncle Ezra's Radio Station	8:15
The Colonial Quartet	Pick and Pat	Music	The Voice of Firestone	
The Speech Doctor				8:45
The House of Melody	The Alemite Half-Hour	News	Fibber McGee and Molly	9pm
		Mal Hallett Orchestra		9:15
Helen Hayes in Bambi	The Morgan Family	Dance Orchestra	The Champions	9:30
				9:45
Musical Celebrities		Al Kavelin Orchestra	The Richfield Reporter	10pm
		House Undivided	Stringin' Along	10:15
	Legion Wrestling	Sterling Young Orchestra	Jimmy Grier Orchestra	10:30
				10:45

EVENING — WINTER, 1937

Tuesday

	BLUE	CBS	MBS	NBC
5pm	What's in a Word	The Hammerstein Music Hall	Music	Magic Fire
5:15	Paul Martin Orchestra			Along About Sundown
5:30	News	Jack Armstong, the All-American Boy	Listen to This	Music
5:45	Records	Little Orphan Annie		Tommy Harris Orchestra
6pm	Ben Bernie, the Old Maestro	White Fire	Tom Sawyer, comment	Music
6:15		News	Sing Time	Screen Week
6:30	Husbands and Wives	Benny Goodman's Swing School		The Packard Hour, Fred Astaire
6:45			Drums	
7pm	The Armco Iron Master		Sinfonietta	
7:15				
7:30	King's Cowboy Revue	Strange As It Seems	Dance Orchestra	Jimmy Fidler, gossip
7:45	The House of Peter McGregor	The Male Chorus Parade		The CHB House Party
8pm	News	Poetic Melodies	The Court of the People	Amos 'n' Andy
8:15	Lum and Abner	Renfrew of the Mounted		Sidewalk Interviews
8:30	The Log Cabin Dude Ranch	The Lifebouy Program, Al Jolson	Freddy Martin Orchestra	Johnny Presents
8:45				
9pm	Music	Watch the Fun Go By, Al Pearce	News	Death Valley Days
9:15			Horace Heidt Orchestra	
9:30	The University Explorer	The Town Crier	Music	Good Morning Tonight
9:45	Headlines from Home	The Morgan Family		
10pm	Musical Celebrities			The Richfield Reporter
10:15			House Undivided	The Packard Parade
10:30		Dance Orchestra	Sterling Young Orchestra	Dance Orchestra
10:45				

EVENING — WINTER, 1937

Wednesday

BLUE	CBS	MBS	NBC	
The Better Business Bureau	Popeye, the Sailor	The Voice of the Philosopher	One Man's Family	5pm
Music	The Junior Nurse Corps			5:15
News	Jack Armstrong, the All-American Boy	Tony D'Orazi, cartoons	Organ Recital	5:30
Moving Stories of Life	Little Orphan Annie	Piano Duo	Music	5:45
The Professional Parade	Chesterfield Presents	Tom Sawyer, comment		6pm
		Federal Housing Authority Talk	The Old Observer	6:15
	The Palmolive Beauty Box Theater	Nibs White, songs	Thrills	6:30
		Drums	The Old Observer	6:45
The Library of Congress Concert	Gangbusters	Musical Importations	Your Hit Parade	7pm
		Music		7:15
King's Cowboy Revue	Music	The Lone Ranger	Music	7:30
Music	News			7:45
News	Poetic Melodies	Music	Amos 'n' Andy	8pm
Lum and Abner	Renfrew of the Mounted		Uncle Ezra's Radio Station	8:15
Music	Burns and Allen	Louisiana Hayride	Winning of the West	8:30
				8:45
Los Angeles Orchestra	Calling All Cars	News	Town Hall Tonight, Fred Allen	9pm
		Eddy Duchin Orchestra		9:15
Waltz Time	The Morgan Family	Emerson Dill Orchestra		9:30
		Jimmy Dorsey Orchestra		9:45
Musical Celebrities		Ted Fiorito Orchestra	The Richfield Reporter	10pm
	Tommy Tucker Orchestra	House Undivided	Ed Fitzpatrick Orchestra	10:15
		Sterling Young Orchestra	The Haven of Rest	10:30
	Dance Orchestra			10:45

EVENING — WINTER, 1937

Thursday

	BLUE	CBS	MBS	NBC
5pm	Public Affairs	Wilbur Hatch Orchestra	Piano Team	The Royal Gelatin Hour, Rudy Vallee
5:15		The Junior Nurse Corps	Invisible Trails	
5:30	News	Jack Armstong, the All-American Boy	Guy Lombardo Orchestra	
5:45	The Stamp Club	Little Orphan Annie	Stories of Life	
6pm	Angelus	Major Bowe's Original Amateur Hour	Tom Sawyer, comment	Barnum Was Right
6:15	Music		Legislative Keyhole	H. Bedford Jones, talk
6:30	America's Town Meeting of the Air		Hawaiian Serenade	
6:45			Drums	You and Your Government
7pm		True Adventures	George Fisher, gossip	The Kraft Music Hall, Bing Crosby
7:15			World Affairs	
7:30	King's Cowboy Revue	The March of Time	Music	
7:45	News			
8pm	Dr. Kate	Poetic Melodies	Calling All Cars	Amos 'n' Andy
8:15		Renfrew of the Mounted		The Standard Symphony Hour
8:30	The Maxwell House Showboat	The Cavalcade of America	Thomas Lee Presents	
8:45				
9pm		Ted Fiorito Orchestra	News	
9:15			Benny Goodman Orchestra	Ben Alexander, stories
9:30	The University Explorer	The Town Crier	Velos and Yolanda, songs	Carl Omeron, songs
9:45		The Morgan Family		Jack Randolph, songs
10pm	Musical Celebrities		Al Kavelin Orchestra	The Richfield Reporter
10:15			House Undivided	Records
10:30			Sterling Young Orchestra	Jimmy Grier Orchestra
10:45		Dance Orchestra		

EVENTING — WINTER, 1937

Friday

BLUE	CBS	MBS	NBC	
Lady Counselor	Broadway Varieties	Cesare Sidero Directs	Blue Skies	5pm
The Radio Book Club			Organ Recital	5:15
News	Jack Armstrong, the All-American Boy	The Grummits		5:30
Music	Little Orphan Annie		Music You Love	5:45
	Hollywood Hotel	Tom Sawyer, comment	Music	6pm
		The Story Teller		6:15
Twin Stars, Brancato and Clair		Nibs White, songs		6:30
		Drums	The Old Observer	6:45
Public Affairs	Philadelphia Symphony Orchestra	The Witch's Talk	The First Nighter Program	7pm
				7:15
King's Cowboy Revue	Strange As It Seems	The Lone Ranger	The Pontiac Varsity Show	7:30
Elza Schallert Interviews	News			7:45
News	Mortimer Gooch	Music	Amos 'n' Andy	8pm
Lum and Abner	Renfrew of the Mounted		Uncle Ezra's Radio Station	8:15
Singin' Sam, the Barbasol Man	Chesterfield Time		The Court of Human Relations	8:30
The Speech Doctor				8:45
Universal Rhythm	Russ Hughes, sports	News	Carefree Carnival	9pm
	Guy Lombardo Orchestra	Music		9:15
Harbor Lights	Carl Ravel Orchestra	Leo Reisman Orchestra	Music	9:30
	The Hollywood Legion Fights			9:45
Musical Celebrities		Sammy Kaye Orchestra	The Richfield Reporter	10pm
		House Undivided	Music	10:15
		Sterling Young Orchestra	Jimmy Grier Orchestra	10:30
	Dance Orchestra			10:45

EVENING — WINTER, 1937

Saturday

	BLUE	CBS	MBS	NBC
5pm	Music	The Modern Masters	Music	Ed Fitzpatrick Orchestra
5:15				
5:30	News	The Columbia Workshop		The Three Cheers
5:45	Meredith Willson Orchestra			
6pm	Music	The Nash Program	Keyboard and Console	The Musical Grab Bag
6:15			Horace Heidt Orchestra	
6:30	Jack Meskin Orchestra	Your Pet Program		Shell Chateau, Joe Cook
6:45				
7pm	Nickelodeon	Your Hit Parade	Music	
7:15				
7:30	Raine Bennett's Island Cruises	Music		Paducah Plantation, Irwin S. Cobb
7:45				
8pm	The National Barn Dance	Dance Orchestra		Music
8:15			Ted Weems Orchestra	
8:30		The Hollywood Barn Dance	The Juvenile Revue	Dance Orchestra
8:45				
9pm	Ed Wynn,, the Perfect Fool		News	Jerry Blain Orchestra
9:15			Shep Fields Orchestra	
9:30	News		Dick Jergens Orchestra	Ben Bernie, the Old Maestro
9:45	The Four Blackbirds		Dance Orchestra	
10pm	Command Performance			Headlines from Home
10:15				Frank Andrews, news
10:30		Tommy Tucker Orchestra	Sterling Young Orchestra	Jimmy Grier Orchestra
10:45		Dance Orchestra		

DAYTIME — WINTER, 1937

Sunday

	BLUE	CBS	MBS	NBC
8am	Records	Music	The Northwestern Reviewing Stand	Ward and Muzzy, piano
8:15			Music	The Church Quarter-Hour
8:30	Paul Carson, organ	Major Bowes' Capitol Family		The World is Yours
8:45				
9am	Moscow Sleigh Bells		The Cadic Tabernacle Choir	The Southernaires Quartet
9:15	Dr. Caldecott, health			
9:30	The Radio City Music Hall	The Salt Lake Tabernable Choir	The Music-Art Quartet	The University of Chicago Round Table
9:45				
10am		The CBS Church of the Air	The Chapel Singers	Physical Well-Being
10:15				Songs You Love, Muriel Wilson
10:30	Our Neighbors	Josiah Stamp, talk	Views of the News	Melody Matinee
10:45		Eddie Dunstedter, organ	Frank Tavaglione, songs	
11am	The Magic Key of RCA	Music of the Theater	Trails of Yankee Trade	Choral Voices
11:15			Colonel Evans, comment	Nick Harris
11:30			Men of Destiny	The Beaux Arts Trio
11:45		The Aeolians		
12pm	Better Speech	New York Philharmonic Orchestra	Songs	The Metropolitan Opera Auditions
12:15	Dr. Brainard, health		Music	
12:30	Gale Page, songs		Three Leagues from Jerusalem	Grand Hotel
12:45	Dorothy Dreslin, songs		Looks at Books	
1pm	National Vespers		Harold Stokes Orchestra	Sunday Serenade
1:15				

DAYTIME — WINTER, 1937

Monday-Friday

BLUE	CBS	MBS	NBC	
News	Keeping Fit in Hollywood	Talk and Music	Financial Service	8am
Vagabonds Orchestra			Howdy Folks / Cross Cuts of the Day	8:15
Vic and Sade	Eddie Albright, organ			8:30
The Gospel Singer	Music / Dr. Allen Dafoe, health	Music / House Undivided	Music / The Voice of Experience	8:45
Music / Honeyboy and Sassafras	The Gumps	Music / Howard Lanin Orchestra	News	9am
Music / Language Lesson	Between the Bookends		The Story of Mary Marlin	9:15
Talk and Music	The Romance of Helen Trent	The Monticello Party Line	Talk and Music / How to Be Charming	9:30
	Rich Man's Darling	Talk and Music	Talk and Music	9:45
News	Betty and Bob	Music / Music from Texas	Talk and Music / The Mystery Chef	10am
Music / Norman V. Young, talk	Modern Cinderella	Music / The Hollisters	Mrs. Wiggs of the Cabbage Patch	10:15
	Hymns of All Churches / Betty Crocker, cooking	Midday Service	John's Other Wife	10:30
Music / Dot and Will	John K. Watkins, news		Just Plain Bill	10:45
Music / Words and Music	Big Sister	Our Neighbors	Ann Warner Chats / The Standard School Broadcast	11am
	The American School of the Air	Music		11:15
The National Farm and Home Hour		For the Ladies	Talk / One Girl in a Million	11:30
	The Story of Myrt and Marge		Stock Market Report	11:45
	Talk and Music / Magazine of the Air	News	Pepper Young's Family	12pm
		Talk and Music	Ma Perkins	12:15
Talk and Music	Music	Ben Sweetland, comment	Vic and Sade	12:30
		Music	The O'Neills	12:45
	Fletcher Wiley, talk	Talk and Music	Music / The Weekday Special	1pm
				1:15

DAYTIME — WINTER, 1937

Sunday

	BLUE	CBS	MBS	NBC
1:30	Senator Fishface and Professor Figgsbottle		Music	Musical Camera
1:45				
2pm	We, the People	The CBS Church of the Air	Freddy Martin Orchestra	Ry-Krisp Presents Marion Talley
2:15				
2:30	Stoopnagle and Budd	Music	Ted Weems Orchestra	Dr. Casselbury, health
2:45				Music
3pm	The Catholic Hour	The Park Avenue Penners	Arnold Johnson Orchestra	Barnstormers Drama
3:15				
3:30	The Golden Gate Park Band	The Chevrolet Program	The Hollywood Theater	A Tale of Today
3:45				
4pm	The Helen Traubel Program	Reunion of the Stars	Classics	The Hall of Fame
4:15				Crashing Headlines
4:30	Believe It or Not		The Listener Speaks	The Sperry Special
4:45				

DAYTIME — WINTER, 1937

Monday-Friday

BLUE	CBS	MBS	NBC	
News	Pietro Pontrelli Orchestra			1:30
Music / Young Hickory	News		Talk and Music / Grandpa Burton	1:45
The Classic Hour	Music / The Women's Forum	Music	Music	2pm
	Music / Almanac	The Johnson Family		2:15
	News Through a Woman's Eyes	Music		2:30
	Talk and Music			2:45
Talk and Music	The Western Home Hour	Feminine Fancies	Women's Magazine of the Air	3pm
				3:15
		Talk and Music		3:30
Happy Kitchen				3:45
Talk and Music	The Newlyweds	News	Talk and Music / Easy Aces	4pm
	Talk and Music	Talk and Music	Music	4:15
		The Radio University	Music / The Helen Traubel Program	4:30
	Music / Hometown Sketches	Music	Pictorial	4:45

DAYTIME — WINTER, 1937

Saturday

	BLUE	CBS	MBS	NBC
8am	Madge Marley, songs	New York Philharmonic Children's Concert	Music	Our American Schools
8:15	Organ Recital			Financial Service
8:30	The Magic of Speech		News	Bromley House, songs
8:45			House Undivided	Meditations
9am	Call to Youth		The Collegiate Cowboy	News
9:15	Genia Fonarovia, songs		Gaylord Carter, organ	County Medical Association Talks
9:30	The National Farm and Home Hour	The Federation of Women's Club		Rex Battle Orchestra
9:45		News	Howard Lanin Orchestra	
10am		The Monitor Children's Program		The Mystery Chef
10:15		Jack and Jill, songs	Newark Symphony Orchestra	Music
10:30	News	Buffalo Presents	Midday Service	
10:45	Music			
11am	The Metropolitan Opera	Dancepators	Emerson Gill Orchestra	Stars of Tomorrow
11:15		Eddie Albright, organ		
11:30		Music	Music	Campus Capers
11:45				
12pm		Down by Hermans	News	Walter Logan's Musicale
12:15			Sammy Kaye Orchestra	
12:30		Tour in Tone	Music	The Weekend Revue
12:45				
1pm		The Captivators		
1:15				
1:30		Pietro Pontrelli Orchestra	Howard Lanin Orchestra	Golden Melodies
1:45		News		

DAYTIME — WINTER, 1937

Saturday

	BLUE	CBS	MBS	NBC
2pm		Eddy Duchin Orchestra	Woody Herman Orchestra	Top Hatters Orchestra
2:15	The Classic Hour			
2:30		Fiddlers Six	Dance Orchestra	Stringtime
2:45		Dance Orchestra		
3pm		Allen Roth Orchestra	Surnames	Lee Gordon Orchestra
3:15			The Music Parade	
3:30		Dance Orchestra	Music	News
3:45		The Swing Club	Alfred Karger, songs	Religion in the News
4pm			News	Song Stories
4:15		Officer of the Day	March On	The Hampton Institute Singers
4:30		Sunset Serenade	Louisiana Hayride	
4:45				Thornton Fisher, sports

EVENING — SPRING, 1937

Sunday

	BLUE	CBS	MBS	NBC
5pm	The General Motors Promenade	Twin Stars, Broderick and Moore	Father Charles Coughlin, religion	Do You Want to Be an Actor
5:15				
5:30		Moments You Never Forget	Sunshine Melodies	
5:45			Public Affairs	
6pm	The Rippling Rhythm Revue	The Ford Sunday Evening Hour	Music	The Manhattan Merry-Go-Round
6:15				
6:30	Walter Winchell's Jergens Journal			The American Album of Familiar Music
6:45	Choir Symphonette			
7pm	California Concert	The Gillette Community Sing	Rev. Fuller, religion	Gladys Swartout, songs
7:15				
7:30				Music
7:45		Radio Headlines		
8pm	Records	Texaco Town, Eddie cantor	The University Explorer	The Fitch Jingle Program
8:15	The Chapel Quartet		Buried Treasure	Treasure Island
8:30	The Reader's Guide	Jay Freeman Orchestra		The Jello Program, Jack Benny
8:45			Music	
9pm	The Chamber Music Ensemble		News	The Passing Parade
9:15			Dance Orchestra	The Night Editor
9:30	News			One Man's Family
9:45	Records	Modern Miracles		
10pm		The Temple Square Program	Ted Fiorito Orchestra	The Richfield Reporter
10:15	Musical Celebrities			Bridge to Dreamland
10:30		Dance Orchestra	House Undivided	
10:45			Dance Orchestra	

EVENING — SPRING, 1937

Monday

BLUE	CBS	MBS	NBC	
Music	News	Romance in Rhythm	Music	5pm
	The Junior Nurse Corps			5:15
News	Jack Armstrong, the All-American Boy	Cassandra	Famous Songs	5:30
Sports	Little Orphan Annie	Spelling Bee	Junior News	5:45
Good Time Society	The Lux Radio Theater	Page One Parade	Monday Melodies	6pm
		Meet Some People		6:15
S. O. S.		Sports	Burns and Allen	6:30
		Tom Sawyer, comment		6:45
The Championis	Lady Esther Serenade	Music	The Carnation Contented Hour	7pm
		George Fisher, gossip		7:15
King's Cowboy Revue	The Old Observer	The Lone Ranger	Hawthorne House	7:30
Albert Bergman, legal talk	Easy Aces			7:45
Music	Scattergood Baines	Drums	Amos 'n' Andy	8pm
Lum and Abner	Pretty KItty Kelly	Pageant of Melody	Uncle Ezra's Radio Station	8:15
The Colonial Quartet	Pick and Pat	The In-Laws	The Voice of Firestone	8:30
Music		The Townsend Plan		8:45
The House of Melody	The Alemite Half-Hour	News	Fibber McGee and Molly	9pm
		Records		9:15
Dr. Kate	Music	Dance Orchestra	Vox Pop	9:30
	News			9:45
Musical Celebrities	Legion Wrestling	Bob McGraw Orchestra	The Richfield Reporter	10pm
		House Undivided	The Voice of Hawaii	10:15
		Sterling Young Orchestra	Jimmy Grier Orchestra	10:30
	Pietro Pontrelli Orchestra			10:45

EVENING — SPRING, 1937

Tuesday

	BLUE	CBS	MBS	NBC
5pm	Husbands and Wives	The Hammerstein Music Hall	Lee Shelley Orchestra	Magic Fire
5:15				Josef Hornik Orchestra
5:30	News	Jack Armstong, the All-American Boy	Listen to This	Music
5:45	The Stamp Club	Little Orphan Annie		
6pm	Ben Bernie, the Old Maestro	Paul Lammoreaux Orchestra	Page One Parade	An Invitation to Dance
6:15		News	Music	Screen Week
6:30	Music / Public Affairs	Benny Goodman's Swing School		The Packard Hour, Fred Astaire
6:45			Tom Sawyer, comment	
7pm	Music		Sinfonietta	
7:15				
7:30	King's Cowboy Revue	Pietro Pontrelli Orchestra	Fred Stark's Pop Party	Jimmy Fidler, gossip
7:45	Masterpieces of Melody	The Male Chorus Parade		The CHB House Party
8pm	Music	Scattergood Baines	Drums	Amos 'n' Andy
8:15	Lum and Abner	Pretty Kitty Kelly	Music	The Martinez Brolthers, songs
8:30	Dr. Peter Puzzlewit	The Lifebouy Program, Al Jolson	The In-Laws	Johnny Presents
8:45			Musical Moments	
9pm	Music	Watch the Fun Go By, Al Pearce	News	Death Valley Days
9:15			Carl Hoff Orchestra	
9:30	The University Explorer	The Town Crier	Vocal Varieties	Good Morning Tonight
9:45	Music	News	George Hamilton Orchestra	
10pm	Musical Celebrities	Whte Fires of the South Seas	Dance Orchestra	The Richfield Reporter
10:15			House Undivided	The Voice of Hawaii
10:30		Harry Owens Orchestra	Sterling Young Orchestra	Dance Orchestra
10:45		Ted Fiorito Orchestra		

EVENING — SPRING, 1937

Wednesday

BLUE	CBS	MBS	NBC	
Rackets of Today	Federal Housing Authority Talk	The Voice of the Philosopher	One Man's Family	5pm
Humoresque	The Junior Nurse Corps			5:15
News	Jack Armstrong, the All-American Boy	Cassandra	Music	5:30
Moving Stories of Life	Little Orphan Annie	Melody Muse	Organ Recital	5:45
String Symphony	Chesterfield Presents	Page One Parade	Music	6pm
		George Duffy Orchestra		6:15
	The Palmolive Beauty Box Theater	Sports	Thrills	6:30
		Tom Sawyer, comment		6:45
Music	Gangbusters	Romance and Roses	Your Hit Parade	7pm
				7:15
King's Cowboy Revue	Man to Man	The Lone Ranger		7:30
California Safety Talk	Easy Aces		Song Stories, Jim Kemper	7:45
Music	Scattergood Baines	Drums	Amos 'n' Andy	8pm
Lum and Abner	Pretty Kitty Kelly	Dance Orchestra	Uncle Ezra's Radio Station	8:15
Viennese Echoes	Laugh with Ken	The In-Laws	Winning of the West	8:30
The California College Series		The Best of the Week		8:45
Los Angeles Orchestra	Calling All Cars	News	Town Hall Tonight, Fred Allen	9pm
		Music		9:15
Waltz Time	Musical Moments	Dance Orchestra		9:30
	News			9:45
Musical Celebrities	Fiesta		The Richfield Reporter	10pm
	Dance Orchestra	House Undivided	The Four Blackbirds	10:15
		Sterling Young Orchestra	The Haven of Rest	10:30
	Ted Fiorito Orchestra			10:45

EVENING — SPRING, 1937

Thursday

	BLUE	CBS	MBS	NBC
5pm	James Samuel Lacy, talk	News	Music and You	The Royal Gelatin Hour, Rudy Vallee
5:15	Music	The Junior Nurse Corps		
5:30	News	Jack Armstong, the All-American Boy	Guy Lombardo Orchestra	
5:45	The Stamp Club	Little Orphan Annie		
6pm	New American Music	Major Bowe's Original Amateur Hour	Page One Parade	Barnum Was Right
6:15			Irish Minstrel	
6:30	America's Town Meeting of the Air		Sports	Jack Dempsey's Fight Series
6:45			Tom Sawyer, comment	
7pm		True Adventures	The Witch's Tale	The Kraft Music Hall, Bing Crosby
7:15				
7:30	King's Cowboy Revue	The March of Time	Musical Revue	
7:45	Music		Drums	
8pm	Back Seat Driver	Scattergood Baines	Calling All Cars	Amos 'n' Andy
8:15	The All-Star Cycle	Pretty Kitty Kelly		The Standard Symphony Hour
8:30	The Maxwell House Showboat	The Cavalcade of America	The In-Laws	
8:45			Musical Moments	
9pm		Jerry Cooper and Music	News	
9:15		The Captains of Industry	Modern Miracles	Not for the Ladies
9:30	Short Story Playhouse	The Town Crier	Dance Orchestra	Dance Orchestra
9:45		News		
10pm	Musical Celebrities	Lud Gluskin on the Air	Bob McGraw Orchestra	The Richfield Reporter
10:15			House Undivided	An Invitation to Dance
10:30		Harry Owens Orchestra	Sterling Young Orchestra	Jimmy Grier Orchestra
10:45		Ted Fiorito Orchestra		

EVENING — SPRING, 1937

Friday

BLUE	CBS	MBS	NBC	
Irene Rich Dramas	Broadway Varieties	W. P. A. News	Meskin's Musical News	5pm
Al Gayle Orchestra		John Brown University Talk		5:15
News	Jack Armstrong, the All-American Boy	Cassandra	Organ Recital	5:30
The Radio Book Club	Little Orphan Annie	Your Radio Columnist	Junior News	5:45
The Harlem All-Colored Revue	Hollywood Hotel	News	Music	6pm
		World Affairs		6:15
Coronet on the Air		Sports	The US Army Band	6:30
		Tom Sawyer, comment		6:45
The Raleigh-Kool Program, Jack Pearl	Philadelphia Symphony Orchestra	Dance Orchestra	The First Nighter Program	7pm
				7:15
King's Cowboy Revue	The Old Observer	The Lone Ranger	The Pontiac Varsity Show	7:30
Elza Schallert Interviews	Easy Aces			7:45
The Speech Doctor	Scattergood Baines	Drums	Amos 'n' Andy	8pm
Lum and Abner	Pretty Kitty Kelly	Dance Orchestra	Uncle Ezra's Radio Station	8:15
Singin' Sam, the Barbasol Man	Chesterfield Time	The In-Laws	The Court of Human Relations	8:30
The University Explorer		Dance Orchestra		8:45
Records	Russ Hughes, sports	News	Carefree Carnival	9pm
	Music	Carl Hoff Orchestra		9:15
Detective Mysteries	Radio Headlines	Dance Orchestra	Money Mysteries	9:30
	The Hollywood Legion Fights			9:45
Musical Celebrities			The Richfield Reporter	10pm
		House Undivided	The Southern Harmony Four	10:15
		Sterling Young Orchestra	Jimmy Grier Orchestra	10:30
	Ted Fiorito Orchestra			10:45

EVENING — SPRING, 1937

Saturday

	BLUE	CBS	MBS	NBC
5pm	The Three Cheers	Professor Quiz	Benay Venuta's Variety Program	Stars of Tomorrow
5:15				
5:30	News	Dance Orchestra		Musical Echoes
5:45	Meredith Willson Orchestra			
6pm	Paul Carson, organ	The Nash Program	Page One Parade	Rhythm and Romance
6:15			Rhythm Cocktails	
6:30	Meskin's Musical News	Your Pet Program	Old Time Meller-Drama	Shell Chateau, Joe Cook
6:45				
7pm	Southern California Colleges Music Series	Your Hit Parade	Hawaii Serenades	
7:15				
7:30	Raine Bennett's Island Cruises		Tony D'Orazi, cartoons	Paducah Plantation, Irwin S. Cobb
7:45		Universal Rhythm	Saturday Serenade	
8pm	The National Barn Dance		Dance Orchestra	Jimmy Joy Orchestra
8:15		The Juvenile Revue		
8:30		Johnny Presents		The Gilmore Circus
8:45				
9pm	Ed Wynn, the Perfect Fool	The Hollywood Barn Dance	News	Hollywood Extras on the Air
9:15			Dick Stabile Orchestra	
9:30	News		Paul Whiteman Orchestra	Phil Harris Orchestra
9:45	Music	News	Les Hite Orchestra	
10pm	Command Performance	The Hollywood Barn Dance	Sterling Young Orchestra	Headlines from Home
10:15				Paul Pendarvis Orchestra
10:30		Harry Owens Orchestra	Ted Fiorito Orchestra	Jimmy Grier Orchestra
10:45		Ken Allen Orchestra	Herman Waldman Orchestra	

DAYTIME — SPRING, 1937

Sunday

	BLUE	CBS	MBS	NBC
8am	Records	Organ Moods	The Northwestern Reviewing Stand	Ward and Muzzy, piano
8:15			Music	The Church Quater-Hour
8:30	The Iodent Dress Rehearsal	Major Bowes' Capitol Family		The World is Yours
8:45				
9am	Dr. Caldecott, health		The Cadic Tabernacle Choir	Paramount on Parade
9:15	Songs			
9:30	The Radio City Music Hall	The Salt Lake Tabernable Choir	The Voice of Prophecy	The University of Chicago Round Table
9:45				
10am		The CBS Church of the Air	Martha and Hal, songs	Dorothy Dreslin, songs
10:15			Music	The Garden Guide
10:30	Our Neighbor	Paris News Exchange		Dreams of Long Ago
10:45		Headlines and History	Trails of Yankee Trade	
11am	The Magic Key of RCA	Songs	Palmer House Ensemble	Nick Harris
11:15		Music of the Theater	The Key Men Quartet	The Hour Glass, Jerry Brannon
11:30			Great Music at the Church	Thatcher Colt Mysteries
11:45		Alvin Wilder, news		
12pm	Howard Bell, talk	New York Philharmonic Orchestra	The Hall of Song	Music
12:15	Choral Voices			
12:30	Alistair Cooke, comment			The Widow's Sons
12:45	Songs		Music	
1pm	National Vespers			Romance Melodies
1:15				

DAYTIME — SPRING, 1937

Monday-Friday

BLUE	CBS	MBS	NBC	
Talk / Vagabonds Orchestra	Keeping Fit in Hollywood	Andy and Virginia, songs	Financial Service	8am
Music / Larry Larson, organ		Music	The Church Quarter-Hour	8:15
Vic and Sade	Eddie Albright, organ		Cross Cuts of the Day	8:30
The Gospel Singer	Talk / Dr. Allen Dafoe, health		Music / The Voice of Experience	8:45
Music / Honeyboy and Sassafras	The Gumps	Talk and Music	News	9am
Music / Language Lesson	Columbia Almanac	Sycamore Street	The Story of Mary Marlin	9:15
Talk and Music	The Romance of Helen Trent	The Monticello Party Line	Talk and Music / How to Be Charming	9:30
	Our Gal Sunday	We Are Four	Talk and Music	9:45
News	Betty and Bob	Norma Young, talk	Music / The Mystery Chef	10am
Ann Cook, songs	Modern Cinderella	Talk and Music / Dr. A. F. Payne, psychology	Mrs. Wiggs of the Cabbage Patch	10:15
We Love and Learn	Hymns of All Churches / Betty Crocker, cooking	Merrymakers Orchestra	John's Other Wife	10:30
Talk and Music	John K. Watkins, news		Just Plain Bill	10:45
Talk and Music	Big Sister	Palmer House Ensemble	Ann Warner Chats / The Standard School Broadcast	11am
	The American School of the Air	House Divided	Music / The Standard School Broadcast	11:15
The National Farm and Home Hour		Music	Talk and Music	11:30
	The Story of Myrt and Marge		Music / Hollywood in Person	11:45
	Mary Lee Taylor, cooking / Magazine of the Air	Ben Sweetland, comment	Pepper Young's Family	12pm
		News	Ma Perkins	12:15
Talk and Music	Hometown Sketches	Music / Howard Lavin Orchestra	Vic and Sade	12:30
	Talk and Music		The O'Neills	12:45
	Fletcher Wiley, talk	Talk and Music	Music / California Kitchen	1pm
				1:15

DAYTIME — SPRING, 1937

Sunday

	BLUE	CBS	MBS	NBC
1:30	Senator Fishface and Professor Figgsbottle			Musical Camera
1:45				
2pm	We, the People	The CBS Church of the Air	Freddy Martin Orchestra	Ry-Krisp Presents Marion Talley
2:15			Rabbi Magnin, religion	
2:30	Stoopnagle and Budd	Rainbow Ends	Freddy Martin Orchestra	Know Your America
2:45		Let's Get Together		The Tune Transgressor
3pm	The Catholic Hour	The Park Avenue Penners	The 1937 Radio Show, Ray Knight	
3:15				Smilin' Ed McConnell, songs
3:30	The Golden Gate Park Band	The Chevrolet Program	Help Thy Neighbor	A Tale of Today
3:45				
4pm	The Helen Traubel Program	Reunion of the Stars	Louisiana Hayride	Headline Crashing
4:15	Musical Moods			Stars on Parade
4:30	Believe It or Not		Music for Today	The Sperry Special
4:45				

DAYTIME — SPRING, 1937

Monday-Friday

BLUE	CBS	MBS	NBC	
News	Pietro Pontrelli Orchestra	Variety Program	Follow the Moon	*1:30*
Talk and Music	Aunt Jenny's True Life Stories		The Guiding Light	*1:45*
The Story of Mary Martin	Music / The Women's Forum	Music	Music / Hello, Peggy	*2pm*
The Classic Hour	News	Music / The Johnson Family	Music	*2:15*
	News Through a Woman's Eyes	Talk and Music	The Dorin Sisters, songs	*2:30*
	Talk and Music		Pictorial	*2:45*
Talk and Music	The Western Home Hour	Feminine Fancies	Women's Magazine of the Air	*3pm*
				3:15
		Talk and Music		*3:30*
				3:45
	The Newlyweds		Talk and Music	*4pm*
	Talk and Music			*4:15*
Music / The Haven of Rest	Happy Family		Talk and Music / The Helen Traubel Program	*4:30*
	Talk and Music	Music / The In-Laws		*4:45*

DAYTIME — SPRING, 1937

Saturday

	BLUE	CBS	MBS	NBC
8am	Madge Marley, songs	Cincinatti Conservatory Symphony	Andy and Virginia, songs	Our American Schools
8:15	The Church Quarter-Hour			Financial Service
8:30	The Magic of Speech		The US Army Band	Doc Whipple, talk
8:45				Songs
9am	Call to Youth	The Captivators	Women of the World	News
9:15		Orientale	Organ Recital	County Medical Association Talks
9:30	The National Farm and Home Hour	The Federation of Women's Club		The National Federation of Music Clubs
9:45		News	Howard Lanin Orchestra	
10am		The Monitor Children's Program		The Mystery Chef
10:15		Eddie Albright, organ	Steve Severn's Pet Club	Whitney Ensemble
10:30	News	Eddie Elkin Orchestra	Carnegie Tech Symphony Orchestra	Campus Capers
10:45	Music			
11am	Music	The Federation of Women's Club	Sylvia Oyde Orchestra	The Metropolitan Opera
11:15		Music		
11:30	Walter Blaufuss Orchestra		Palmer House Ensemble	
11:45			Len Saldo, organ	
12pm	Music	Down by Hermans	Music	
12:15			News	
12:30		Department of Commerce Series	Horse Racing	
12:45		Music		
1pm	Club Matinee, Ransom Sherman	Bull Session		
1:15	News			
1:30	Spelling Bee		Howard Lanin Orchestra	
1:45				

DAYTIME — SPRING, 1937

Saturday

	BLUE	CBS	MBS	NBC
2pm		News	Music	
2:15		The Singing Strings		
2:30	The Classic Hour	California Legislature Talk		Josef Honik Orchestra
2:45		The Singing Waiters		
3pm		Chamber of Congress Musicale	The Story Teller	Tophatters Orchestra
3:15			Unmasking the Rackets	
3:30	Home Symphony Orchestra	Officer of the Day	Enoch Light Orchestra	Alma Kitchell, talk
3:45		Bob Feld Orchestra	Music	Religion in the News
4pm	Message of Israel	The Saturday Night Swing Club	Salon Moderne	Music
4:15				The Haven of Rest
4:30	Tea Time	The Weekend Potpourri	Michael Zarin Orchestra	
4:45			Palmer House Ensemble	The ABC of NBC

EVENING — SUMMER, 1937

Sunday

	BLUE	CBS	MBS	NBC
5pm	The Rippling Rhythm Revue	Universal Rhythm	Hi There Audience, Ray Perkins	The Manhattan Merry-Go-Round
5:15				
5:30	Walter Winchell's Jergens Journal		Dance Orchestra	The American Album of Familiar Music
5:45	Cabbages and Kings			
6pm	The National Music Camp	The Lewisohn Stadium Concerts	Kay Kyser's Surprise Party / The Goodwill Hour	Josef Hornick Orchestra
6:15				
6:30			Rhythm and Romance	King Cowboy's Revue
6:45			John B. Hughes, news	Thesaurus
7pm	The Chapel Quartet	The Gillette Summer Hotel	The Old Fashioned Revival Hour	The Fitch Jingle Program
7:15	Music			Treasure Island
7:30	Dance Orchestra	Jay Freeman Orchestra		The Jello Program, Jane Froman
7:45				
8pm	The Reader's Guide	Texaco Town	Dance Orchestra	Music
8:15				
8:30	Dance Orchestra	Modern Miracles	Eddy Duchin Orchestra	One Man's Family
8:45		Music		
9pm	Music	Nocturne	News	The Passing Parade
9:15		Al Lyons Orchestra	Dance Orchestra	The Night Editor
9:30	News		Joe Sanders Orchestra	Carlos Molina Orchestra
9:45	Music	George Hamilton Orchestra		
10pm	Musical Celebrities	The Ten o'Clock Wire	Music	The Richfield Reporter
10:15		The Temple Square Program		Bridge to Dreamland
10:30			Larry Kent Orchestra	
10:45		Dance Orchestra		

EVENING — SUMMER, 1937

Monday

BLUE	CBS	MBS	NBC	
Music	Columbia's Shakesphere	Music	News	5pm
Sports			Famous Songs	5:15
Streamlined Shakesphere / The O'Neil Cycle			The Hour of Charm	5:30
				5:45
	Lady Esther Serenade	The In-Laws	The Carnation Contented Hour	6pm
Music		Frank Watanabe and the Professor		6:15
The National Radio Forum	Neck o' the Woods	Sports	Burns and Allen	6:30
		John B. Hughes, news		6:45
The Colonial Quartet	Scattergood Baines	The Pageant of Melody	Amos 'n' Andy	7pm
Lum and Abner	Boake Carter, news	Meet Some People	Uncle Ezra's Radio Station	7:15
King's Cowboy Revue	Pick and Pat	The Lone Ranger	The Voice of Firestone	7:30
Paul Sabin Orchestra				7:45
Safety First	The Alemite Half-Hour	Dance Orchestra	Fibber McGee and Molly	8pm
Jesse Crawford, organ				8:15
The Symphonettes	School Days	The Backyard Astronomer	Vox Pop	8:30
News		The Townsend Plan		8:45
The House of Melody		News	Hawthorne House	9pm
	Dance Orchestra	Drama		9:15
News		Happy Felton Orchestra	The Monday Night Special	9:30
Meskin's Musical News	Easy Aces	Joe Sanders Orchestra		9:45
Musical Celebrities	The Ten o'Clock Wire	Eddy Duchin Orchestra	The Richfield Reporter	10pm
	White Fires of Inspiration		Ben Klauson, songs	10:15
		The Witch's Tale	Jimmy Grier Orchestra	10:30
	Dance Orchestra			10:45

EVENING — SUMMER, 1937

Tuesday

	BLUE	CBS	MBS	NBC
5pm	Ben Bernie, the Old Maestro	Cassandra	The Grant Park Concerts	News
5:15				The Beaux Arts Trio
5:30	The Lee Murray Players	Jack Oakie's College	Music	The Packard Hour
5:45	The Radio Book Club			
6pm	The Other Americas	The US Navy Band	The In-Laws	
6:15			Frank Watanabe and the Professor	
6:30	Jose Rodriguez Orchestra	Charflie Hamp, organ	Sports	Jimmy Fidler, gossip
6:45	Norman Thomas, talk	Leaves in the Wind	John B. Hughes, news	Vic and Sade
7pm	Music	Scattergood Baines	Sing Time	Amos 'n' Andy
7:15	Lum and Abner	Dance Orchestra		King's Cowboy Revue
7:30	Professor Puzzlewit		Music	Johnny Presents
7:45		Club Romance		
8pm	George Olsen Orchestra	Watch the Fun Go By, Al Pearce		Death Valley Days
8:15				
8:30	Concert Favorites	The Randalliers		Good Morning Tonight
8:45		On the Air	Gus Haenshen Orchestra	
9pm	Russian Rhapsody		News	Thrills
9:15		Dance Orchestra	The Hollywood Sunshine Girls	
9:30		Al Lyons Orchestra	Tommy Tucker Orchestra	The Music Parade
9:45	Music	George Hamilton Orchestra		Carlos Molina Orchestra
10pm	Musical Celebrities	The Ten o'Clock Wire	Jack Denny Orchestra	The Richfield Reporter
10:15		The Art of Converstion		Miss Fisher Directs
10:30			Larry Kent Orchestra	George Olsen Orchestra
10:45		Dance Orchestra		

EVENING — SUMMER, 1937

Wednesday

BLUE	CBS	MBS	NBC	
Rackets of Today	Chesterfield Presents	Dance Orchestra	News	5pm
Music		Crime Clinic	The Beaux Arts Trio	5:15
	The Palmolive Beauty Box Theater	Ed Fitzgerald and Company	Music	5:30
Moving Stories of Life			Junior News	5:45
Dance Orchestra	Gangbusters	The In-Laws	Your Hit Parade	6pm
Carol Weyman, songs		Frank Watanabe and the Professor		6:15
The NBC Minstrels	Design in Harmony	Sports		6:30
	Dr. Barr, health	John B. Hughes, news	Hedda Hopper, gossip	6:45
Music	Scattergood Baines	Melodies from the Sky	Amos 'n' Andy	7pm
Lum and Abner	Boake Carter, news	Jose de Corsey Orchestra	Uncle Ezra's Radio Station	7:15
Cabbages and King	Laugh with Ken	The Lone Ranger	Olsen and Johnson	7:30
The California Safety Council				7:45
Jesse Crawford, organ	Magazine of the Air	Guy Lombardo Orchestra	Town Hall Tonight, Walter O'Keefe	8pm
	Dance Orchestra			8:15
The March of Progress		Dance Orchestra		8:30
Music				8:45
Waltz Time	Calling All Cars	News	The Frank Morgan Show	9pm
		Charles Gaylord Orchestra	Alias Jimmy Valentine	9:15
Dr. Kate	Al Lyons Orchestra	Joe Sanders Orchestra	Screen Week	9:30
	Easy Aces		Will Hollander Orchestra	9:45
Musical Celebrities	The Ten o'Clock Wire	Eddy Duchin Orchestra	The Richfield Reporter	10pm
	Your Witness		Glen Hurlburt Orchestra	10:15
		Larry Kent Orchestra	The Haven of Rest	10:30
				10:45

EVENING — SUMMER, 1937

Thursday

	BLUE	CBS	MBS	NBC
5pm	The Robin Hood Dell Concerts	Major Bowes' Original Amateur Hour	Music	News
5:15				Wesley Tourtellotte, organ
5:30	America's Town Meeting of the Air		Pat Barnes' Opera House	Helen Colley, songs
5:45				You and Your Government
6pm		True Adventures	The In-Laws	The Kraft Music Hall, Bob Burns
6:15			Frank Watanabe and the Professor	
6:30	The Picadilly Music Hall	The March of Time	Sports	
6:45			John B. Hughes, news	
7pm	Carlos Molina Orchestra	Scattergood Baines	Know Your State	Amos 'n' Andy
7:15	Paul Sabin Orchestra	Lloyd Pantages Covers Hollywood	Dance Orchestra	The Maxwell House Showboat
7:30	Eddie Varza Orchestra	Dance Orchestra	Music	
7:45				
8pm	Henry Busse Orchestra	George Hamilton Orchestra	Calling All Cars	
8:15				The Standard Symphony Hour
8:30	Garwood Van Orchestra	Dance Orchestra	Eddy Duchin Orchestra	
8:45		Captains of Industry	Gus Haenchen Orchestra	
9pm	Murder Will Out	Jan Garber Orchestra	News	
9:15			Highlights of Life	Alias Jimmy Valentine
9:30	News	Al Lyons Orchestra	Dance Orchestra	Jimmy Grier Orchestra
9:45	Viennese Echoes			Mark Fisher Orchestra
10pm	Musical Celebrities	The Ten o'Clock Wire	Eddy Duchin Orchestra	The Richfield Reporter
10:15		Fiesta		The Music Parade
10:30			Larry Kent Orchestra	Archie Loveland Orchestra
10:45		Benny Goodman Orchestra		

EVENING — SUMMER, 1937

Friday

BLUE	CBS	MBS	NBC	
Music	Hollywood Hotel	Music	News	5pm
			The Beaux Arts Trio	5:15
The Grant Park Concerts		Sammy Kaye Orchestra	Kenneth Spencer, songs	5:30
			Junior News	5:45
The Raliegh-Kool Program, Jack Pearl	Hobard Bosworth, gossip	The In-Laws	The First Nighter Program	6pm
	Designs in Harmony	Frank Watanabe and the Professor		6:15
Music	Public Affairs	Sports	Jimmy Fidler, gossip	6:30
		John B. Hughes, news	Roy Campbell's Royalists	6:45
Mindways	Scattergood Baines	David Brockman Presents	Amos 'n' Andy	7pm
Lum and Abner	Boake Carter, news		Uncle Ezra's Radio Station	7:15
The Drama Hour	Hal Kemp Orchestra	The Lone Ranger	The Court of Human Relations	7:30
				7:45
Elza Schallert Interviews	New Horizons	Dance Orchestra	Carefree Carnival	8pm
The Speech Doctor				8:15
Records	George Hamilton Orchestra	The Voice of Prophecy	Believe It or Not	8:30
				8:45
Traffic Interview	Sports	News	Don Fernandos Orchestra	9pm
Ricardo and His Caballeros	Jan Garber Orchestra	Drama	Alias Jimmy Valentine	9:15
News	Eddie Fitzpatrick Orchestra	Joe Sanders Orchestra	Bill Roberts, news	9:30
Music	Easy Aces		Jesse Crawford, organ	9:45
Musical Celebrities	The Ten o'Clock Wire	Eddy Duchin Orchestra	The Richfield Reporter	10pm
	Al Lyons Orchestra		Sports	10:15
		Larry Kent Orchestra	Jimmy Grier Orchestra	10:30
	Benny Goodman Orchestra			10:45

EVENING — SUMMER, 1937

Saturday

	BLUE	CBS	MBS	NBC
5pm	Education Today	Maurice Winnick Orchestra	Louisiana Hayride	The Robin Hood Del Concerts
5:15	Josef Hornick Orchestra			
5:30	Meskin's Musical News	Hollywood Showcase	Ectasy	Emery Deutsch Orchestra
5:45				
6pm	Music	Your Hit Parade	El Paso Orchestra	Jamboree
6:15			George Fisher, gossip	
6:30			Sports	King's Cowboy Revue
6:45		Patti Chapin, songs	John B. Hughes, news	The Music Parade
7pm	The National Barn Dance	Bunny Berrigan Orchestra	Contrasts	Carlos Molinas Orchestra
7:15				
7:30		Johnny Presents	Enrico Madriguera Orchestra	The Gilmore Circus
7:45				
8pm	Paul Whiteman Orchestra	Professor Quiz	Dance Orchestra	Hollywood Extras on the Air
8:15				
8:30	George Olsen Orchestra	The Juvenile Revue	Eddy Duchin Orchestra	William Farmers Orchestra
8:45				
9pm	Raine Bennett, rhymes	Al Lyons Orchestra	News	Don Fernando Orchestra
9:15		The Hollywood Barn Dance	Larry Kent Orchestra	
9:30	News		Tommy Tucker Orchestra	Paul Sabin Orchestra
9:45	The Concert Recital Series			Headines from Home
10pm	Command Performance	The Ten o'Clock Wire	Joe Sanders Orchestra	Jimmy Grier Orchestra
10:15		Jan Garber Orchestra		
10:30		Sterling Young Orchestra	Larry Kent Orchestra	Archie Loveland Orchestra
10:45				

DAYTIME — SUMMER, 1937

Sunday

	BLUE	CBS	MBS	NBC
8am	Sacred Concert	Major Bowes' Capitol Family	The Cadic Tabernacle Choir	The Hour Glass, Jerry Brannon
8:15				
8:30	The Radio City Music Hall	The Salt Lake Tabernacle Choir	Salon Moderne	The University of Chicago Round Table
8:45				
9am		The CBS Church of the Air	Music	The Church Quarter-Hour
9:15				Dorothy Dreslin, songs
9:30	Musical Pilgrimage	Talk	The Voice of Prophecy	Dreams of Long Ago
9:45	Music	Poet's Gold		
10am	The Magic Key of RCA	St. Louis Serenade	Music	Health Talk
10:15				Sunday Drivers
10:30		Living Stories of the Bible		Thatcher Colt Mysteries
10:45				
11am	Music	Everybody's Music	Songs	Chatauqua Symphony Orchestra
11:15			Just Between Us	
11:30			Dance Orchestra	
11:45				
12pm	National Vespers	Spelling Bee	Radioland Orchestra	Romance Melodies
12:15				
12:30	Senator Fishface and Professor Figgsbottle		The Alpine Village Concerts	The World is Yours
12:45				
1pm	There Was a Woman	Our American Neighbors	Dance Orchestra	Paul Martin Orchestra
1:15				Nick Harris
1:30	The Helen Traubel Program	The CBS Church of the Air		Paul Carson, organ
1:45				

DAYTIME — SUMMER, 1937

Monday-Friday

BLUE	CBS	MBS	NBC	
Talk and Music	Keeping Fit in Hollywood	Andy and Virginia, songs	Financial Service	*8am*
Grace and Scotty, songs	Eddie Albright, organ	Music / Zeke Clemens, songs	The Story of Mary Marlin	*8:15*
Music	Music	Music	Music / The Three Marshalls	*8:30*
	Ma Perkins	We Are Four	News	*8:45*
We Love and Learn	Betty and Bob	Music / The Homemakers	Music / The Mystery Chef	*9am*
Music / Language Lesson	Hymns of All Churches / Betty Crocker, cooking	Music / Tom, Dick and Harry, songs	Mrs. Wiggs of the Cabbage Patch	*9:15*
Talk and Music	Arnold Grimm's Daughter	Merrymakers Orchestra	John's Other Wife	*9:30*
	Hollywood in Person		Just Plain Bill	*9:45*
News	Big Sister	Music / Norma Young, talk	Talk and Music	*10am*
Cross-Cuts of the Day	Aun Jenny's True Life Stories	House Undivided		*10:15*
Talk and Music	Edwin C. Hill, news	Sycamore Street	Talk and Music / How to Be Charming	*10:30*
	The Story of Myrt and Marge	Just Like Home	Ann Warner Chats	*10:45*
Talk and Music	Mary Lee Taylor, cooking /	Talk and Music	Pepper Young's Family	*11am*
	Music / Magazine of the Air		Ma Perkins	*11:15*
The National Farm and Home Hour	Fletcher Wiley, talk		Vic and Sade	*11:30*
			The O'Neills	*11:45*
	Talk and Music	Ben Sweetland, comment	Talk and Music	*12pm*
	Pretty Kitty Kelly	News	The Gospel Singer	*12:15*
Stock Market Reports	Talk and Music	Music	Talk and Music	*12:30*
Club Matinee, Ranson Sherman	News		The Guiding Light	*12:45*
	The Women's Forum		Talk and Music	*1pm*
	Talk and Music	Radioland Orchestra		*1:15*
News	News Through a Woman's Eyes	Music		*1:30*
The Classic Hour	Talk and Music			*1:45*

DAYTIME — SUMMER, 1937

Sunday

	BLUE	CBS	MBS	NBC
2pm	The Catholic Hour	Dance Orchestra	Dancing Moods	The Music Parade
2:15				
2:30	The Golden Gate Park Band	Chicagoans Orchestra	Fun in Swingtime, Tim and Irene	A Tale of Today
2:45				
3pm	California Concert	The Columbia Workshop	Help Thy Neighbor	The Argentine Trio
3:15				A Pair of Pianos
3:30	Werner Janssen Orchestra	The Sunday Players	The Romance of Transportation	The Beaux Arts Trio
3:45			Cesare Sedero Directs	The Jingle Town Gazette
4pm	Music	The Singing Strings	Dance Orchestra	The Chase and Sanborn Hour
4:15		Music		
4:30		Idylls of the King		
4:45				

DAYTIME — SUMMER, 1937

Monday-Friday

BLUE	CBS	MBS	NBC	
	Music	Talk and Music	Women's Magazine of the Air	2pm
	The Catalina Islander			2:15
	The Newlyweds			2:30
	Music			2:45
Ann Cook, songs	The Western Home Hour	Feminine Fancies	Pictorial	3pm
Music			Talk and Music / Hello, Peggy	3:15
Memory Lane		Talk and Music	Music / The Passing Parade	3:30
Music			Music	3:45
Music / Good Time Society / Husbands and Wives / Irene Rich Dramas	Music / The Cavalcade of America / Broadway Varieities	Music / Jazz Nocturne	Music / One Man's Family / The Royal Gelatin Hour , Rudy Vallee /	4pm
				4:15
Music / The Haven of Rest	Music	Talk and Music / Let's Visit	Talk and Music	4:30
	Music / Moving Stories of Real Life			4:45

DAYTIME — SUMMER, 1937

Saturday

	BLUE	CBS	MBS	NBC
8am	Call to Youth	Jack Shannon, songs	Andy and Virginia, songs	The Continentals
8:15	The Three Marshalls	Eddie Albright, organ	Sports	
8:30	George Hessberger Orchestra	George Hall Orchestra	The California Board of Education	Music
8:45			Music	News
9am	Our Barn	The Captivators		The Mystery Chef
9:15		The Federation of Women's Clubs		County Medical Association Talks
9:30	The National Farm and Home Hour	Buffalo Presents	Happy Felton Orchestra	Josef Hornick Orchestra
9:45				
10am		The Monitor Children's Program	Sylvia Cyde, songs	Your Host is Buffalo
10:15		Ann Leaf at the Organ		
10:30	News		Palmer House Ensemble	Golden Melodies
10:45	Music	Tours in Tone	The Theater Club	
11am		Down by Herman's	Music	Concert Miniatures
11:15				
11:30	Ricardo and His Caballeros	Department of Commerce	Sports	The Weekend Revue
11:45		Clyde Barrie, songs		
12pm	Club Matinee, Ransom Sherman	Dictators Orchestra	News	
12:15			Horse Racing	
12:30		Federal Housing Authority Talk		Willy Bryant Orchestra
12:45		News		
1pm	Music	The Great Lakes Concerts	Radioland Orchestra	Music
1:15			Public Affairs	
1:30		Public Affairs		Kaltenmeyer's Kindegarten
1:45		Ben Salvo Orchestra		

DAYTIME — SUMMER, 1937

Saturday

	BLUE	CBS	MBS	NBC
2pm	The Classic Hour	Sports	Len Salvo Orchestra	Norman Cloutiers Orchestra
2:15			Sally Jo Nelson, songs	Sports
2:30		Ralph Ricard, piano	The Four Californians	Alma Kitchell, talk
2:45		Bob Crosby Orchestra	Sports	The Art of Living
3pm	Message of Israel		Palmer House Ensemble	El Chico
3:15		Song Time	Happy Felton Orchestra	
3:30	Music	Music	Guatemala Miramba Orchestra	Public Affairs
3:45				
4pm		The Saturday Swing Session	Phil Harris Orchestra	Ernest Gills Orchestra
4:15	Nola Day, songs			
4:30	Edwin Franko Goldman Band	The Weekend Potpourri	David Brockman Orchestra	The Haven of Rest
4:45				

EVENING — FALL, 1937

Sunday

	BLUE	CBS	MBS	NBC
5pm	The General Motors Concert	The Columbia Workshop	Music	The Chase and Sanborn Hour
5:15				
5:30		David Ross' Birthday Party	Dance Orchestra	
5:45				
6pm	The Hollywood Playhouse	The Ford Sunday Evening Hour	Guess What	The Manhattan Merry-Go-Round
6:15			The Deep South	
6:30	George Fisher, gossip		The Forum	The American Album of Familiar Music
6:45	Cabbages and Kings		John B. Hughes, news	
7pm	The Zenith Foundation	Showcase	Dance Orchestra	Hawthorne House
7:15				
7:30	Vocal Varieties	Headlines and Bylines	The Old Fashioned Revival Hour	Carefree Carnival
7:45	Cherrio's Musical Mosaics			
8pm	Irene Rich Dramas	Lloyd Pantages Covers Hollywood		Interesting Neighbors
8:15	The Colonial Quartet	Thru the Centuries		I Want a Divorce
8:30	The Beaux Arts Trio	Cab Calloway Orchestra	Music	The Jello Program, Jack Benny
8:45				
9pm	Dance Orchestra	Modern Miracles	News	The Night Editor
9:15		Henry King Orchestra	The Passing Parade	Treasure Island
9:30		Red Norvo Orchestra	Lady Esther Serenade	One Man's Family
9:45	The University Explorer			
10pm	Phil-Harmonia	The Ten o'Clock Wire	Freddy Martin Orchestra	The Richfield Reporter
10:15		The Melody Hour	Ted Weems Orchestra	Bridge to Dreamland
10:30		Dance Orchestra	News	
10:45			Dance Orchestra	

EVENING — FALL, 1937

Monday

BLUE	CBS	MBS	NBC	
Music	Maurice Winnick Orchestra	P. M. Gaylord Orchestra	Gladys Swartout, songs	5pm
Sports		The Astronomer		5:15
The Music Parade	Hawaiian Noon	Jack Denny Orchestra	Vanity Fair	5:30
News	Little Orphan Annie			5:45
Philadelphia Symphony Orchestra	The Lux Radio Theater	Jack Armstrong, The All-American Boy	Lum and Abner	6pm
		The Phantom Pilot Patrol	The Two Keys	6:15
		Sports	The Hour of Charm	6:30
		John B. Hughes, news		6:45
Behind Prison Bars	Lady Esther Serenade	Glen Gray Orchestra	The Carnation Contented Hour	7pm
		Did You Know That		7:15
The National Radio Forum	Music	The Lone Ranger	Burns and Allen	7:30
				7:45
Whatsit Land	Scattergood Baines	Henry Weber's Musical Revue	Amos 'n' Andy	8pm
Lum and Abner	Boake Carter, news		Uncle Ezra's Radio Station	8:15
The Colonial Quartet	Pick and Pat	Mysteries	The Voice of Firestone	8:30
Magnolia Blossoms		The Townsend Plan		8:45
The University Explorer	The Alemite Half-Hour	News	Fibber McGee and Molly	9pm
Music		The Round Towner		9:15
Memory Lane	Tommy Tucker Orchestra	Dance Orchestra	Vox Pop	9:30
				9:45
Phil-Harmonia	The Ten o'Clock Wire	Dick Stabile Orchestra	The Richfield Reporter	10pm
	White Fires of Inspiration	Room Service	R. S. Ames, comment	10:15
		News	Jimmy Grier Orchestra	10:30
	Dance Orchestra	Dance Orchestra		10:45

EVENING — FALL, 1937

Tuesday

	BLUE	CBS	MBS	NBC
5pm	Husbands and Wives	Big Town	Jazz Nocturne	Helen Colley, songs
5:15				Kids Kabaret
5:30	Mindways	Strings	Symphonic Strings	Kelsey Orchestra
5:45	Moving Stories of Life	Little Orphan Annie		The Voice of Hawaii
6pm	Ben Bernie, the Old Maestro	Rube Applebury	Jack Armstong, the All-American Boys	Lum and Abner
6:15		Strings	The Phantom Pilot Patrol	Alias Jimmy Valentine
6:30	The Roy Shield Revue	Jack Oakie's College	Sports	Mardi Gras
6:45			John B. Hughes, news	
7pm	Violin Recital	Benny Goodman's Swing School	Sing Time	
7:15	Choir Symphonette			
7:30	Music	Calling All Cars	The Witch's Tale	Jimmy Fidler, gossip
7:45				Four Stars Tonight
8pm	Whatsit Land	Scattergood Baines	Music	Amos 'n' Andy
8:15	Lum and Abner	Man to Man		Vocal Varieities
8:30	Your Neighbor	The Lifebouy Program, Al Jolson	Room Service	Johnny Presents
8:45			Vic Arden Orchestra	
9pm	Preview	Watch the Fun Go By, Al Pearce	News	Death Valley Days
9:15			Whispering Jack Smith, songs	
9:30	Dance Orchestra	Sam Balter, sports	Did You Know That	Good Morning Tonight
9:45	The University Explorer	Ted Fiorito Orchestra	Henry King Orchestra	
10pm	Phil-Harmonia	The Ten o'Clock Wire	Dance Orchestra	The Richfield Reporter
10:15		The Art of Conversation		The Steinie Bottle Boys
10:30			News	Jimmy Grier Orchestra
10:45		Dance Orchestra	Burke Orchestra	

EVENING — FALL, 1937

Wednesday

BLUE	CBS	MBS	NBC	
Eddy Duchin Orchestra	Maurice Winnick Orchestra	Music	One Man's Family	5pm
				5:15
Sid Skolsky, sports	Hawaiian Moon	Jimmy and Gyp, songs	News	5:30
News	Little Orphan Annie	Public Affairs	The Buckaneers	5:45
Hits and Bits	Chesterfield Presents	Jack Armstong, the All-American Boys	Lum and Abner	6pm
		The Phantom Pilot Patrol	Alias Jimmy Valentine	6:15
The NBC Minstrels	They Won't Forget	Sports	Thrills	6:30
	Strings	John B. Hughes, news		6:45
Raine Bennett, rhymes	Gangbusters	Horace Heidt Orchestra	Your Hit Parade	7pm
				7:15
Marching Along	Hobby Lobby	The Lone Ranger		7:30
Music			I Want a Divorce	7:45
Whatsit Land	Scattergood Baines	Meet Some People	Amos 'n' Andy	8pm
Lum and Abner	Boake Carter, news	Neutral Thousands	Uncle Ezra's Radio Station	8:15
Public Affairs	Texaco Town, Eddie Cantor	Did You Know That	Olsen and Johnson	8:30
		Dr. McCoy, health		8:45
Dance Orchestra	The Cavalcade of America	News	Town Hall Tonight, Fred Allen	9pm
		The Round Towner		9:15
	Styles	Dance Orchestra		9:30
	Vic Arden Orchestra	Drama		9:45
Phil-Harmonia	The Ten o'Clock Wire	Dick Joy Orchestra	The Richfield Reporter	10pm
	Your Witness	Room Service	Everybody's Music	10:15
		News	The Haven of Rest	10:30
		Kay Kyser Orchestra		10:45

EVENING — FALL, 1937

Thursday

	BLUE	CBS	MBS	NBC
5pm	Music	Maurice Winnick Orchestra	Dance Orchestra	The Royal Gelatin Hour, Rudy Vallee
5:15	News			
5:30	The March of Time	Football Review	Henry King Orchestra	
5:45		Little Orphan Annie		
6pm	Music	Major Bowe's Original Amateur Hour	Jack Armstong, the All-American Boy	John Marvin, songs
6:15			The Phantom Pilot Patrol	Alias Jimmy Valentine
6:30			Sports	King's Cowboy Revue
6:45			John B. Hughes, newsr	Bill Roberts, news
7pm	Jamboree	Tish	The Forum	The Kraft Music Hall, Bing Crosby
7:15			Room Service	
7:30		We, the People	Henry Weber's Musical Revue	
7:45				
8pm	Whatsit Land	Scattergood Baines	Calling All Cars	Amos 'n' Andy
8:15	Elza Schallert Interviews	The Kate Smith Hour		The Standard Symphony Hour
8:30	News		Sam Hayes, news	
8:45	Dr. Kate		Vic Arden Orchestra	
9pm			News	
9:15	Football Review	Ted Fiorito Orchestra	Whispering Jack Smith, songs	The Maxwell House Showboat
9:30	Lou Bring Orchestra	Red Norvo Orchestra	Did You Know That	
9:45	The University Explorer		Henry King Orchestra	
10pm	Phil-Harmonia	The Ten o'Clock Wire	Dick Joy Orchestra	
10:15		On the Air	The Round Towner	The Richfield Reporter
10:30		Dance Orchestra	News	Winston Giles Orchestra
10:45			Dance Orchestra	

EVENING — FALL, 1937

Friday

BLUE	CBS	MBS	NBC	
Stringtime	The Hammerstien Music Hall	Music	Helen Colley, songs	*5pm*
The Book Club		The Fashion Parade	The Rumpus Room	*5:15*
Gladys Swartout, songs	Hawaiian Moon	Jimmy and Gyp, songs	Freddy Martin Orchestra	*5:30*
News	Little Orphan Annie	Pictures	Moving Stories of LIfe	*5:45*
The Pontiac Varsity Show	Hollywood Hotel	Jack Armstong, the All-American Boy	Lum and Abner	*6pm*
		The Phantom Pilot Patrol	Football Forecast	*6:15*
Tommy Dorsey Orchestra		Sports	King's Cowboy Revue	*6:30*
		John B. Hughes, news	Music	*6:45*
Madison Square Garden Boxing	The Song Shop	David Brockman Presents	The First Nighter Program	*7pm*
				7:15
		The Lone Ranger	Jimmy Fidler, gossip	*7:30*
	Next Step Forward		Dorothy Thompson, news	*7:45*
Whatsit Lamd	Scattergood Baines	Music	Amos 'n' Andy	*8pm*
Lum and Abner	Boake Carter, news		Uncle Ezra's Radio Station	*8:15*
Vocal Varieities	Chesterfield Time	The Voice of Prophecy	The Court of Human Relations	*8:30*
Music				*8:45*
Dr. Kate	Russ Hughes, sports	News	Jimmy Davidson Orchestra	*9pm*
	Music	The Round Towner		*9:15*
Ho Hum			Dance Mysteries	*9:30*
Dance Orchestra	Vic Arden Orchestra	Sports		*9:45*
Phil-Harmonia	The Ten o'Clock Wire	Dick Stabile Orchestra	The Richfield Reporter	*10pm*
	Digest		The Steinie Bottle Boys	*10:15*
		News	Jimmy Grier Orchestra	*10:30*
	Dance Orchestra	Dance Orchestra		*10:45*

EVENING — FALL, 1937

Saturday

	BLUE	CBS	MBS	NBC
5pm	Ted Lewis Orchestra	Maurice Winnick Orchestra	Hi There Audience, Ray Perkins	Josef Hornik Orchestra
5:15				
5:30	Linton Wells, news	Sports	Sylvia Froos, songs	The Haven of Rest
5:45	Music	Marshall Grant, organ		
6pm	Education Today	Rube Applebury	Music	Special Delivery
6:15	Football Resume	Twilight Comes		
6:30	Music	Saturday Night Serenade	Sports	King's Cowboy Revue
6:45			John B. Hughes, news	Pat Bishop, songs
7pm	Gunsmoke Law	Your Hit Parade	Music	
7:15				Marching Along
7:30	Dance Orchestra			The Gilmore Circus
7:45		The Juvenile Revue		
8pm	The National Barn Dance			Four Stars Tonight
8:15		Victor Young Orchestra		Drama
8:30		Johnny Presents		Dance Orchestra
8:45				
9pm	Music	Professor Quiz	News	Believe It or Not
9:15			Your State	
9:30		Sports	Henry King Orchestra	The Log Cabin Jamboree, Jack Haley
9:45		Dance Orchestra	Did You Know That	
10pm	Phil-Harmonia	The Hollywood Barn Dance	Clarence Williams Orchestra	Dance Orchestra
10:15			Room Service	
10:30			News	Raine Bennett, rhymes
10:45		Red Norvo Orchestra	Dance Orchestra	Winston Giles Orchestra

DAYTIME — FALL, 1937

Sunday

	BLUE	CBS	MBS	NBC
8am	Music	The CBS Church of the Air	The Northwestern Reviewing Stand	Bon Jour
8:15			Music	The Silver Flute
8:30		Major Bowes' Capitol Family		
8:45			The American Radio Warblers	The Church Quarter-Hour
9am	Garden Talk		Music	Dorothy Dreslin, songs
9:15	The Southenaires Quartet			
9:30	The Radio City Music Hall	The Salt Lake Tabernable Choir	Pages from Experience	The University of Chicago Round Table
9:45			It's a Racket	
10am		The CBS Church of the Air	Music	Howard Bell, songs
10:15				Music
10:30	Pilgrimage	Poet's Gold	News	
10:45	Al Gayle Orchestra	Eddie Dunstedter, organ	Psychiana	John Holmes, sports
11am	The Magic Key of RCA	Romany Trail	Music	Sunday Drivers
11:15				
11:30		Music		Way Down Home
11:45				
12pm	There Was a Woman	Everybody's Music	Piano	Tapestry Musicale
12:15			Music	
12:30	Senator Fishface and Professor Figgsbottle		The Song Shop	Bicycle Party
12:45			The Sands of Time	
1pm	National Vespers		Music	Romance Melody
1:15				Hair Raisers
1:30	Beth Chamber, songs			The World is Yours

DAYTIME — FALL, 1937

Monday-Friday

BLUE	CBS	MBS	NBC	
Music	Eddie Albright, organ	Music / Andy and Virginia, songs	Financial Service	8am
Birthday Bill	Houseboat	Music	The Church Quarter-Hour	8:15
Talk and Music	Kitty Keene, Inc.		News	8:30
	Ma Perkins		The Gospel Singer	8:45
	Talk / Mary Margaret McBride, talk	Sycamore Street	Music	9am
News	Edwin C. Hill, news	Music		9:15
Talk and Music	The Romance of Helen Trent	Norma Young, talk	David Harum	9:30
	Our Gal Sunday	We Are Four	Talk and Music	9:45
Cross-Cuts of the Day	Betty and Bob	The Monticello Party Line		10am
	Hymns of All Churches / Betty Crocker, cooking	Music / Dr. A. F. Payne, psychology	Mrs. Wiggs of the Cabbage Patch	10:15
Talk / We Love and Learn	Arnold Grimm's Daughter	Music	John's Other Wife	10:30
Talk and Music	Hollywood in Person		Just Plain Bill	10:45
Talk and Music	Big Sister	House Divided	Talk and Music / The Standard School Broadcast	11am
Ann Cook, songs	Aunt Jenny's True Life Stories	First Love	Music / The Standard School Broadcast	11:15
The National Farm and Home Hour	The American School of the Air	Music		11:30
			Music / The Mystery Chef	11:45
	Talk / Mary Lee Taylor, cooking	Ben Sweetland, comment	Pepper Young's Family	12pm
	Magazine of the Air	News	Ma Perkins	12:15
Stock Market Reports	Talk and Music	Talk and Music	Vic and Sade	12:30
Music	The Newlyweds		The O'Neills	12:45
Club Matinee, Ransom Sherman	The Story of Myrt and Marge		Music / Hello, Peggy / Ann Warner Chats	1pm
	Pretty Kitty Kelly		The Guiding Light	1:15
	News		The Story of Mary Marlin	1:30

DAYTIME — FALL, 1937

Sunday

	BLUE	CBS	MBS	NBC
1:45	The Ranch Boys			
2pm	The Metropolitan Opera Auditions	The Silver Theater	Let's Visit	Ry-Krisp Presents Marion Talley
2:15				
2:30	Sunshine Melodies	Reunion of the Stars	Dance Orchestra	Time of Your Life
2:45			Rabbi Magnin, religion	
3pm	The Catholic Hour	The Park Avenue Penners	Thirty Minutes in Hollywood, George Jessel	Barnstormers Drama
3:15				
3:30	Dance Orchestra	Romantic Rhythms	Fun in Swingtime, Tim and Irene	A Tale of Today
3:45				
4pm	The Classic Hour	Vick's Open House	Help Thy Neighbor	Professor Puzzlewit
4:15				
4:30	Seein' Stars	The Gulf Headliners, Phil Baker	Ted Weems Orchestra	The Sperry Special
4:45				

DAYTIME — FALL, 1937

Monday-Friday

BLUE	CBS	MBS	NBC	
	Music / Dr. Allen Dafoe, health		News	1:45
The Classic Hour	Follow the Moon		Talk and Music	2pm
	The Life of Mary Southern	The Gumps		2:15
	Talk and Music	The Johnson Family		2:30
		The Widder Jones		2:45
Talk and Music	The Western Home Hour	Feminine Fancies	Women's Magazine of the Air	3pm
				3:15
	Music	Talk and Music		3:30
				3:45
	Fletcher Wiley, talk	News	Talk and Music	4pm
		The In-Laws		4:15
	Talk and Music	Memory Chest		4:30
		This Side of Twenty		4:45

DAYTIME — FALL, 1937

Saturday

	BLUE	CBS	MBS	NBC
8am	Toy Symphony Orchestra	Cincinatti Conservatory Symphony	Andy and Virginia, songs	The Florence Hale Radio Forum
8:15	Birthday Bill		Varieties	The Church Quater-Hour
8:30	Our Barn		The US Army Band	News
8:45				Cobwebs
9am	Call to Youth	Music	The California Board of Education	Continental Orchestra
9:15	News	The Federation of Women's Club	This Wonderful World	County Medical Association Talks
9:30	The National Farm and Home Hour	George Hall Orchestra	Music	Rex Battle Orchestra
9:45		Federal Housing Authority Talk	Songs	
10am		The Monitor Children's Program	Music	Happy Jack Turner, songs
10:15		Songs	News	The Escorts and Betty
10:30	Club Mattnee, Ransom Sherman	Buffalo Presents	Dick Stabile Orchestra	Campus Capers
10:45				
11am		Sports	Dance Orchestra	Your Host is Buffalo
11:15			The Three Graces	
11:30	Panico Orchestra		Palmer House Ensemble	Music
11:45				
12pm	Sports		Sports	Sports
12:15				
12:30				
12:45				
1pm				
1:15				
1:30			News	
1:45			Music	

DAYTIME — FALL, 1937

Saturday

	BLUE	CBS	MBS	NBC
2pm			Sports	
2:15				
2:30				
2:45				
3pm	Nikolai Rakov Orchestra			
3:15				
3:30	Songs			
3:45	Hi Hats			
4pm	Message of Israel			
4:15				
4:30	Wenreddie Varzo Orchestra			
4:45				

Bear Manor Media

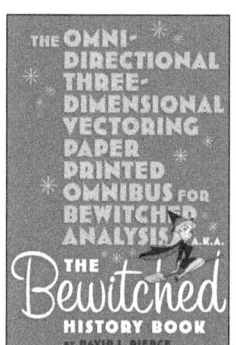

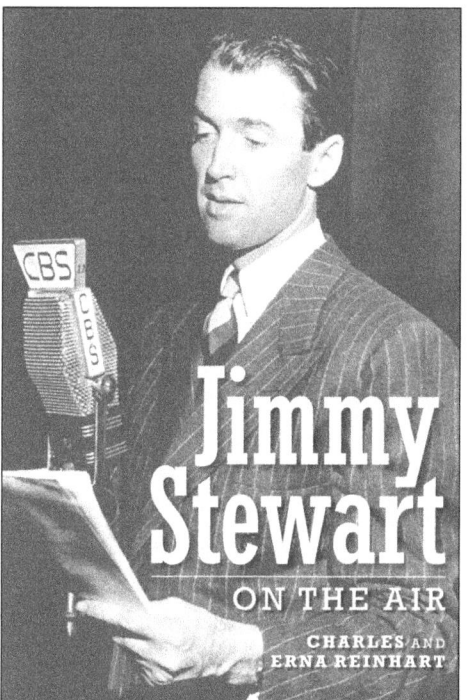

Classic Cinema.
Timeless TV.
Retro Radio.

WWW.BEARMANORMEDIA.COM

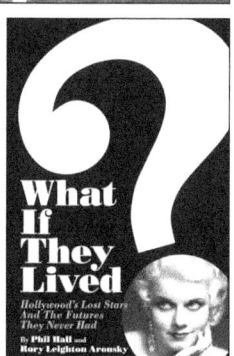

www.ingramcontent.com/pod-product-compliance
Lightning Source LLC
Chambersburg PA
CBHW050322230426
43663CB00010B/1706